CW01162465

Real Vanilla:

Nature's Unsung Hero

**The Rather Large
Story of LittlePod®**

Janet Sawyer MBE BEM

UNICORN

This book is dedicated to my grandson, Joshua, and all of the LittlePodders in Generation Alpha, who will grow up to hopefully reach the 22nd century. May they, with constant vigilance and guardianship, protect our forests for future generations. We cannot pay back but we can pay on.

Vanilla hugs, Nonna Janet x

JANET SAWYER MBE BEM
Managing Director & Founder of LittlePod

Fifteen years ago, I launched LittlePod at Hampton Court. It was a period in which the world was experiencing one of the worst economic recessions in a lifetime. Since then, there have been many more challenges, none greater than those that we face today.

It has been my privilege to develop a sustainable, award-winning company, and to mentor so many talented and conscientious teams of people, who have helped to build the reputation that LittlePod has today. Each team has been perfect for each phase of LittlePod's development. I thank them all, each and every one, for the commitment and energy they have given.

CONTENTS

06	**Foreword**
08	**Introduction**
10	**Chapter 1:** From Barren Land to Paradise
20	**Chapter 2:** 'We are Family'
42	**Chapter 3:** Education and the Environment
56	**Chapter 4:** The Future of Farming
66	**Chapter 5:** The Vanilla Farmer's Daughter
80	**Chapter 6:** Our Doctor in Madagascar
94	**Chapter 7:** Saving the Orchid
104	**Chapter 8:** Memories of a Lost Village
120	**Chapter 9:** A Promise to Dr Made
134	**Chapter 10:** Arts and Culture
144	**Chapter 11:** A Tribute to Trust
162	**Chapter 12:** Vanilla and Wellbeing
172	**Chapter 13:** The Importance of an Education
180	**Chapter 14:** Keep it REAL
196	**Chapter 15:** Our Man in Belém
208	**Chapter 16:** A Promise Fulfilled
218	**Acknowledgements**
222	**Picture Credits**

FOREWORD
by Dr Vik Mohan

Dr Vik Mohan is a practicing GP, planetary health pioneer, storyteller and teacher. He combines his expertise as a doctor with a passion for biodiversity conservation to support frontline communities to live sustainably.

I remember the day very clearly: 8th July, 2013. While I was busy making a note of everything that had been donated for the upcoming auction, a warm and chatty Janet Sawyer arrived at my house in Exeter with a hamper packed with exciting-looking goodies. The ingredient that made these goodies so special was real vanilla, sourced from a country that, for seemingly different reasons, held a special place in both our hearts.

A GP by profession and a conservationist at heart, I had found an exciting way of using my skills as a doctor in service to our natural world. Working alongside fishing communities on the southwest coast of Madagascar in my role as Medical Advisor to the marine conservation organisation Blue Ventures, I had discovered a huge unmet need for healthcare, and we were working to address that need.

Janet, whose own interest in Madagascar stemmed from its vanilla-growing tradition, having founded LittlePod three years earlier, could instantly see the value of what I was trying to do. I was encouraging Blue Ventures to act holistically in support of the communities who are the stewards of our precious marine life. The communities with whom we were working are among the most vulnerable and underserved on the planet. How could we expect them to engage in the complex long-term work of protecting our oceans if their more pressing needs were not met? By integrating health services into our suite of offerings to communities, not only were we helping to improve the health of some of the world's hardest-to-reach communities, we were also unlocking their ability to engage in marine conservation.

Janet, whose interest in vanilla extended far beyond simply the procurement of this precious commodity, shared my passion for ensuring that these rural communities in Madagascar were able to live in harmony with their natural environment.

The hamper of LittlePod ingredients that arrived at my door in 2013, which was to be auctioned to raise money for the community health programme, was Janet's first offer of support. Janet later offered to donate 10 per cent of all of LittlePod's online sales to help support me to continue do my important work in Madagascar – a generous gesture that made a great difference, and an arrangement that remains in place to this day.

By the time I left Blue Ventures in 2024, what started in one fishing village in southwest Madagascar had grown into a movement that served nearly one million people across five countries. Janet has been a steadfast and valued supporter of my work throughout this journey. At a personal level, in an approach that mirrors her approach with her own staff at LittlePod, Janet has been a valuable source of support for me.

Real Vanilla: Nature's Unsung Hero explores the lives of vanilla farmers around the world, an interesting parallel with my own interest in artisanal fishers in the coastal tropics. In a world where the provenance of the food we eat is of increasing interest and importance, this book takes us on a journey to the varied sources of that most precious of food products: real vanilla. It shines a light on the challenges, successes and wisdom of those who skilfully cultivate the vanilla orchid. It demonstrates how thoughtful vanilla production can benefit both people and planet and help foster resilience to climate change.

Having left Blue Ventures, I am now working with Planet Indonesia, a fantastic conservation organisation concerned with communities across the Indonesian Archipelago. In another interesting parallel, Janet is supporting vanilla growers in Bali. Our respective stories remain intertwined.

This book provides rich insights into the approach that the LittlePod farmers are taking to vanilla farming – an approach that ensures good crop yields and the restoration of biodiversity. It is about the people behind the magical vanilla flavour that so many of us cherish. It captures an ethos that we both hold dear: to put communities first.

These communities are the stewards of some of the planet's richest biodiversity and producers of so much of our food. Whatever our goal, whether it's biodiversity conservation, climate resilience or sustainable food production, we must focus on and uphold the rights of frontline communities. It is so important to us all.

Real Vanilla: Nature's Unsung Hero

INTRODUCTION
by Janet Sawyer MBE BEM

Founded in 2010, LittlePod is a natural ingredients company specialising in REAL vanilla. Nestled among the rolling hills of East Devon on the beautiful Jurassic Coast, we reach out to support farming communities in the equatorial regions and to educate consumers worldwide about the value of REAL vanilla to the planet and its people.

As the title suggests, the rather large story of LittlePod covers the larger canvas of the company journey. Donald Winnicott, in his book *The Child, the Family and the Outside World*, shows the interconnectedness of a child's world. At the centre is the child, encircled by its family. At the centre of our circle is LittlePod, surrounded by all those who have driven our Campaign for Real Vanilla for the last fifteen years.

The outer circle is the outside world. In the child's case this encompasses the school and all those people who are there to support the family and the child. In the case of LittlePod, it is represented by our supporters and our customers, consumers and companies at home and abroad, and all those who value vanilla and its importance to the environment.

This book introduces the reader to various people within those circles. They all contribute to LittlePod from different positions in the supply chain. Together they make up the human chain who we fondly refer to as our LittlePodders.

Wherever LittlePod takes me, whether it be trade shows, talks, demonstrations or dinner parties, there are three fundamental questions that I am constantly faced with. They are:

Vanilla, what is it? How do I use it? and the third, the most enigmatic question of all... How did you get into vanilla in the first place?

It is my hope that this book will answer these questions and enlighten the reader.

At the heart of the story is a little flower. Its life and mine have become entwined for the last fifteen years. If you are inspired by the rather large story of LittlePod, I hope that you will join our Campaign for Real Vanilla.

Opposite: This is REAL vanilla – LittlePod's natural paste and extract

01
From Barren Land to Paradise

'Agape' – love, wonder, divine – this is the word that comes to me to describe the magical sensation I feel.

Standing here in Bali among the trees laden with vanilla vines wrapped over their branches, staring at the evidence of a culmination of thirteen years' labour of love, I was experiencing an atavistic sense of belonging to the ecosystem.

I am visiting the farm set up in 2014 by Dr Made Setiawan as the LittlePod collaborative orchard. I can identify the coconut trees as I gaze up seeing them silhouetted against an azure sky. However, I need the help of the young men who are gathered around Made 2. (We call him this so as not to confuse him with Dr Made, 'Made 1'; 'Made' means second son in Bali). Working with Made 2 under the leadership of Muhammad Syirazi – known here simply as Syiraz – these young men are interns, graduate students with a keen interest in the future of their environment. Their command of the English language is very good: 'This is coffee, this is mangosteen. Here is nutmeg and cinnamon.' They are enthusiastically educating me about the forest floor.

I am enticed over to see the cacao. The young man is holding out the brown-red cacao pod to me and looking proudly at it. I am not sure what to say as I walk toward the trees. There, hanging in what is a canopy vine, strung over the cacao tree, is a delicate little pale orchid flower opening before our eyes. There are estimated to be around 35,000 species of orchids, but the vanilla vine is the only one that produces an edible fruit, known as a vanilla bean pod. With a huge smile, Made 2 directs me to the flower and allows me to take a small twig to transfer the pollen, which he has taken by reaching the reproductive area between the anther cap and the stigma; he shows me how to find the ridge behind the rostellum and gently massage it in with my thumb.

Vanilla is an epiphyte that clings to other plants. Like some other orchids it is hermaphroditic: it has both male and female reproductive organs, allowing self-pollination. However, most orchids have complex mechanisms to avoid self-pollination. It is a wondrous sight and very important that we hand pollinate this flower immediately, as it only opens for a day and there is only an eight-hour window for hand pollination. Left wild, the pollination would need the help of a hummingbird or perhaps a passing insect that could reach inside the flower.

I press the stamen and stigma together. The deed is done. The flower has been pollinated, not by a bee but by a human hand. This process is known as 'the marriage'.

The vanilla flower has been pollinated in this way since 1841, when a young orphaned African slave called Edmond Albius made the discovery in a garden on the Île de la Réunion in the western Indian Ocean (then a French colony), not unlike the one I am standing in.

Top: Made 2 with a cacao pod at the LittlePod orchard in Bali
Bottom: Hand pollinating the vanilla orchid

From Barren Land to Paradise

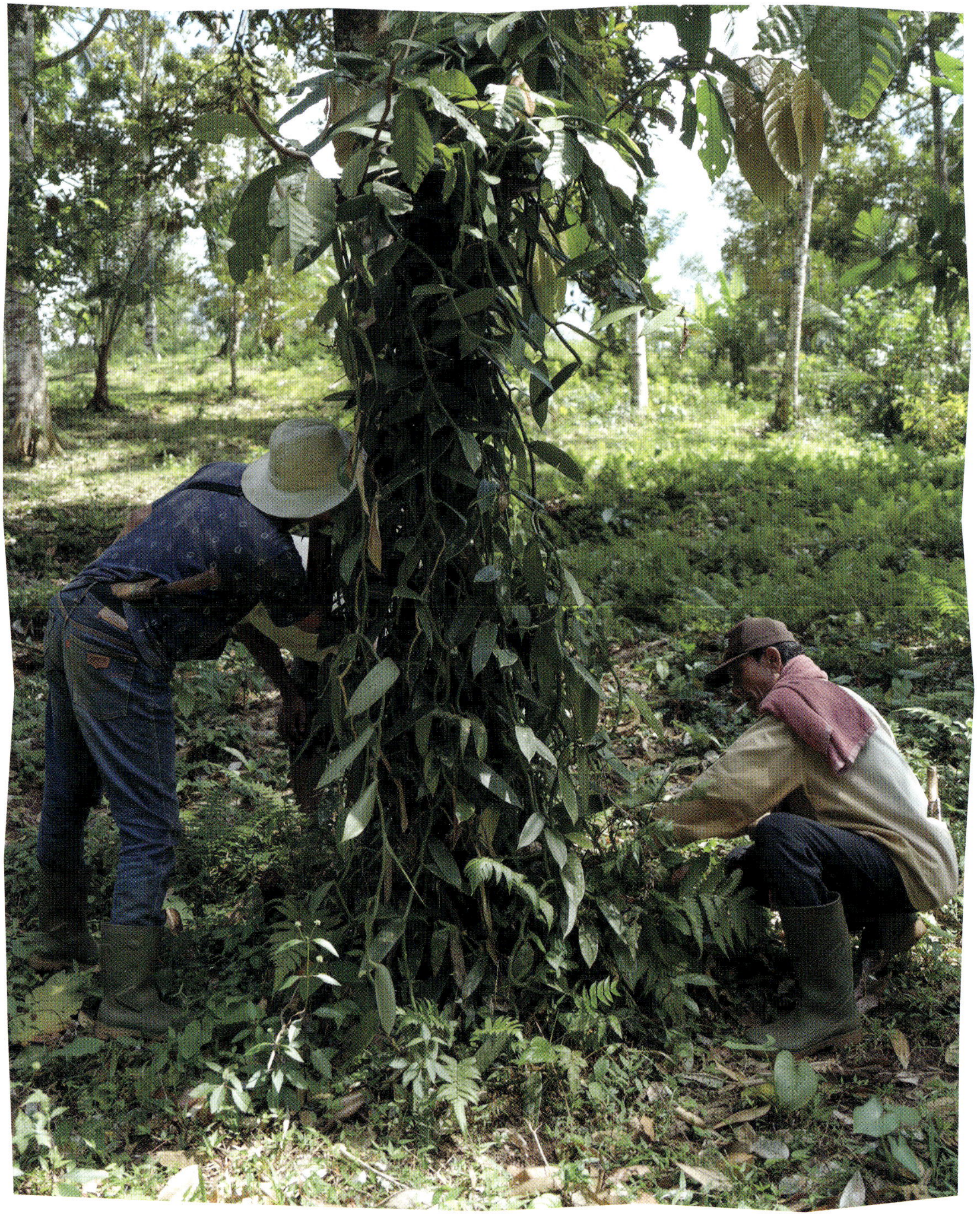

His discovery changed the course of history for the story of vanilla. By perfecting the technique of hand pollination to fertilise the flower Edmond revolutionised the cultivation of vanilla and made it profitable to grow vanilla outside Mexico, where the Melipona bee was the natural pollinator. The indigenous Totonac people of east-central Mexico, an artistic and peace-loving community, are credited with cultivating the orchid, making an intoxicating drink from vanilla pods and chocolate which was known as 'the drink of the Gods'. When the warring Aztecs arrived, the Totonacs were taxed to destruction. The Aztecs claimed their right to vanilla and used it as a natural aphrodisiac. Montezuma was famed for satisfying his many wives.

However, recent archaeological evidence unearthed in the Babylonian destruction layer in Jerusalem (586 BCE) found thirteen amphorae, five bearing the rosette stamp indicating that the content was related to the kingdom of Judah's royal economy. Some of the jars contained wine which was spiced with vanilla. Could the story of the Queen of Sheba's visit to Jerusalem bringing exotic gifts to Solomon show that the elite enjoyed spices and fragrances imported from afar? Vanilla would have had to be imported from the tropical environments of India or East Africa. Soil samples show that there may have been desert caravans trading much earlier than thought, and the kings of Judah would have drunk vanilla wine! Maybe that is why a start-up company in Israel is desperately trying to grow vanilla in greenhouses and to grow it fast. Is it going to produce a vanilla wine branded from the kings of Judah?

Opposite: Tending the vanilla vines at the LittlePod orchard in Bali

It is important to remember that the farmers we are working with in Bali are growing vanilla on tutor trees of all kinds in the orchard forest to improve soil and aid forest regeneration.

Queen Elizabeth in Tudor England encouraged the kings of France to cultivate vanilla on the Île de la Réunion. She had been introduced to it by an apothecary called Hugh Morgan. The food at the time was very bland; when the Queen tasted vanilla she adored the flavour and insisted on having it in everything!

All these historical facts are crowding my mind, and I am overcome with more agape and with the intense pleasure of being in this garden of Eden. As Made 2 thoughtfully walks me around his orchard forest I am overwhelmed with the fecundity of this place. It has been in my imagination for over a decade, and here I am now experiencing it for the first time.

I call to Syiraz and the interns and ask, 'Can you tell me the names of the trees please?' I wish that I had more tacit knowledge of this environment. 'Yes, of course', the interns chorus back to me. 'Come and see.' I am so impressed with these young men. They show such commitment to the regeneration of the rainforest. 'It is not just regeneration that is needed, but restoration', they say.

We step into the interior of this rainforest orchard. I recognise the orange trees, as we had visited a village farm the day before where the vanilla was hanging in a honey-scented orange grove. We could even see the condition of the soil, resplendent with mycorrhizal fungi, normally not visible due to the practice of monoculture planting. While monoculture is advantageous for efficiency and crop predictability, there are some serious disadvantages. Monoculture planting can lead to loss of biodiversity, and there is a susceptibility to pests and disease, particularly fusarium, which devastated the vanilla farms here in Bali in the past through wet weather conditions and continuously digging the same ground, weakening the soil and destroying rootstocks.

In monoculture plantings to maintain harvest yields farmers must use fertiliser, which can harm the environment. The United Nations' goals for sustainability include moving away from monoculture planting to more natural polyculture methods which enrich the soil. And scientists have found that planting vanilla vines in a hectare of soil results in more biodiversity than with any other plant.

This is why I am here in this beautiful forest orchard. I have come finally to meet the farmers who are reaping the rewards of their pioneering polyculture planting techniques. It has not been easy.

It takes five years to produce a vanilla pod. It takes three and a half years to flower. The flowering season is around six weeks. Each flower must be hand pollinated within an eight-hour window. It begins to swell, and takes nine months to produce a long green pod. This orchard does not smell of vanilla, because vanilla pods must be harvested and then cured and conditioned to become the long black vanillin-rich pods we use in our kitchens. The process of drying and conditioning can take up to eighteen months. It is the most labour-intensive crop in the world.

Dr Made and his village farmers have kept the faith over thirteen years as pioneers of their polyculture method, growing vanilla in a way to mimic the natural world, and the results are all around me in what they proudly call 'the LittlePod Orchard' – a name Dr Made and the farmers insisted upon since LittlePod funded the saplings that created this abundance of vanilla. It is a huge tribute to the trust that has been needed between us all over a long period of time, and I am excited today because we are having a gathering at the house of Made 2 here on the farm. David, my partner, and Paul Gilder, LittlePod's media manager, have been taken to the other side of the forest to collect coconuts and see the inter-planting among the rice fields and the undulating landscape.

Made 2 and I share a silent relationship of two people who recognise each other by their actions. Words are not needed. Today is a very special day indeed. 'Look, Janet', Syiraz is begging me over. 'These are all tutor trees for vanilla', he says. 'This is mango, here is cloves, snake fruit, mangosteen, cacao, nutmeg, durian (which I note has a rather revolting smelling fruit), avocado, coffee, moringa (a fast-growing tree known as the medicinal miracle tree), tulip tree, candlenut (look out, seriously poisonous), bauhinia trees; multiple species including butterfly tree, orchid tree and pink bauhinia.' 'And there', whispers one of the interns, 'is the frangipani tree. This is the symbol of Bali's cultural and spiritual heritage and is the national flower of Bali. It has a decadent scent and delicate, lovely colours.' 'I noticed one outside the door of my hotel room', I tell them. 'The hotel staff told me it is a symbol of kindness and purity.'

Oh, I mused, if only the rest of the world was like this, and that the environment was appreciated as much as these people here with me now revere theirs. I begin to reflect on previous experiences of exotic locations I have known.

It is not my first time visiting a vanilla farm, however.

Left: Getting to know Syiraz in Indonesia
Right: The precious vanilla orchid flowers for just one day

From Barren Land to Paradise   17

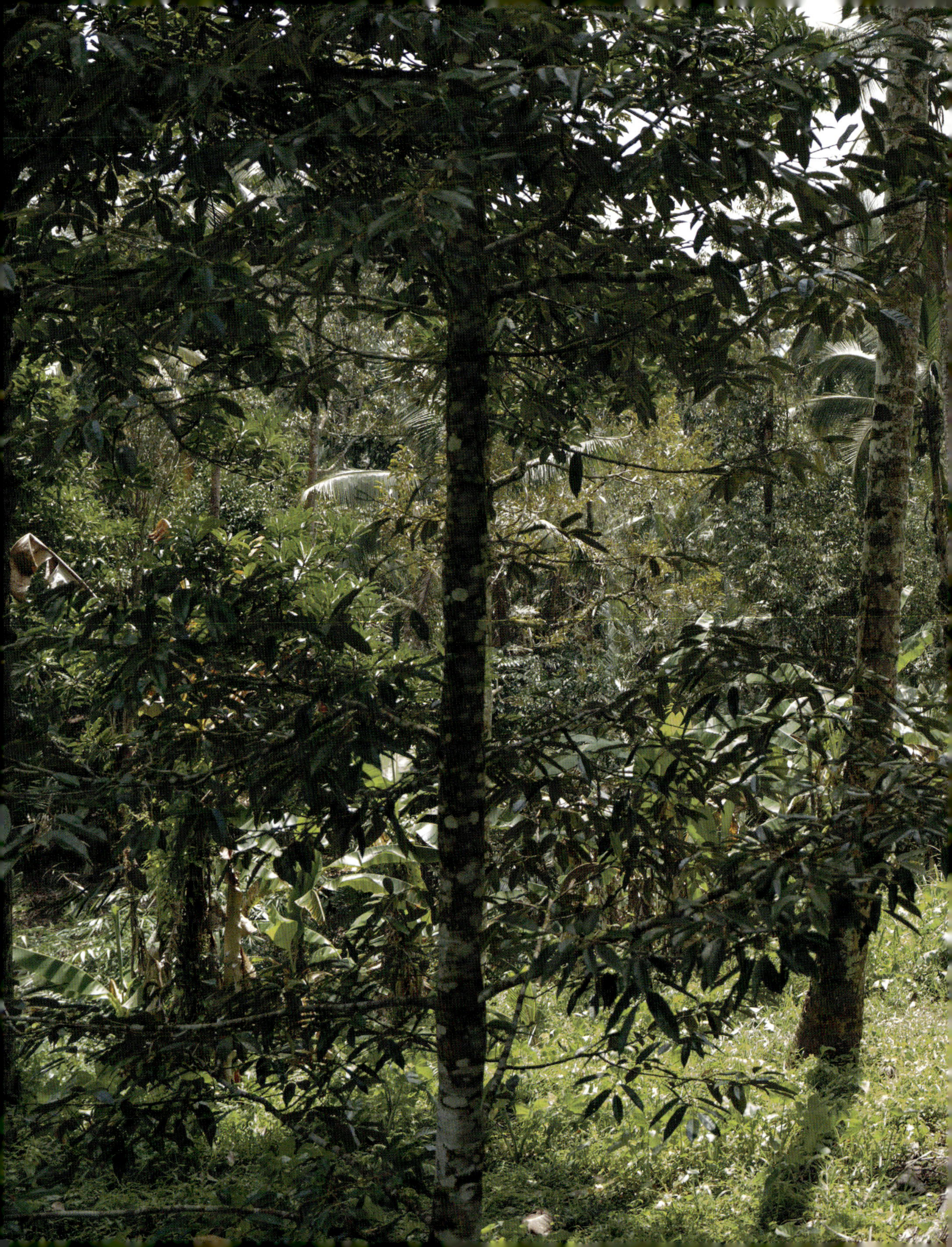

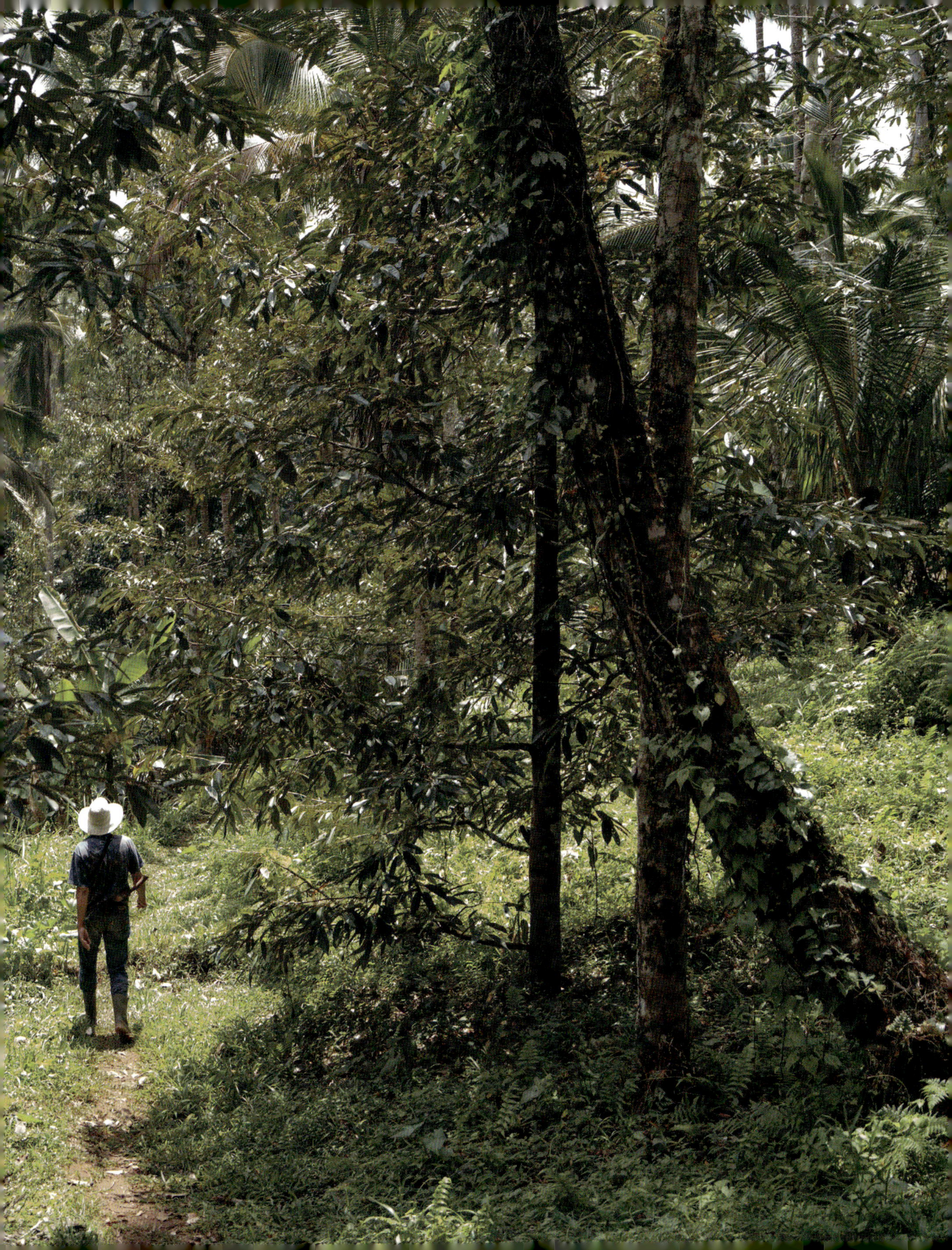

02
'We are Family'

I've seen the vanilla flower opening before.

It was in 2019, when I went to Tanzania to participate in the Vanilla Symposium at Moshi in the foothills of Kilimanjaro. I had been taken to visit two subsistence farmers' homes several hours' drive from the conference centre.

I had decided to attend the Symposium because I knew the company hosting the event. In 2011 a man had contacted me to ask if we could meet up in London. He was starting a vanilla project in Tanzania and wanted to discuss the possibility of LittlePod, my fledgling company, and Natural Extracts Industries, his start-up company, working together.

When we met it was clear that Juan Guardado was driven to make his project a success. He wanted to be with his wife, a doctor who had set up an Aids clinic in the region. And he wanted to contribute something to the community infrastructure, to improve the lives of the people among whom he was to be living. I was awed by his desire to change his life. He had been working in the world of multinational companies, and this was out of his comfort zone. It was a love story as I saw it. He was clearly devoted to his wife, and she had led him to do something rather brave and entrepreneurial.

It was not possible to offer any assistance at the time when we met because I was still learning about vanilla and my own company was new. It was challenging enough to embark on this unknown journey into the world of vanilla. However, we kept in touch, and eight years later in 2019 when I heard that Juan's company were hosting a special symposium where vanilla farmers, researchers and other vanilla companies were gathering from across the globe, I knew I had to go. I wanted to see Juan and find out how he had got on.

Opposite: Taken during our time in Tanzania, the vanilla orchid in flower

22 Real Vanilla: Nature's Unsung Hero

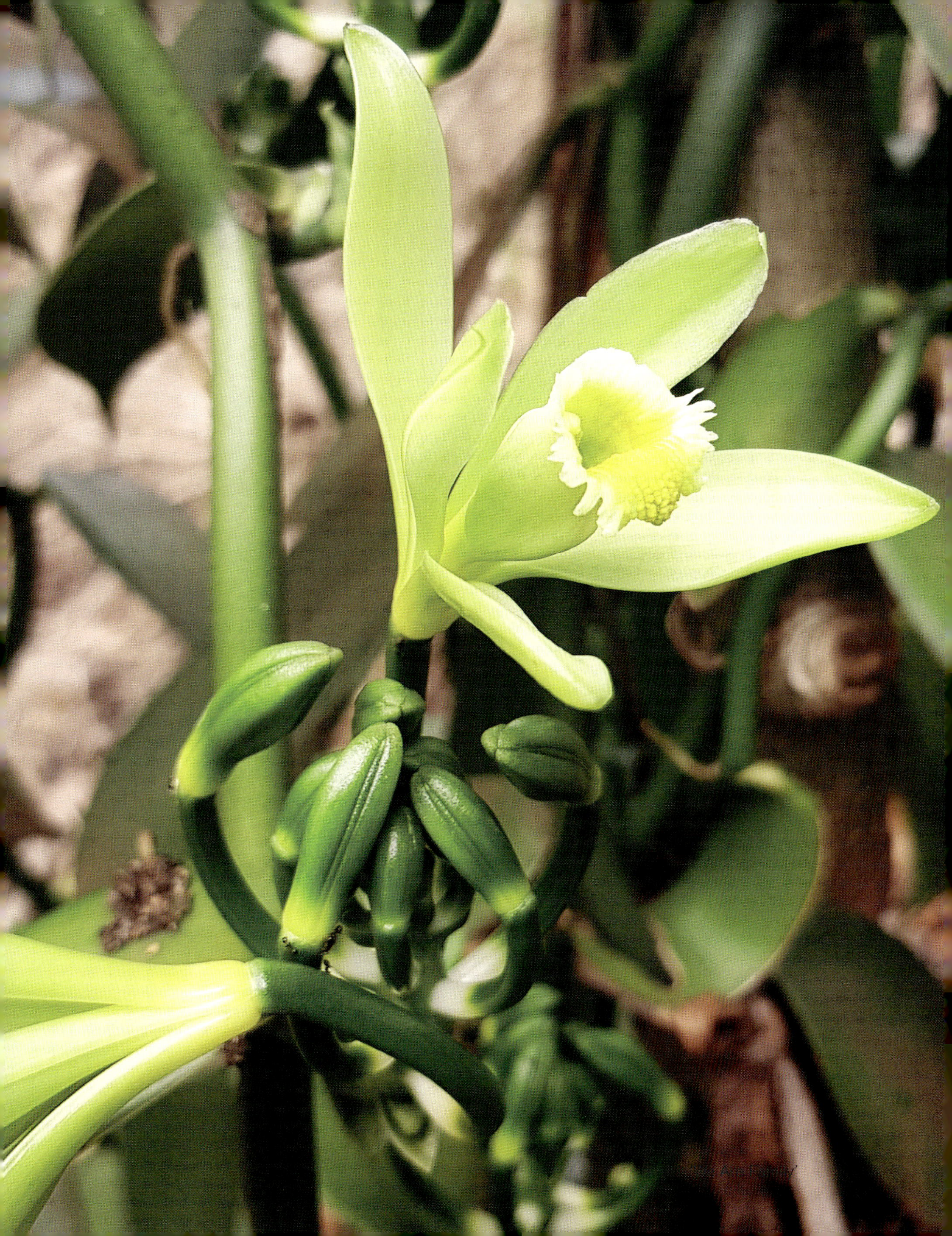

Some time after the conference, Paul, LittlePod's media manager, was keen to interview Juan to see what he recollected from then and the earlier time. He started by asking him about his involvement with vanilla. Juan told him, 'I started NEI (Natural Extracts Industries) at the end of 2011. The business model from the beginning was set up like a social enterprise, although legally that concept doesn't really exist in Tanzania. The purpose was to bring economic development to rural communities. The way to do that is to create shared values, to add value at the origin, and then share that by paying more, essentially. Vanilla just happened to be a coincidence, shall we say. It was a happy coincidence because vanilla has such a lot of positive environmental factors. It needs canopies, you need to protect the trees. It uses space that is not used by other crops because it's under the canopy and therefore needs other plants around it to thrive. That canopy creates soil moisture and improves soil health. It's naturally organic, you're not using fertilisers or chemicals to grow it. There is a lot of positive reinforcement that comes just from growing vanilla. If you grow it in the right way.'

'Did you grow it the right way?' Paul asked him.

'That has evolved in what we are doing today', Juan continued. 'This is more of an agroforestry practice, regenerating plots. Maybe there are plots of maize and corn that are so depleted that the farmers need to keep feeding them fertilisers, which are expensive. We're generating those plots with forest and putting vanilla under it and things like that. It has evolved like that from there. We started with about 30 farmers and now we are managing around 12,000 in our own network. It has grown laterally, with a huge geographic coverage.

'Unlike LittlePod, we're purely b2b (business-to-business). We work with the flavour houses and the food and beverage manufacturers. We don't work a lot on getting our brand out there. It's all about the product and the quality.'

'What kind of results have you seen?' Paul was eager to know.

'We have seen a lot of farmer transformations. We work directly with the farmers; there are no middlemen involved. It's a tight-knit community, a close relationship. We also work closely with many other stakeholders around here, with the government, the Bureau of Standards, the East African community, because vanilla is grown in multiple countries. We are on the technical committee.'

Paul was keen to know more about the infrastructure, and questioned Juan further. 'How do you define the framework, what standards should be used, what regulations should be in place for growing vanilla in the region?'

'There's a lot that we have done for vanilla in this corner of the world', Juan said. 'We have worked with many NGOs and donor organisations to try new things and benefit farmers. We did a large project on rainwater harvest capture, putting the water that lands on your roof into tanks for later use. We've done work with savings groups, self-help groups, women's empowerment, trying to employ more youth, so many different things. We do a lot and so much of our ethos is shared with LittlePod.'

'Is that why you have an affinity with Janet?' Paul enquired.

'We got to know each other well when Janet

came to Kilimanjaro for the vanilla conference we held in 2019. That was special. She got to see a little bit more of what we stood for. I remember Janet so well. We had a one-year-old at that time and she brought him a small gift. It was unexpected. It was a little wooden car carrier. We still have it around. It was sweet, special. It cemented what we stood for.

'That was when Janet met Irine, who is the daughter of one of our farmer champions. Together we decided to help her out. LittlePod financed Irine's studies, and we put the action on the ground to make sure that the money all went where it was supposed to go. Irine thrived. (*For the story of Irine and more about the Symposium, see Chapter 5.*) It's representative of the broader network and the work that we do. Corporates call it a supply chain. We call it family. Our farmer network, the people we work with. We see and feel their pain every day. We help where we can. We can't help every Irine out there, not with 12,000 farmers and their families, 60,000 people. But it shows what you can do when you really work closely with your stakeholders.'

Paul was struck: 'That was a special collaboration. The success of that project spurred Janet on to find ways in which LittlePod could be a useful voice, especially around education.'

'Yes', said Juan. 'Since that time, we've seen LittlePod do wonderful things. We've seen the awards they have achieved and heard about Made in Indonesia. It's all part of the same ethos – that we all must try to make the world a better place. At NEI we have a slogan. We say, "Developing a better world one flavour at a time."'

'Well, I am sure that Janet would endorse that', Paul concluded.

26   Real Vanilla: Nature's Unsung Hero

Later, when I read Paul's interview I could remember that visit as if I were still there. Meeting Juan again after almost a decade had been a joy. He now had his wonderful one-year-old son. I remember the gift I brought for Hugo, a set of little wooden cars. From our arrival at Kilimanjaro airport to the final safari this was to be ten unforgettable days.

To me, Juan had grown in stature. Was it because he had now become a father, or could it be because of the circumstances of living alongside people with whom he was sharing his daily life? Or could it be because of the responsibility he felt for having created this hope for a prosperous future? Perhaps all of that and more. I respect his integrity and can see that still glowing.

Working conditions for Juan are not easy. There is a lot to contend with. Permissions to gain from government officials, expectations of the farmers, having to use a generator that packs up regularly. But despite all those difficulties he organised the most brilliant symposium.

I had not attended the conference alone. Olly, LittlePod's CEO, had come with me. He was going to present a poster paper at the conference on the state of vanilla knowledge in the UK. It was an eye opener for both of us to meet vanilla farmers from across the globe, some of whom were planting vanilla for the first time. It was also great serendipity, because I was looking to work with a new vanilla supplier from Madagascar, as my friend Nash – Naushad – had decided to sell his company and retire *(please see chapter 10 to find out more)*. I had depended on him up to this point.

I did not want to go to Madagascar myself. I sponsored a local doctor in Exeter, Vik Mohan, who was a co-founder of the charity Blue Ventures in Madagascar that worked on women's health projects, including the vanilla-growing areas. From 2013, 10 per cent of our online sales were donated to Vik. He would go to Madagascar twice a year and send a report to us or take part in our International REAL Vanilla Day events *(more will be told about Vik and his time in Madagascar in Chapter 6)*. Now Vik has left Blue Ventures in Madagascar and is working with a charity called Planet Indonesia. This is very near to LittlePod's heart too. We continue to sponsor his efforts.

Vik is a very decent and humane individual who has given up much of his own life to improve life chances for others. When I think of him I am reminded of a line in a poem by Francis Thompson, which had resonated with me when I felt very selfishly down after my father's death: 'For we are born in other's pain, and perish in our own.' I have always tried to be proactive since then, which is why I admire and want to support people like Vik.

Opposite: Inspecting the vanilla vines in Tanzania in 2019

It was crucial that I meet a new vanilla supplier that I could trust.

I had tried to work with a young woman who had been to college in the UK and had returned to Madagascar with the intention of setting up her own vanilla business. She wanted to sell vanilla to the UK, where she had studied. It all went well for the first three orders. Then one day I had a telephone call from her to say that she was in hospital and could not fulfil the order, but that her brother, who was an engineer in Aberdeen, would help. Please would I place the money in the Western Credit Union for him? Every new business owner must suffer from naivety at some point along the way. Thank goodness I was stabbed wide awake early on. I followed through with her instructions and even spoke with her brother a few times on the phone before placing the money in the Credit Union. It was £800. The fraud squad told me later that I had got off lightly. Apparently, this type of scammer is willing to wait a couple of years until trust is built up and then they go for the big numbers! I felt sick to my stomach at the idea. I also felt sad, because I truly thought I was doing the best thing supporting a young woman start-up in Madagascar.

A few years later I bumped into a Malagasy lady who has her own vanilla company. We met up occasionally at trade shows. I asked her how she got on importing her vanilla from Madagascar. She told me 'They rip me off.' I was so shocked to hear this. 'They do this to you. In a way, I am so glad to hear this', I said, and told her of my experience and that I was sure it was because I was an outsider. She reassured me that it is simply how it is. They learnt their ways from the West, from the speculators who ripped them off. 'We live with the consequences of our actions', I say. 'Survival is the name of the game', she intoned.

Left: Catching up with Juan at the Vanilla Symposium in 2019
Right: Meeting Irine – the vanilla farmer's daughter

I was heartened when ten years later I received an official letter from the fraud squad to say that a US company who had gone after these criminals and caught them had taken the Western Union to court and that a cheque was enclosed to reimburse me for my loss. Karma, I thought.

From that experience I knew that I would have to find someone I could trust from whom I could purchase our Madagascan vanilla, and being here at the conference was the perfect opportunity to meet that person. Hurrah, we did, and that relationship is still as secure as it was six years ago.

It is so important to know your vanilla supplier. Theft is the greatest threat to vanilla. It is a high value commodity and therefore sorely fought after. There are gangs who organise young children to be let loose in the vanilla farms in the dead of night to fleece the crops. It is a dangerous activity for both sides, because farmers protect their crops with guns and patrol all night during the harvest season. If the bean pods are harvested too soon before the yellowing of the tip then they could easily suffer from mould. Picking early might get extra money, but later in the supply chain those pods will have to be discarded or they will ruin all the crop.

'We Are Family'

I know a gardener living near me in Devon who used to be a Royal Marine. He was stationed off Madagascar and Mozambique to patrol the pirate areas. Northern Madagascar supplies 80 per cent of the world's vanilla. There is a history of vanilla being moved from Papua New Guinea and Indonesia through Madagascar and sold as Madagascan for a better price. It is important to know if your supplier is registered. Madagascar has the reputation for producing the best vanilla. This is because the old colonial style companies who have been managing vanilla plantations there for over a century have invested in top of the range curing systems. The farmers are on a dollar a day, but during the boom periods in the vanilla industry a farmer can make enough money to send a child to school.

The problem is that Madagascar is still one of the poorest countries in the world. Nash explained to me that the farmers are able to earn the money, but that there is nothing for them to buy with it. He told me that he had seen farmers flaunting their wealth in the good times by rolling up dollar notes and smoking them. There are inherent environmental problems born out of climate change, and it is prone to frequent disasters due to its geographical location. Global warming has had a detrimental effect on the land, and cyclones are becoming increasingly common. El Niño used to take place roughly every ten years, but now it is happening almost every third year.

Children are still not protected from traffickers. It is rather like the county lines groups in the UK who use young people to distribute drugs. In Madagascar highwaymen will hold up the DHL lorries and other hauliers who are transporting commodities including vanilla from northern regions to the capital, Antananarivo, for shipping out. There is a lot of corruption. Monoculture is killing the earth.

There has long been a fight against poverty in Madagascar. Although only 3 per cent of Madagascan forests are left, it still has abundant natural resources and is recognised as one of the top five biodiversity hotspots worldwide. How was LittlePod going to get this message across to our customers?

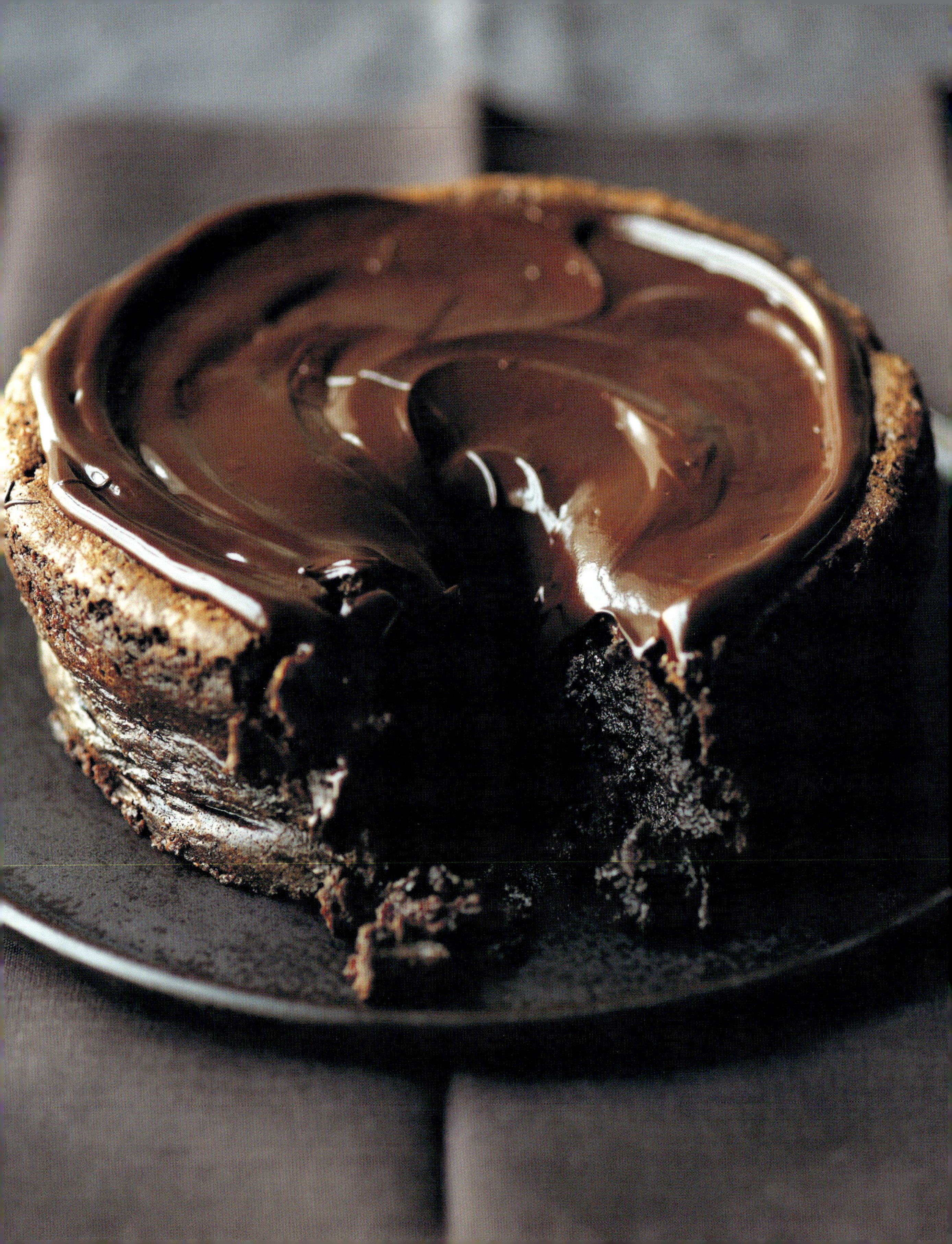

The year 2014 was LittlePod's fourth anniversary, and a local café called Bumble & Bee in Exmouth in East Devon agreed to host an event for National Real Vanilla Day. Liz, who was working with LittlePod at the time, collected members of a steel band that she belonged to called Street Heat who had played at carnivals all over the world, and they warmed up a cold October day. Joe, who also worked with LittlePod at the time, brought his wonderful travelling Fun Kitchen to do demonstrations in the park. We also had a group of parkour performers from Exeter who did a fabulous demonstration, even jumping over my head!

Hilary Bradt MBE had published a remarkable guide to Madagascar (then in its 11th edition), and took groups of intrepid eco tourists there. She had recently retired to East Devon, and I asked if she would give a talk about her travel company and the thirty-six tours that she had organised. Hilary told the audience how poor people are in Madagascar, and the everyday challenges they must deal with. She explained that vanilla is a high value commodity for them. She then regaled her audience with the diversity of life and the unusual animals that live there. I was tempted to go to Madagascar with her. She was about to do one final tour before retiring, but looking at my physique she suggested that it might be a bit challenging for me. I was disheartened not to see the flora and fauna of Madagascar, especially the ancient avenue of baobab trees.

Hilary was brilliant. I had met her at the Women's Institute's centenary celebrations in Harrogate the year before. I had been invited to give a talk there too. There was a hilarious moment when I was presenting the LittlePod products to these forthright ladies (ever since the former Prime Minister Tony Blair was slow handclapped by the ladies of the WI their reputation as a formidable audience has been legendary). I was demonstrating how to make the LittlePod signature cake, our Chocolate and Beetroot Fudge Cake that had been noted in Woman magazine as 'Fit for a Queen' during Queen Elizabeth II's Diamond Jubilee. I turned to put the cake in an oven which the show planners had mocked up. Unfortunately, the oven and the mocked-up wall had not been tied securely. I opened the door of the oven and as I pulled it towards me the whole wall came towards me too! It was almost a health and safety nightmare, but the ladies helped to push the wall, oven intact, upright again. I twizzled around to my audience and said, 'Ladies, I am proud to be here today to celebrate a hundred years with the Makers and Bakers, Movers and Shakers of the WI.' We all laughed, and I received a tumultuous applause as we all saved the day!

Opposite: LittlePod's signature Chocolate and Beetroot Fudge Cake

Illegal logging is causing a lot of environmental destruction in Madagascar. The hungry loggers are now hunting rare lemurs for food; in the markets peeled lemurs are for sale alongside eels and fruit bats. In 2023 the southern region suffered its first famine from climate change.

Approximately 4.7 million people, or 42 per cent of the population of Madagascar's southern, south-eastern and northern regions, will need humanitarian assistance in 2025 due to the lasting effects of past cyclones, an anticipated intense cyclone season, and a continuous high level of food insecurity.

The population has doubled since 1990, and the last thirty plus years have seen topsoil washed away in red rivers to the sea. Astronauts have seen Madagascar and described it as 'bleeding to death'.

There is so much raiding of resources: sapphires and the like are sold to unscrupulous dealers who get rich quick from these precious stones. Villages have no infrastructure, electricity, sanitation or running water. Huts are made up of sticks and rusty tins; most people only sleep in these makeshift homes, and spend the day outside.

I do not want to be a pampered tourist, knowing the conditions of so much of the population. Then again, people like Hilary add to the economy. It really requires a balance of the right kind.

If only the world would buy REAL vanilla and move away from synthetic vanillin, then people in Madagascar would have a high value commodity to sell and a chance to determine their own livelihoods. It should give the vanilla farmers, who are mainly women, a higher wage, full-time education for the children, and freedom from controlling monopolies. If the world turns away because they don't want to see the problems, then we will all suffer. A sustained economic growth for vanilla would mean less destruction of the rainforest.

It is not a case of donating money. It is a case of trade. Proper trading laws and proper transparency would enable Madagascar and other countries to sell to the West and grow their economies, and eco-tourism would be more attractive. One big problem is food insecurity. However, if it is more cost-effective to chop down the forests and grow foods that wreck the earth, but the West will buy, then that is what will happen.

In 2018 LittlePod was given a substantial accolade. I was invited to the Foreign Office in London to receive the Board of Trade Award in recognition of LittlePod's outstanding contribution to international trade and investment. Olly and I were featured on the side of a bus that toured the country with the message 'If we can, you can'. We had agreed to be used as an example of a small company that had been trading abroad since 2010. My daughter saw me on the screen in the lounge at Belfast airport and was amazed.

I was so heartened when I heard the Rt Hon. Dr Liam Fox MP (Secretary of State for International Trade and President of the Board of Trade) who was presenting the awards say that he felt that the way to help third world economies is to trade with them. I wholeheartedly agree. He was an excellent ambassador for the UK in that role, and I was very sad that he was unceremoniously denied the job after the change of prime ministers in 2019.

I was also invited to attend a fantastic banquet held at the Mansion House which Liam Fox's department organised. There were seven hundred guests, mostly representing businesses from the UK but also from China, and the then-Director General of the World Trade Organization, Roberto Azevêdo. It was an evening in which businesses were gathered and made to feel part of the new trade strategy and the new phase of world trade.

I sat next to the owner of a food machinery manufacturing company. I was able to ask him about the new automated machine we had ordered from Italy. He knew the company and the bespoke service they offered and was able to reassure me that I had negotiated a fair price. We worked with a UK company called Adelphi whose engineers were overseeing the process. On the opposite side of my table there was a UK company that designs space rockets and another company that had developed new security technology. That evening had all the hallmarks of a new era of growth and prosperity. Sadly, it was a mirage. I think part of the problem with commerce and trade is that these types of industries are often looked down on. If we are to attract young people into the manufacturing industries and trading generally then those realms have to be seen to be valued. Somehow trade is not thought of as a desirable occupation. And yet in all surveys when people are asked if they fancy running their own company a huge percentage say it is their dream. Well, dreams can be realised.

36 Real Vanilla: Nature's Unsung Hero

I started LittlePod in the 'empty nest' stage of my life. I was fifty-seven. I started with a £10,000 overdraft facility and a promise to set up a Campaign for Real Vanilla. I enlisted the help of graduates who were looking for their first work position, very often not really knowing what they wanted to do in their professional lives. LittlePod gave them their first landing post. I gave them apprenticeships, experience and guidance. They in turn became environmentalists, enthusiastic, computer and media savvy, and loyal LittlePodders.

In the early days of LittlePod my first two interns were Tom, who now has his own studio in London, and Aisha, who later left LittlePod to work for Unilever. Tom had just left university and was looking to become a copywriter. He came over for a cup of tea one day and I told him about my intention to set up my own company. He asked what it would be called.

I had no answer, and said 'Tom, if you can come up with a name and rationale for my company, I will take you through the branding process with Red Rocket, the company I am working with on my branding. It will give you the opportunity to work with an agency.' Tom came back the following week with the name 'LittlePod', and got his first agency experience. His second agency experience was to go to Tanzania to work with the Masai on their new branded secret product. LittlePod always finds a connection.

As each team left a new team came aboard, very often helped to bed in by the outgoing team. I thank them all for their service to LittlePod; I love to hear from them, and I keep them safe in my thoughts.

Opposite: LittlePod's innovative natural vanilla paste in a tube – a little squeeze goes a long way!

My father dropped down dead at fifty (just after his birthday). My mother was dead by fifty. I realised that I was in the vanguard of women who could think about a life post-motherhood in a way that my own mother would not have envisaged. I talked with my friends who told me that they could not summon the energy. They were looking forward to a well-deserved retirement, and they would ask me, 'Where do you get your energy from?' I want to share something with young women who are experiencing peri-menopausal symptoms and feeling that they have no energy left. There is such a thing as post-menopausal zest! I strongly recommend a book called *Beat the Menopause* by Linda Cairns. I made her hormone cake every week and the whole family ate it!

We consumers have far more power than we think we have. The well-earned pound in our pocket is avariciously fought over in the boardrooms of multinationals every day. They are the Goliaths. Companies like LittlePod are the Davids. All businesses were once Davids, I suppose. Davids can succeed in the world of business, but only if they have loyal and trusty customers. In the case of LittlePod we have the support of LittlePodders who love to know about the provenance of their food, who love to produce quality tastes, who want to support the growers and farmers, and who want to be part of our Campaign for Real Vanilla.

When people say 'No, we don't want to purchase stolen vanilla or artificial vanillin' then there is a chance that this opaque industry will no longer be secret. I read an article recently in the Guardian newspaper about Colombia now growing vanilla. This is great news. The more countries that start growing vanilla the better for the environment, and vanilla will eventually be available at a consistent price. However, a ridiculous economic statistic was quoted about the vanilla industry: it said that the industry is 10x that of the chocolate industry, whereas in truth vanilla is 10x smaller than the chocolate industry. With random numbers being bandied about, what are people to believe? Price volatility, insufficient traceability, high prices with low quality, and general concerns about social issues like poverty and child labour have created a sense of urgency for the industry. Origin and authenticity issues are a problem. Economically motivated adulteration, early harvesting and mislabelling are big problems too.

There is hope that the new blockchain technologies will be able to solve some of these difficulties. The real problem is the length of time it takes to produce a vanilla pod. It has always been a boom-and-bust industry. The farmers only plant when the price is high, and the price is always fluctuating. There was a gap in the market for a new product that could offer price stability for chefs and consumers while not compromising on quality. LittlePod had an idea.

When people say 'No, we don't want to purchase stolen vanilla or artificial vanillin' then there is a chance that this opaque industry will no longer be secret.

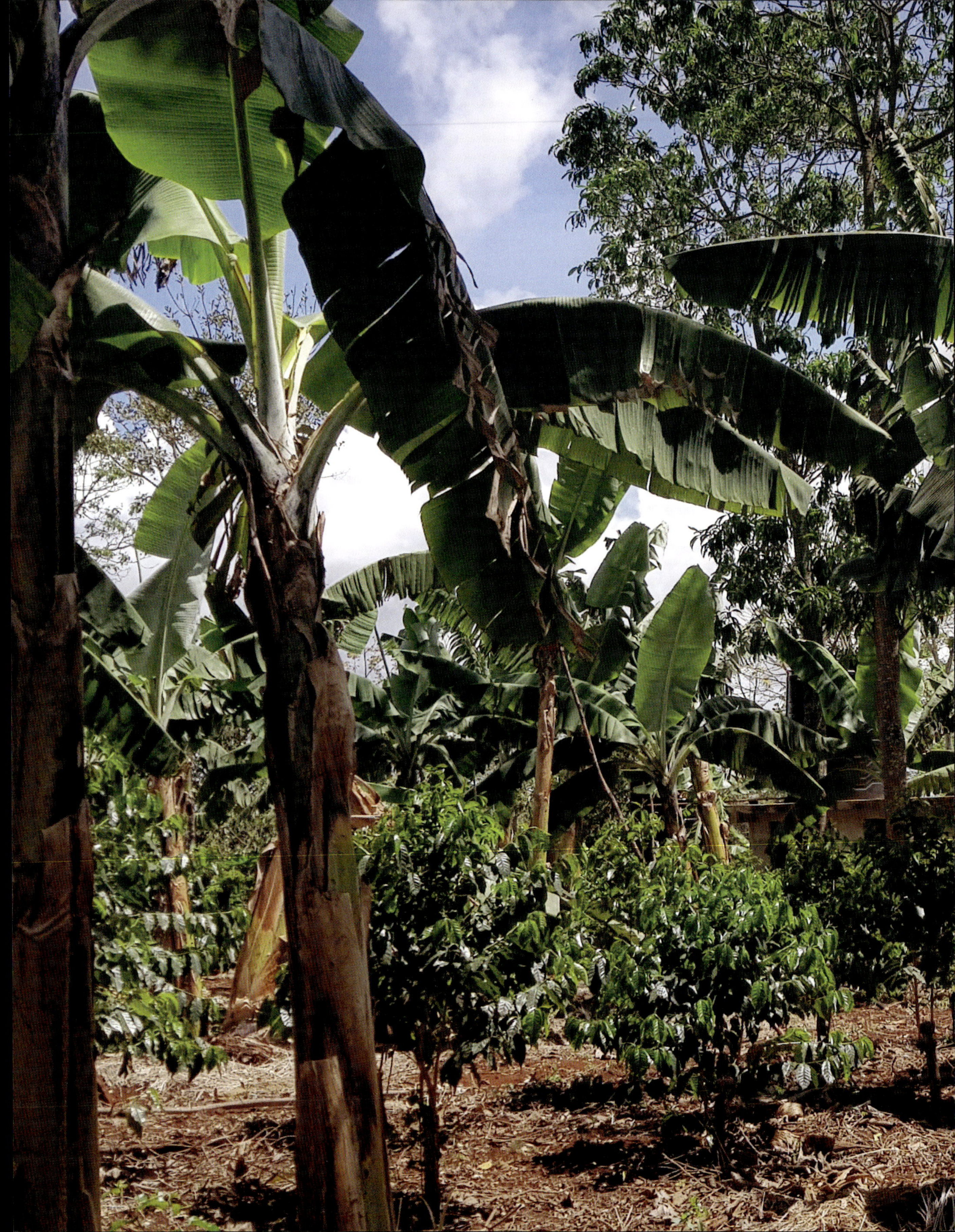

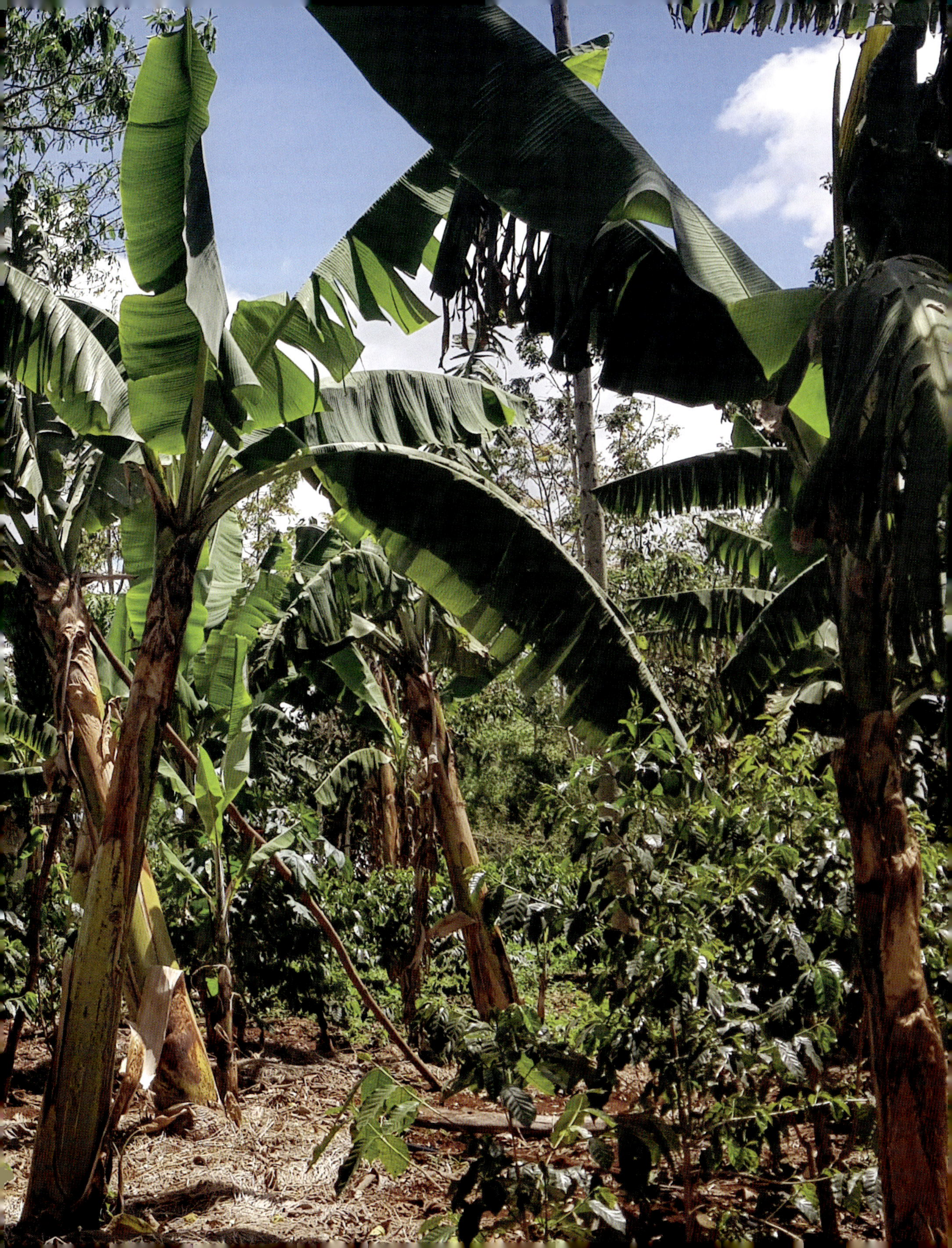

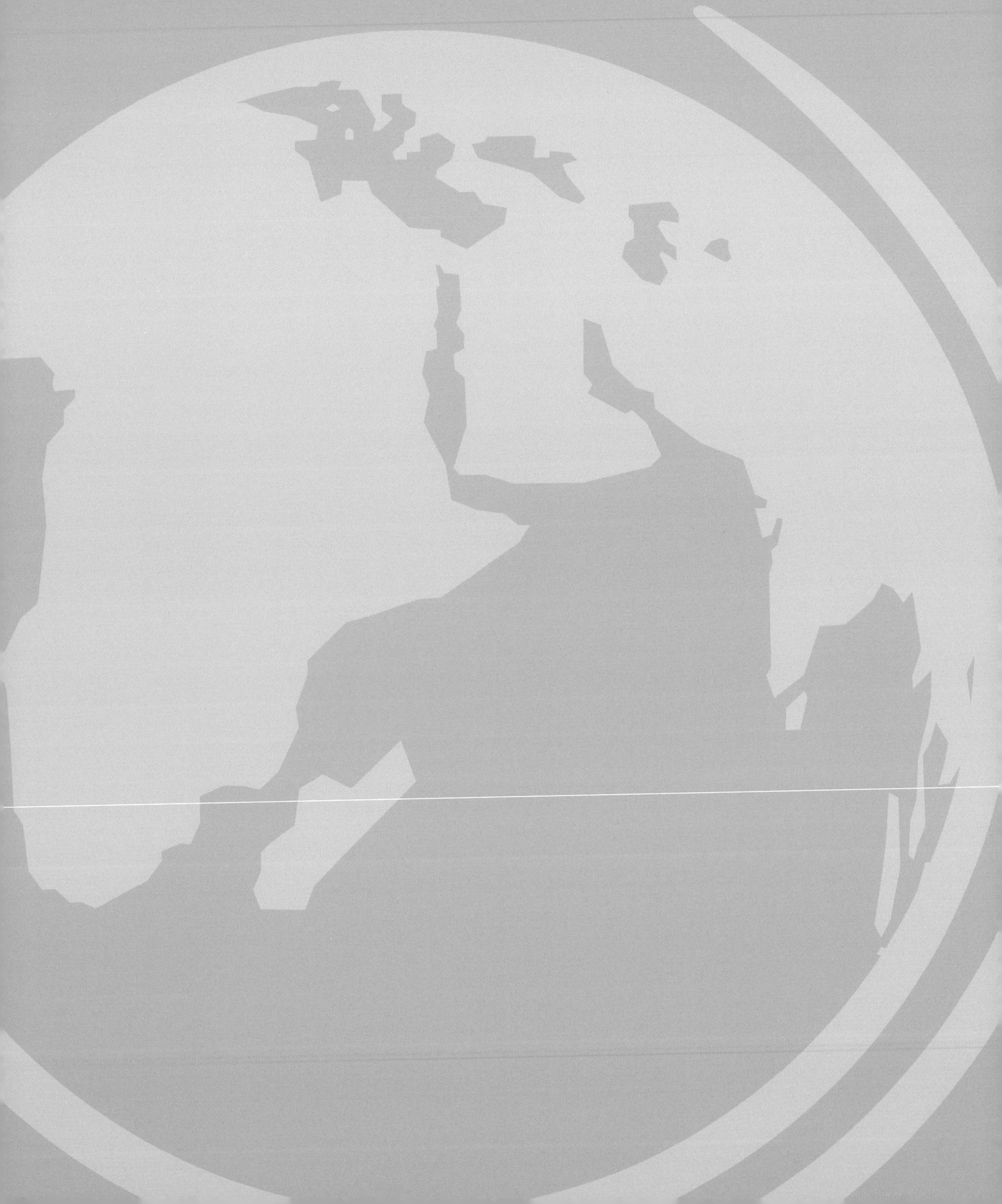

03
Education and the Environment

'Where are you, Janet?' Syiraz is calling me back from my ruminations. I have wandered off in the Bali forest looking at my feet.

Syiraz, a tall, quietly spoken young man, doesn't want me to get lost. I think this is why walking in woodlands, forests, mountains, nature generally, is so good for our mental health. We get to switch off or have a chance to self-indulge in nostalgic memories or to rant to ourselves about injustices.

I remember years ago when I was teaching in a multicultural school near the old Arsenal stadium in North London, I had a little boy in my class called Sam. He was regularly late for school and lived in his own time zone. He wrote what I thought was a poetically descriptive piece, almost a haiku, on the subject of getting lost. This was his story: 'When I walk down the streets in London, I look at my feet. Once, I got lost when I done that.' So many of us can relate to that experience.

'I am still here', I cry back to Syiraz, who is beckoning me to follow him. 'What are you thinking about?' he asks when we catch up.

Syiraz is watching me. I can see him from the corner of my eye. He must think me very strange walking through this forest orchard looking intently at the ground. 'What are you looking for?' his eyes imply.

'Syiraz,' I say, 'I am looking for slime mould. I listen to a radio programme called *In Our Time* presented by a man called Melvyn Bragg. There was an episode that I found totally fascinating. He was interviewing scientists and botanists about slime moulds, which are single-celled organisms that move like amoebas and are found in decaying wood, leaf litter and soil.

'They are the cleaners of the woodlands. They engulf bacteria and organic matter. They are thought to be an example of proto intelligent life, although they do not have a brain, and are very clever especially when they create colonies. At that point they can be seen along a log and can be colourful. They have amazing names such as dog sick slime mould, dog vomit slime, wolf's milk slime and scrambled egg slime!

'Apparently, they are used to help find a way out of mazes or the quickest way to navigate somewhere such as the underground systems. They remember information to navigate the quickest route. They can mimic transportation networks and can choose the healthiest food from a diverse menu. They are used in laboratories to solve complex spatial problems – extraordinary.'

'Yes', replied Syiraz. 'You can see slime mould as it oozes along the forest floor or scales up trees. They are colourful when there is a mass of them. You find slime mould and nematodes that break down the forest floor. They break down decomposing material in the soil which releases nutrients.'

We only have around 70 years' supply of topsoil left. Nearly a quarter of the world's most fertile soil, known as chernozem, is to be found in Ukraine. It takes around 500 years to produce one inch of this type of soil.

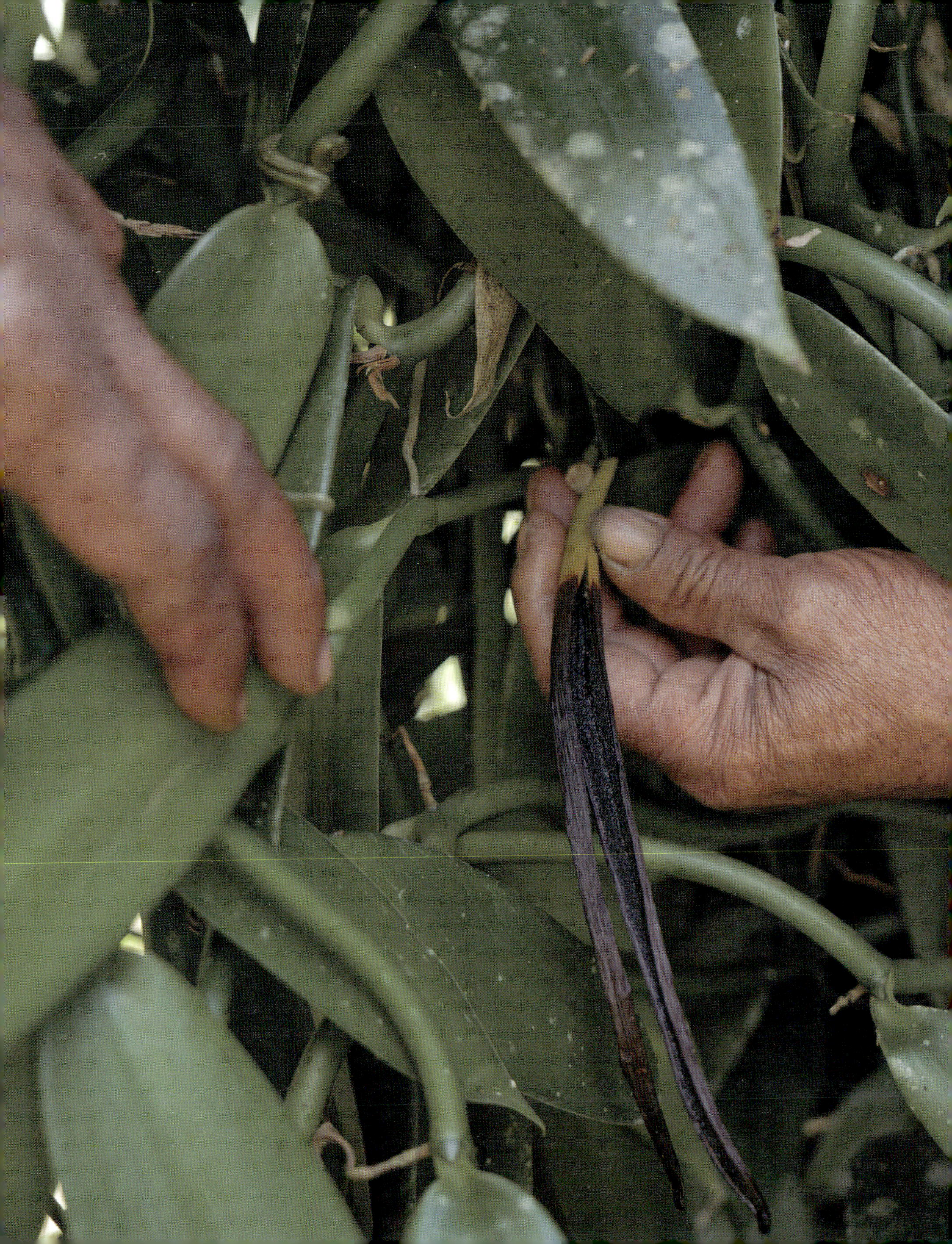

'Gosh, I feel so ignorant, Syiraz,' I say. 'There is so much to learn about healthy soil and soil is so important. If I were in a primary school today, I would certainly be doing a project on soil diversity. We all live on around 12 inches of soil. We grow all our food and gain our nutrients from the quality of soil. However, our soil is dying at a fast rate. Over 80 per cent of the insect biomass has gone, and that's in the last thirty years! If we lose 50 per cent of the remaining bio-organisms we will not be able to revive the soil.

'We must act NOW. Everyone must compost and make soil. We must not use insecticides or chemicals. Monoculture has used soil up thinking it's an infinite resource. But it is not. We need to top it up with organic matter.'

Syiraz tells me that the vanilla orchid is a CAM – a crassulacean acid metabolism synthesiser. CAM plants open their stomata at night. They store the CO_2 in the daytime and release oxygen at night.

I say that the word 'vanilla' is used liberally in the West to mean 'bland and ordinary'. Syiraz looks shocked. 'But it is not ordinary', he says; 'the vanilla orchid is very special. The farmers fall in love with vanilla.'

'This is noted in Tanzania too,' I say, 'where Juan has seen the same love of vanilla. Dr Made says that they get attached to it. It is very good for agroforestry. It aids forest ecosystems to thrive and provides a high-income livelihood for the farmers. It is the second most expensive product on the market after saffron.'

I continue, 'As a child, our garden was given over to planting vegetables. I remember that my parents used to do what is now called companion planting. I remember the marigolds dotted up and down the veg patch. Was that to keep the predators out of the garden?' 'Absolutely', says Syiraz. 'Your parents were doing things properly. They also improve soil health and attract the pollinators. Your parents were probably following the guidance they received from their parents to keep the nematodes in balance.'

'I am a fan of a Scottish writer called George MacDonald', I tell Syiraz. 'He was a nineteenth-century author of fairy stories. He said, "What does it mean to know the name of a thing whose nature one does not know?" I think about my growing-up years in rural Lincolnshire and the natural way my parents lived, in some ways not dissimilar to the farmers here. They knew the nature of things and the names did not matter.

'I did not see a plastic bag until I was around sixteen years old. Up until then when you shopped you took your basket (with some newspaper at the bottom) and items were weighed on old-fashioned scales with brass weights and then popped straight into the basket.

'Once a week at primary school the teacher would take us out as a class on a nature walk. It was a small farming village after all. We would always pass and say hello to Old Captain, the big oak tree where we all gathered to play

Opposite: Checking the crop at the LittlePod orchard

'The vanilla orchid is very special. The farmers fall in love with vanilla.'

Education and the Environment 47

Left: Dr Made
Right: Made 2 at the LittlePod orchard

sometimes. We have an old oak outside our house now at home. It must be about 350 years old, in its prime!'

Now all the interns were here, I explained about Juan. I said he was like Dr Made here in Bali. Before I started my story I answered their questions. It was inevitable that talking about vanilla in Tanzania would arouse their curiosity.

'Well,' I tell them when asked about conditions in Tanzania, 'Juan says that Kilimanjaro is special in lots of ways. He says there's a tradition there of intercropping to a certain extent, or at least of doing integrated farming management not unlike what you have been experimenting with the polyculture planting methods here.'

I tell the story from Juan's perspective. As Juan later told Paul, 'It means you raise the cows for the milk and use the manure for the farm and you try to be organic and plant a variety of things, some of which you eat, some of which you sell. It's a bit of a mishmash but it works. So vanilla works well with those kinds of practices. There are plots of land that we have helped to reforest and regenerate. We learn from them, and they learn from us. Vanilla is a new income stream. It wasn't around before we started doing this. We introduced it to the farmers here. Someone had introduced vanilla here maybe ten or twelve years before us, but it had failed. It was at the time of the previous boom and bust. Whoever was promoting it then never came back. They just left the farmers to their own devices, which was a bit of a disaster. It took a while to convince the farmers to start planting vanilla en masse. I used to go to churches and mosques to "evangelise"

48 Real Vanilla: Nature's Unsung Hero

about vanilla. That's what we called it. We would set up after mass and talk to the population. There was a lot of work to do to convince them.'

Syiraz and the interns are captivated by the story of the Tanzanian farmers. I tell them that just like LittlePod, Juan's company feels that it is crucial to support the farmers. Just like the LittlePod farmers here in Bali, they want to know that the buyer is real. Who is the buyer? They have had their fingers burnt by speculators purchasing once and leaving them high and dry when things got difficult. As the farmers said to Juan, 'A banana, you can sell locally, right? But other types of crops, like vanilla, is different. You need to know that somebody is going to buy it.'

Juan told Paul, 'Showing your face helps. However, it is a leap of faith for the farmers. They don't even see the product. We're the processor, they don't even know how it tastes or what it looks like or how it is used. Sometimes we have taken some end products – cookies or cakes or chocolates that use our vanilla – back to the farmers. They are delighted. But one of the reasons we are the processor (when we started, we wanted the farmers to be the processors) is because the farmers don't have a concept of the end product, how it tastes, the level of quality, the level of consistency that's needed. We couldn't rely on them. We had to do it ourselves. You must be able to imagine the end user, the ultimate high-end gourmet chef. It's a very different context that's needed to make it succeed.'

I say to the interns, 'I am sure you will be able to relate to what Juan said next.' 'When the prices were high, the farmers used to call it the Green Tanzanite. Tanzanite is a precious mineral in Tanzania. Because vanilla grows green, they called it this. It's maybe not quite as special to the farmers here as it is to the LittlePod farmers in Bali, because they haven't grown up with it, they're first-generation vanilla farmers. But it's special in that it's a valuable source of income for them. They're essentially calling it money, right? Instead of the Greenback, it's the Green Tanzanite. But because you spend so much time with it, the farmers do get attached to it. Vanilla is one of those crops that you measure the intensity of with the number of times that you touch the plant over the course of a year. The closest thing that we know is coffee, which you maybe touch four times a year. Maize, corn, you plant it in the ground as a seed and then you go and cut it down. That's it. Vanilla, you must manipulate by hand, maybe twice a month or more. It's highly intensive in that way.

'You can't grow thousands of vanilla vines without being hands on. That level of interaction with the plant makes it feel like something that you're close to.'

Education and the Environment

Juan continues, 'Vanilla is special for many reasons. The flavour. The scent. The aroma. It's very evocative. It brings back memories. It's very complex, like a wine. It's in food that my family enjoys. That's special. The way that it grows is special and the way that it encourages agroforestry and preservation, providing that it's done right. It often isn't the case in Madagascar, where it can cause deforestation. But in the way in which the farmers have benefited from it also, that's special. Scientifically, it's a very interesting crop. I call it the Russian doll of crops.

'There's this never-ending journey to understand it and make better use of it. From that one vanilla stick, we've made two dozen products and by-products and derivatives. So many things that come from it. On many different levels there's something special about this crop.

'People enjoy the flavour too, right? In the end, you're not making a lead acid battery. You're making something that people consume and enjoy. We enjoy growing it and consuming it also. There's a nice story I tell.

'One of our processing sites where we dry the vanilla is next to a hospital. The doctors tell me that the patients are happiest when we're drying the vanilla. There's a visible improvement in everybody's mood. This might not be backed by science, but even anecdotally...

'Once someone sees their neighbour succeeding it's a lot easier to believe in these methods. It's the usual adoption curve. You get a few early adopters and people follow. You see it, you believe it and then you start doing it. But it takes time, five years for the first harvest. You must be patient. There are always people looking to make money, to make a living. The landholding itself in its entirety for a plot is a few acres, one to three acres. Where they grow the vanilla might be a quarter of an acre. They're growing all kinds of fruits, spice trees, bananas, mango, jackfruit, breadfruit. But also ground crops like beans and sunflowers.

'Challenges come from everywhere, but from what we've seen, not now, when the prices are at their lowest, but when the prices are at an average level, the farmers are making a good portion of GDP per capita from vanilla alone. It really is a substantial win. They must be dedicated and committed to it.

'Challenges can come from the climate; we haven't had many diseases with the vanilla, but we've seen the crops around the vanilla get diseases, which can be challenging. Farms decimated and the vanilla suffers because the canopy is gone.

'The support trees are gone. Then there's the market risk, with the pricing and theft, thieves can always come around, usually it's family, by the way, which makes it hard to chase. All kinds of things, there's a lot that can go wrong. For a small farmer there are so many things.

'You're always on the edge. So, you need to diversify as much as possible. That's one of the benefits of vanilla. It's amazing how much they go through to get by, and we're not even dealing with very poor farmers. We're dealing with quite smart business farmers. They know what they're doing. Madagascar has very, very poor farmers. The cocoa farmers in West Africa are very poor; they hardly have a roof over their head. Our farmers have cement houses. It's different. It's much more developed here than in other areas. But still, they

'Vanilla is special for many reasons. The flavour. The scent. The aroma. It's very evocative. It brings back memories. It's very complex, like a wine. It's in food that my family enjoys. That's special. The way that it grows is special and the way that it encourages agroforestry and preservation, providing that it's done right.'

go through ups and down quite regularly.'

Syiraz and the interns are absolutely fascinated to hear what Juan has to say about growing vanilla in Tanzania. It is music to their ears, and they want to hear more.

'We advise on farming as a business. The idea that you must keep good records and know what you're making profits from. You must know where you're spending your cash and what's going to be a good investment. We don't try to manage their lives, but we try to support them as best we can.

'It's quite sad that in terms of a lot of different foods, there is a lack of knowledge and understanding. It's not just vanilla. Consumers around the world have so little understanding of what goes into this and the impact that their choices have. It's asking a lot – everyone has their own problems and concerns, we can't be worried about everything all the time, that would just make us crazy. It would be nice if there was a way for people to be reassured that the choice that they're making is actually doing good for people and the planet.

'Unfortunately, things like Fairtrade are almost meaningless. If you look at what happens, you can show a record of paying the farmer more. But what you don't see is that the farmer has to spend more to get that Fairtrade certification. In their pocket, they're not better off. For me it's less about the consumer being educated and more about companies like LittlePod putting out products that they know are good. Because in the end, we can't all have a piece of the consumers' minds. It's impossible and we shouldn't expect

Top: Putu, one of the LittlePod farmers in Indonesia
Middle: Made 2 and Putu sorting their vanilla pods
Bottom: Irine's family's garden in Tanzania

that as producers.

'We need to work on eco-systems and value chains where everyone knows the deal and can do the right thing. If you put out a good product to a customer at a good price point, they will buy it.

'What I said when I set up the company was that if I can affect 100,000 farmers and there's 1,000 or 10,000 of me or this type of company, then we've got it covered, right? I'm not relying on changing consumers' minds; I'm on the other side. Making sure that I can compete by doing well and by doing good.

'It takes companies like LittlePod and NEI (Natural Extracts Industries, Juan's company) to do the right thing, to start making a change. There's no silver bullet that will make everything better. So, we each need to do our part at every step of the value chain. I do believe in the work that LittlePod does and the values that they put across and how they source right and how they work and treat their people and their suppliers. That is all critical. For me, I'd rather work with LittlePod than with the commodities trader that just wants the cheapest price they can get and just doesn't care about what happens further down the chain. They can put out a good story, it's easy to spin a story, or a product that's cheap and cheerful and that will get the consumer to buy. I'd rather not work with those people.

'I always thought that if we did well enough with this and built a big enough network it would be easier to go into different things. Different crops, cocoa projects for chocolate makers, we're doing a lot more research and development on flavours from East Africa. The concept evolves from creating shared value, giving the farmer more for a single product, and eventually doing it so that the value of their land is much greater than what it would be to deforest it and build houses on it. Trying to find all the different ways to create value from whatever is growing on that land. You must value nature otherwise it's not worth keeping, in the most capitalist sense. That's where we're heading, giving irreplaceable value to nature and to the land.'

Syiraz interrupts: 'Tanzania is a large country, a savannah which is vast. I suppose the difference here in Bali is that we are more intimately involved in what we produce. We know the process from the beginning to the end. We are a smaller island.'

'This is true,' I say, 'which is why this polyculture planting has proved so successful here. It is important though that if vanilla is to be saved to encourage the regeneration of the rainforest, then other places must look to planting vanilla for the future. The value of vanilla is not just as a food source but by its very nature it is of real value to the biodiversity of the rainforest. The real threat to vanilla is the artificial alternative and that the consumer in the West does not know the difference.'

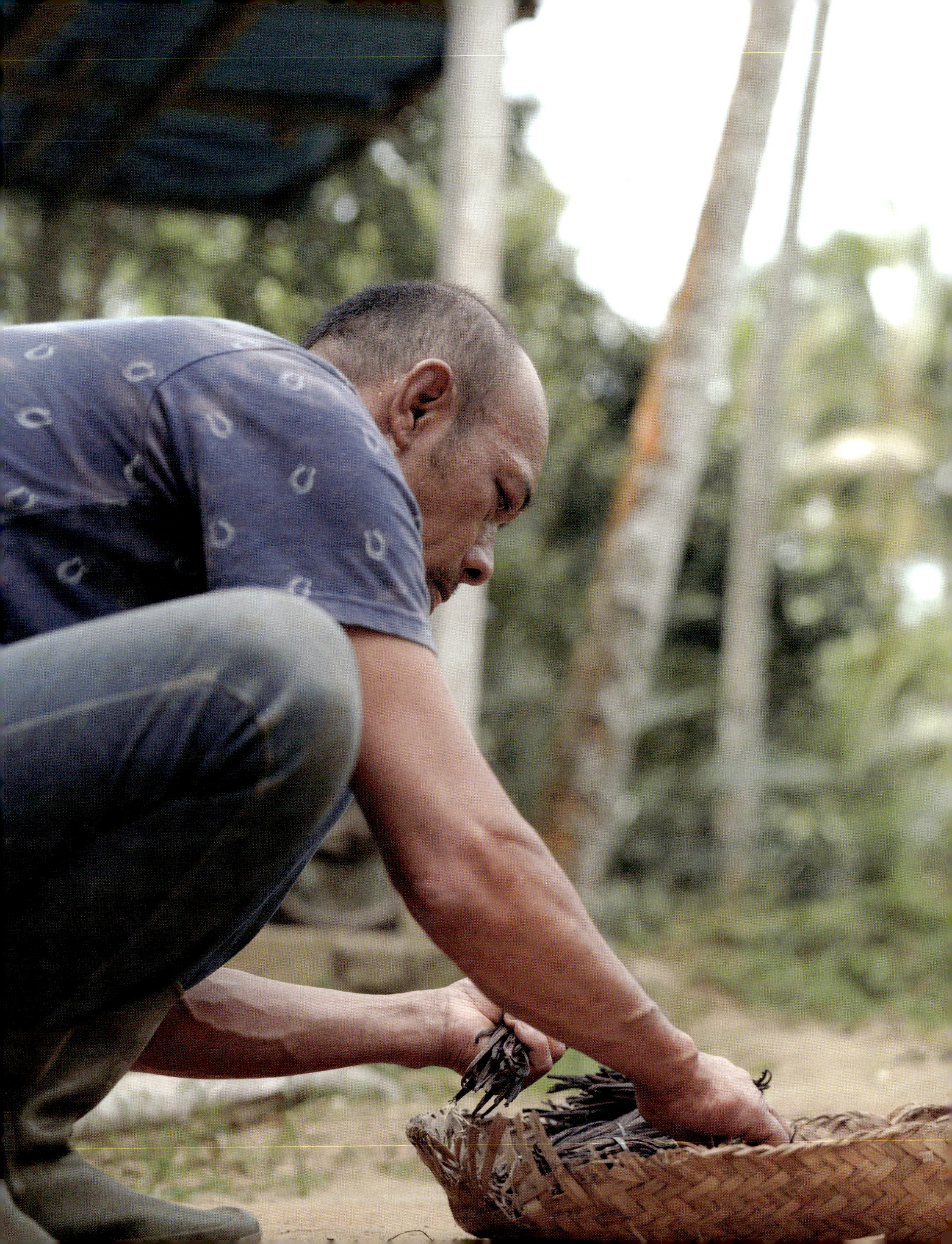

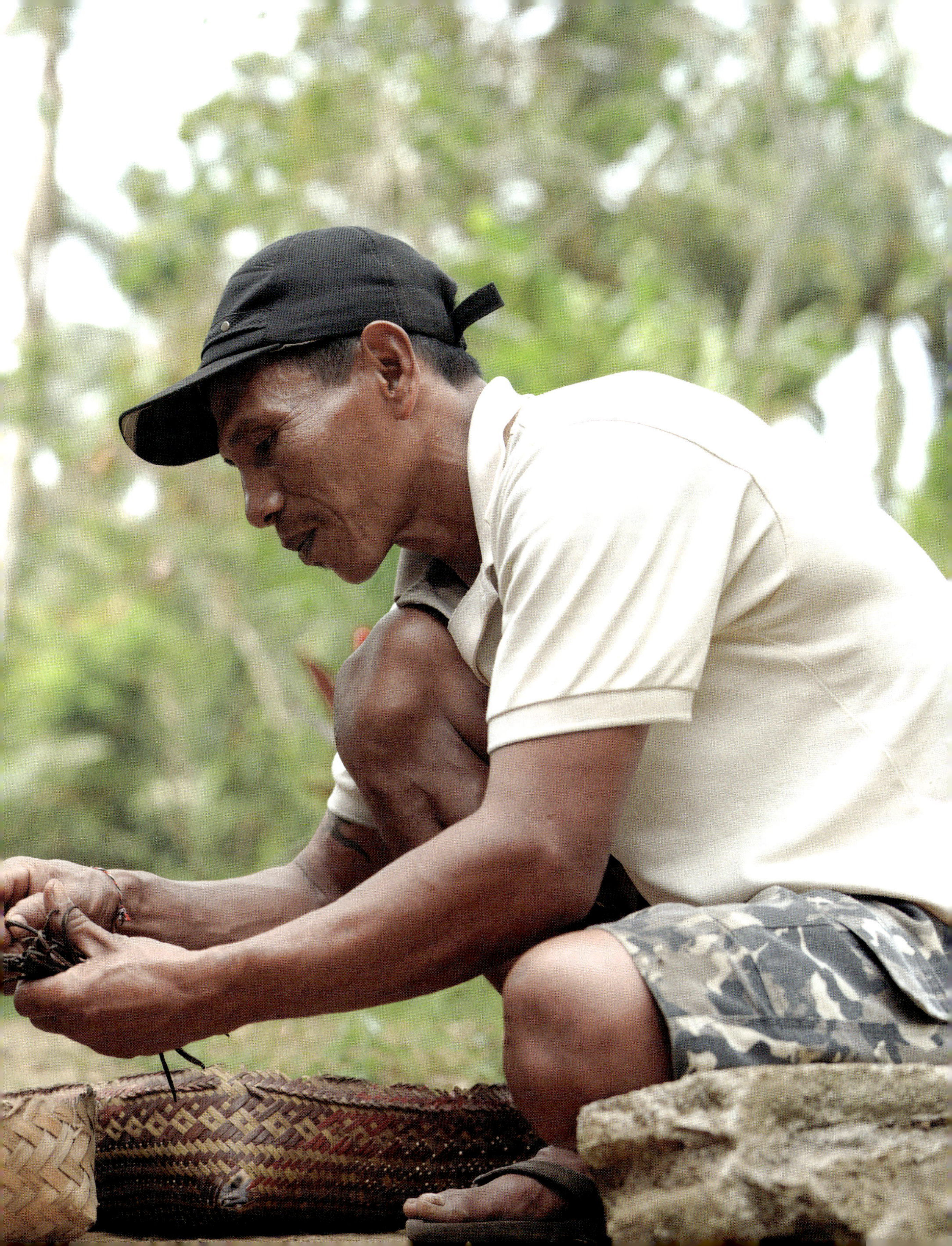

04
The Future of Farming – Dr Made's Protégé

Syiraz is the protégé of Dr Made. He has been to university, and is married with a young daughter. He is part of a generation of young people in Indonesia who are environmentally aware and determined to make a difference for their children's generation.

Speaking to Syiraz, I comment on going to conferences and tell him about my friend Will, who attends the COP conferences. I say, 'I would find those conferences very tedious and hard to bear. How about you?' He replies, 'I think that I would like to go and hear what people have to say. At least people are meeting up. Perhaps it is in the moments between sessions that people meet, and things get done.'

Syiraz tells me that he has been working with Dr Made on a project for his university dissertation. I ask him if it has been published. 'Not yet', he says.

'Would you be prepared for me to share your paper with people, Syiraz?

'Of course. Here is the summary of my report', he says. 'It is *Vanilla: A Bridge Between Conservation and Regenerative Agriculture*, by Muhammad Syirazi, Department of Natural Resources and the Environment at the College of Agriculture and Life Sciences (CALS) of Cornell University.'

Vanilla is more than just a high-value crop – it represents a pathway toward regenerative agriculture and forest restoration. In tropical regions like Indonesia, where deforestation threatens biodiversity and soil degradation reduces productivity, vanilla cultivation in agroforestry systems offers a nature-based solution that integrates economic opportunity with ecological renewal. Unlike monoculture farming, vanilla thrives under canopy cover, making it ideal for forest-integrated agricultural practices. However, despite its potential, the role of vanilla in ecosystem services and community-based conservation remains underexplored. Indonesia faces widespread land degradation and extractive agricultural practices. Conventional farming often relies on chemical-intensive monocultures, leading to soil depletion, biodiversity loss, and increased vulnerability to climate change. While agroforestry provides an alternative, its full potential – particularly vanilla's role in enhancing soil health, supporting biodiversity, and fostering resilient farmer livelihoods – remains insufficiently recognised. From my experience working with forest farmers in Bali, I have witnessed how integrating vanilla into agroforestry systems can create stronger ecosystems and greater economic stability for communities. However, scaling up these practices requires deeper research, policy support, and stronger market incentives.

Our work in Bali, in collaboration with forest farmer communities, focuses on integrating vanilla into agroforestry landscapes to enhance conservation, ecological restoration, and economic resilience. Research on these systems confirms several key benefits.

Key benefits of vanilla farming:

1. Soil Health and Microbial Activity: Rustic agroforestry system where vanilla grows under native forest trees demonstrates higher organic carbon content, phosphorus levels, and microbial diversity compared to polyculture farms that clear natural tree cover (Chavez et al., 2024).

2. Biodiversity Support: Canopy cover and diverse crop integration enhance soil stability, reduce erosion, and create microhabitats for pollinators and other beneficial species (Jose, 2009; Schoeneberger, 2009).

3. Regenerative Livelihoods: By cultivating vanilla alongside cacao, coffee and durian, farmers diversify their income sources while reducing reliance on chemical inputs. This makes farming both more profitable and ecologically restorative.

4. Climate Adaptation: Agroforestry systems store more carbon, regulate local temperatures, and buffer against extreme weather events, making them essential tools for climate resilience.

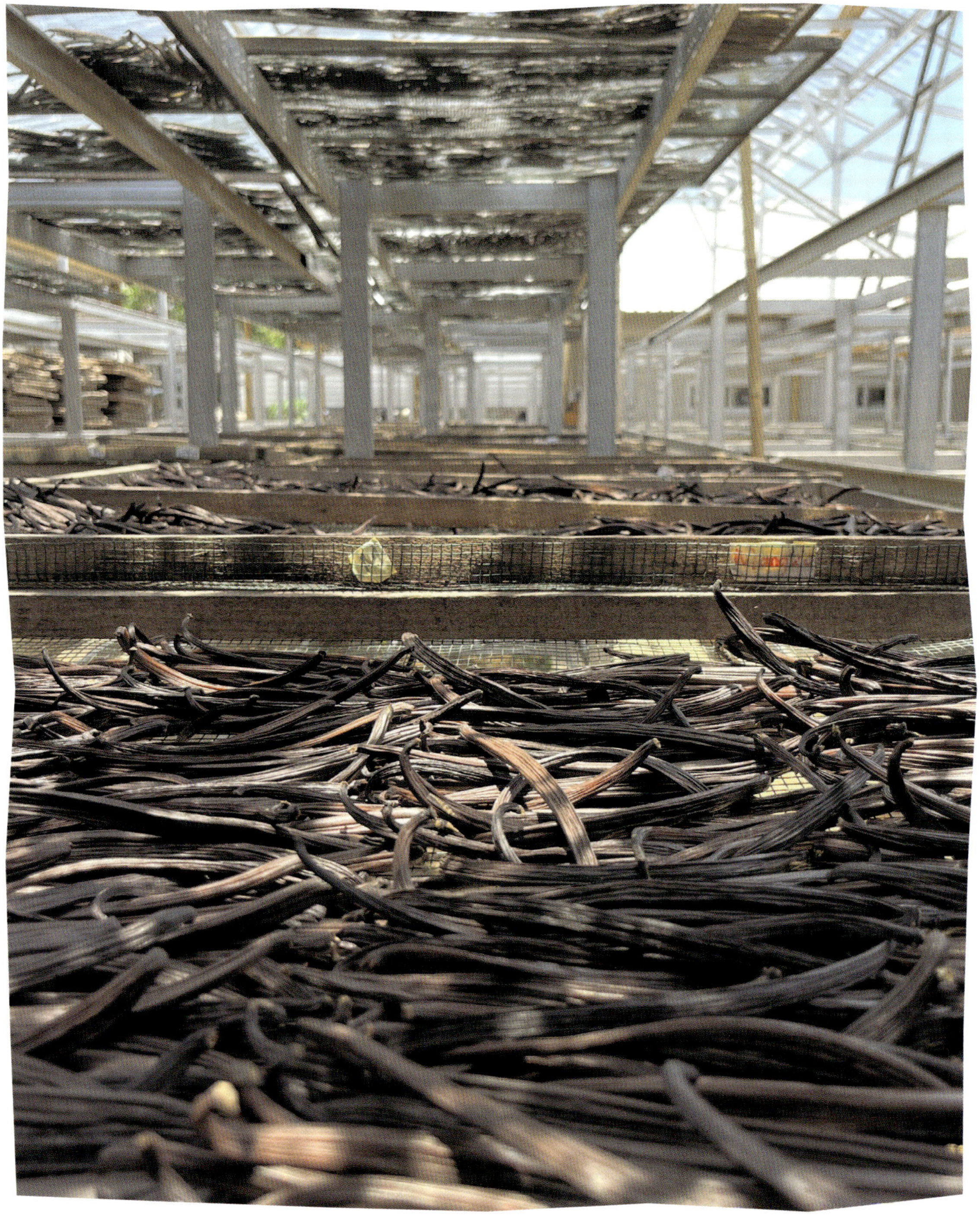

These findings align with research from Madagascar, Colombia and Costa Rica, all reinforcing the fact that vanilla cultivation in tree-shaded systems is a viable model for balancing conservation with agricultural productivity (Dalton, 2019; McTaggart, 1983). Through our collaboration with LittlePod I advocate market-driven conservation by connecting vanilla farmers with ethical buyers. This approach ensures that vanilla sourced from agroforestry systems is recognised, valued, and financially rewarding for farmers who protect forests. By fostering direct partnerships between producers and ethical brands, we increase transparency and promote conservation-conscious vanilla production.

Vanilla agroforestry offers a nature-based strategy to address deforestation, soil degradation, and economic resilience in farming communities. By maintaining tree cover and crop diversity, farmers can enhance ecosystem services, regenerate soil health, and strengthen local economies. However, scaling this model requires policy support, financial incentives, and stronger market demand for regeneratively grown vanilla. Through initiatives like our work in Bali and partnerships with ethical vanilla buyers we are proving that restorative vanilla cultivation is not just possible: it is essential for the future of conservation-driven agriculture. Moving forward, governments, businesses and consumers must prioritise forest-friendly vanilla sourcing to support both ecological restoration and farmer prosperity. With the right strategies, vanilla can become a catalyst for regenerative development, proving that conservation and economic success go hand in hand.

Opposite: Vanilla pods drying in Bali

Thank-you, Syiraz. This report sums up our collaboration very well.

Paul later spoke to Syiraz about his paper and its findings. He told Paul,

'Everything that we're trying to do here in Bali is based on our three main values. Number one is purity of intention, number two is imagination, and number three is always doing it happily. We see these values in the forest farming communities and I've seen them in LittlePod and in Janet. Her intentions are pure, she has great imagination and she's always happy. We share all the same values and that's why we can achieve so much and work so well together.

'I've been passionate about the environment ever since I was a little boy. When I was in high school, I joined a hiking club and walked everywhere there is to walk around Indonesia. The mountains of Java. Bali. Lombok. I decided then that the career I would have would need to involve travelling around, seeing places, and spending time outdoors. I've spent a lot of time in the forest, learning about agriculture and getting to know the farming communities. Not everything that I have seen has been good.

'Even in a short space of time I've seen the environment change and that terrifies me. The mountains of Indonesia are changing, there are more forest fires, and it's hotter for longer each year. I've seen Indonesia changing before my eyes and I don't like it. When we had our daughter, everything changed for me, and I had to act.

'The changes have been so great that I realised that unless we do something immediately, my daughter will not get to see the mountains as I once saw them as a boy. When my wife got pregnant I told her that everything that I do from this point on will be to help fight climate change. I want my daughter to have the same experiences that I had growing up. Unless we make a change, that will not happen.

'I don't like the term "sustainability." We shouldn't be trying to sustain what we have now: we should be aiming to restore things to their best version.

'We were talking about sustainability back in the 1980s, but here we are now, in 2023, still degrading the forest. Deforestation is everywhere and we have to restore, not sustain.

'Like LittlePod, I love real vanilla. It has a huge ecological value. In order to grow it needs cover, which means not chopping down the big trees. If we encourage the farmers to keep growing vanilla – and find a market for their products – the forest communities will leave the big trees alone because there's great value in preserving that environment. Vanilla has great power. People are starting to realise that at last.

'I don't know why people keep telling us that growing vanilla is difficult. It's the laziest form of farming that there is. You don't have to do a lot to grow vanilla because the forest does it all for you. It provides cover, shade and support. It improves the soil and helps water retention. It even provides fertilisation. I always joke with the vanilla farmers and tell them that they're lazy. Yes, you have to do the hand-pollination, but this is the future of farming that I imagine for my children.

'I've learnt such a lot from working with Made and Ketut. When I first met Made I thought he was like a lecturer. He has so much knowledge and great passion for this project. I'm also learning from the forest communities, and I want to gather as much information as I can, put it to

"Vanilla has great power. People are starting to realise that at last."

Left: Sharing stories and smiles with Syiraz in 2023
Middle: Dr Made at the LittlePod orchard
Right: The LittlePod orchard and farmers' village from above

good use and help to make a difference. There's no-one else doing this in Bali. Working together, we have the power to generate change.

'I like to tell my daughter that she can help to make a difference just by eating an ice cream. She's fascinated with vanilla and can't understand how something so black – a vanilla pod – can be used to make something so white – vanilla ice cream! I tell her that all she needs to understand is that by eating a good quality ice cream, made using vanilla from a conservation forest, she is helping the environment. She has come to understand this, and I think that this would be my message to everybody.

'You don't have to be like me, becoming a forester and living it 9–5. You just need to think about the choices you make and the little things that you can do to help make a difference. That's what we're doing in Bali, what LittlePod is doing in the UK and what we're doing together. We just need to keep going, we can drive that change.

'LittlePod has high standards and so do we in Bali. We share those standards, and we share the same values, and I have no doubt that our relationship will continue to grow and grow. It has been great to see the LittlePod team in Bali this week and like everyone who is working here, I'm feeling very positive about our future together.'

'Would you like to see this family shrine?' Syiraz asks me as we pass some railings draped in bougainvillea with bright lipstick-coloured flowers. Walking into the shrine area I can see it is decorated with little parcels of flowers and rice offered on a plate made from banana leaves – offerings in gratitude to the gods. After a moment of silence, the interns turn to Syiraz to say that they can see more farmers gathering down at the house, so we must move on.

'How long will it take me to get down?' I ask.

'About half-an-hour,' replies Syiraz. 'We can talk as we go'.

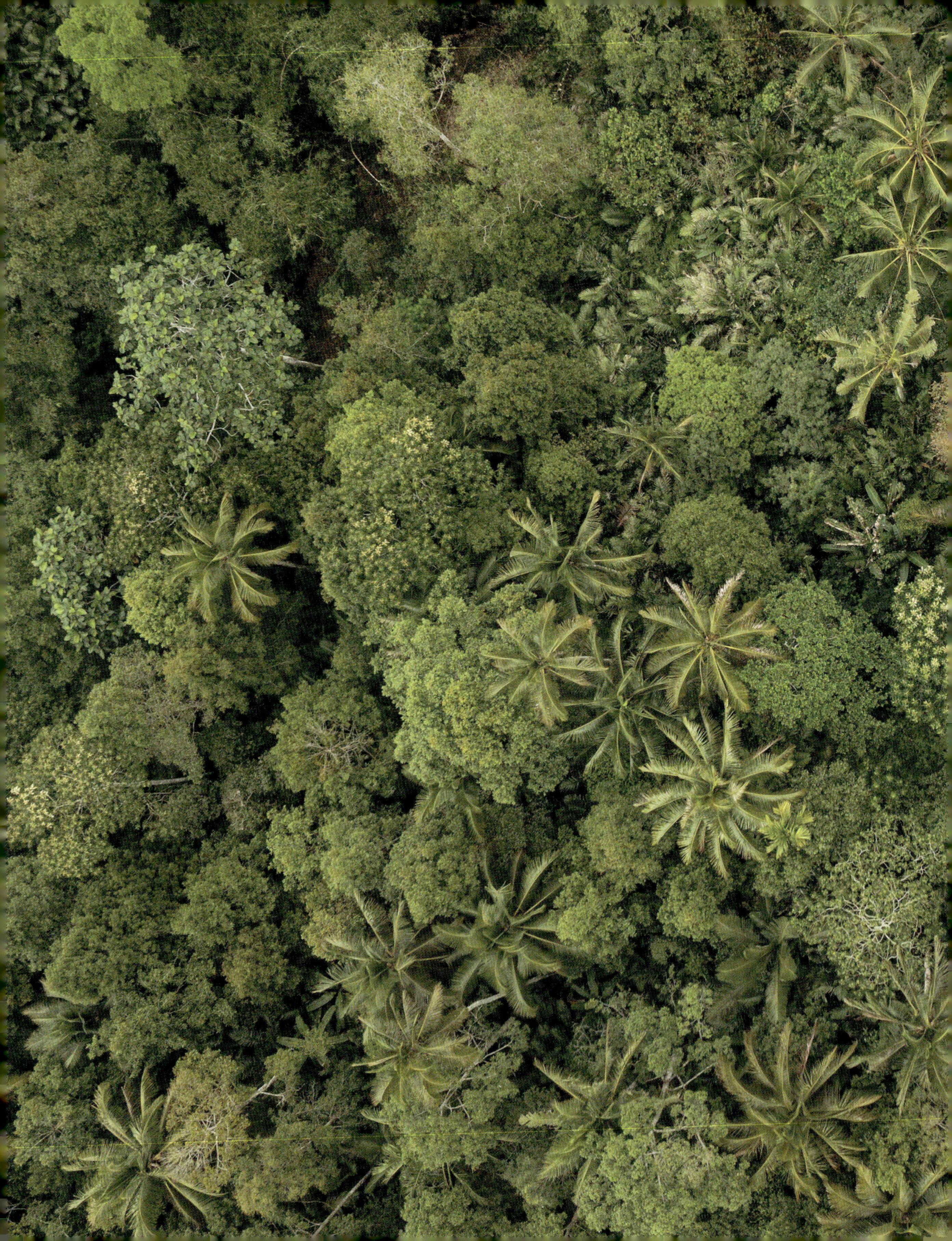

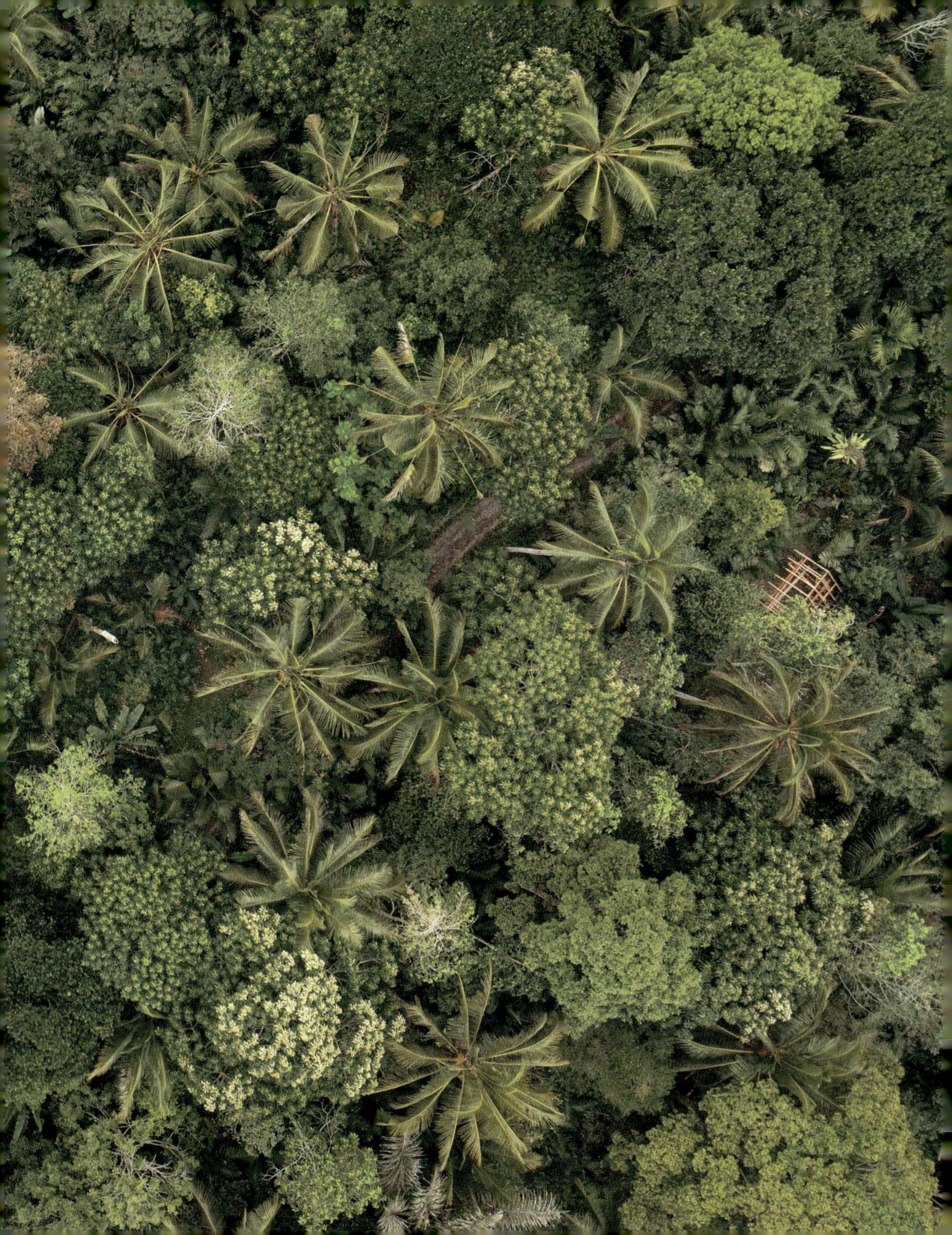

05
The Vanilla Farmer's Daughter

'If you allow me, I will tell you the story of Irine, a subsistence farmer's daughter I met in Tanzania,' I tell the interns. They nod enthusiastically. **'You will have to imagine the scene.**

'First you must know that I once worked as a primary school teacher. It was a vocation for me. I had wanted to be a primary school teacher since the age of eight. I loved my own primary school and all the children there. It was both a refuge and a place of stimulation. Education is so important to me. That is why I am so proud to see you all today. You have all achieved so much going to university and skilling yourselves up since. Yet more than that, you all want to work with Made and the farmers to restore your environment for the next generation, for your own children.

'I was at a Vanilla Symposium in Moshi at the foot of the Kilimanjaro Mountain in 2019. Olly, Littlepod's CEO, came with me. Juan had organised for us to visit a couple of subsistence farmers whose farms had become champion vanilla farms, showing how to cultivate the vine alongside other produce.

'At a remote farm we stopped for lunch, which consisted of sandwiches and an apple that had been packed for the journey. There were some white plastic chairs waiting for us and we sat in the heat; monkeys joined us, peering down from the trees while slowly peeling their bananas. It was here that day that I met Irine Hendry. She had been given the task of taking photographs of the visiting group. The camera was tiny, which seemed incongruous against her tall upright frame decked in her beautiful African colours.

'I suppose I could be described as an intuitive type. When I meet people, even today, I always see them as young children and wonder where in the class I would seat them. My antenna was alert that day as I approached Irine and asked her why she was so happy. '"It is not the task of taking pictures that is making you smile so much today", I said to her. "What else is making you so happy?"

'She looked at me as if to say where have you divined that opinion, then instantly responded, very enthusiastically, and said "Yes, today I've heard that I passed my accountancy degree." It was such an unexpected utterance. I looked around to see where she might have studied for this degree, turning to view a 360-degree perimeter of the savannah farm, with savannah as far as the eye could see. "Oh," she laughed, "I have to walk one and a half hours to my college." The reality hit me.

'The journey here had involved several hours driving on dusty roads and passing makeshift homes, corrugated rooms which slipped by. Of Tanzanian children 2.4 million are orphans. The windows of the bus had been slightly ajar, enough for some air in the stifling sun but not enough to let the dust affect our throats.

'As we walked around the farm I congratulated Irine on her success. I noticed a pomegranate tree at the entrance. I don't know why, but it seemed so festive decked in its baubles of fruit, very appropriate to celebrate the occasion. "What will you do next?" I asked Irine. "Oh, I would love to become a certified public accountant", she said. My attention was interrupted.

'Another agape moment I thought, as my jaw opened, and I saw a wee orchid flower unfold on one of the tutor trees.

'"Where will you go to do that?" I asked, while wishing that I could spot more flowers opening. "Oh, I can't," she replied, "it would take my father ten years to save for me to do that. I will stay here and help my parents on the farm".'

The interns nod sympathetically to this story. It was not long ago that children in Bali left school at twelve years of age to work with their parents, since the income was needed in the family. I continued.

'Well, I was inquisitive and questioned her more, discovering that she was the youngest of six children. One sister was a nurse in Dar es Salaam and two of her siblings were teachers. I called Olly over. Olly had been working with me at LittlePod for a couple of years and had just passed his level three AAT accountancy exams. I wondered how he would respond on hearing Irine's news. "Meet Irine, she's just passed her accountancy degree." Olly did not flinch. His well-mannered schooling showed no hint of surprise, and he congratulated her as if she was a fellow classmate. It was in that moment that I realised something important.

'I am the owner of a small vanilla company, and I can make my own decisions. The teacher in me was awakened. I turned to Irine and exclaimed "Irine, my company, LittlePod, will sponsor you to become a CPA." Her response was to look at me for clarification before jumping up and down on the spot. She then ran off to bring her parents to greet me. They had a dazed look, and in an instant I knew that this was a promise to her parents as much as to her. Irine was unaware of their fear and turned to them, saying "You see this is because I have been a good girl".'

I was suddenly shaken out of my storytelling. Syiraz was talking to me.

'Did she study to become a CPA?' he asked. 'Yes, she did', I answered. 'It was not easy. In the UK it is difficult to pass accountancy exams, especially in corporate finance, if you are not already working in a company. Irine struggled at times and in three years had to retake a couple of the modules. However there came the glorious day when she contacted us to say "I have passed.

I am now a certified public accountant." We tried to get her an internship with LittlePod in the UK, but that was not allowed since she had no-one of note who could sponsor her visit. However, she did find a job, hundreds of miles away from home. She loves her job as an internal auditor. It's a government-paid post.'

Irine emailed recently to say that she has now started a master's course. When I asked why she was going to do this she answered, 'If you have an accountancy degree, and are a qualified CPA with a master's degree, then you can apply to become Head of Department.' Hurrah, I thought, a woman with ambition!

We often call Irine our Voice of Africa. She knows that vanilla is an important crop for the environment because on the day she showed me around her father's farm she pointed to the produce that is benefitting from the canopy plant – adding moisture to the rice growing and protecting the tutor trees, and most importantly enriching the soil, which is improving year on year.

The Vanilla Symposium was held in what used to be a convent. The gardens were clearly tended and planted with vibrant large blousy flowers of every striking colour from bright orange to cobalt blue. The food was nourishing – a choice of meat, fish and rice, and ugali, which is the national dish: it is a stiff dough made from cornmeal, cassava flour and sorghum or millet.

There were two days of interesting presentations on vanilla with specialists from different countries sharing their experiences. We had a workshop on tasting different blends of vanilla using milk as the carrier. The second day ended with a roundtable discussion on the theme of 'How can we increase usage of vanilla?'

On the first night Juan had organised a wonderful dinner at a banana plantation a bus ride away from the centre. It was an authentic tropical experience for Olly and me. I was lucky enough to be seated next to a man called Sir Soekandar Tjandra KBE. When he sadly passed away in August 2024 the tribute said, 'Sir Soekandar was a real down to earth people's man. He was a philanthropist and gave more to the communities. He served with high value and distinction. He was a generous man. He created jobs and helped entire families as a family business with branches in 17 of the country's 19 provinces.' He had been knighted by Queen Elizabeth II, since Papua New Guinea, where he was a significant figure, is a member of the Commonwealth. It joined in 1975 when it became independent.

We had a very light-hearted conversation. Sir Soekandar had a kind face. When I developed a cough due to the dry sandy air, he shared some special throat lozenges that he had brought with him on the journey. They worked, and I gave him a copy of my Vanilla cookbook to take home to his wife, Lady Susan, as a thank-you present.

He grew up in Indonesian Papua, but he started the vanilla business in Papua New Guinea fifty years ago. He told me he had 400,000 mouths to feed and had to produce vanilla 365 days a year. He had grown the company to produce almost 10 per cent of the world's vanilla supply. He also said quietly and defiantly that it was he who set the vanilla prices. When Madagascar sets their price, he can then decide when to cut his prices. I laughed and said that I would never

Top Left: Meeting Irine for the first time in 2019
Top Right: The graduate – three years later in Dar es Salaam
Bottom Left: Hard at work – a woman with ambition
Bottom Right: Back on the farm, Irine's parents checking their crop

The Vanilla Farmer's Daughter

forget this evening, as I had never met an oligarch before! He laughed too.

Whether it is true about the pricing quip I don't know. It is not easy to find out how the pricing structure of vanilla works. This was another reason why working with Dr Made and the orchard was so important to LittlePod. We could be like Sir Soekandar and decide on how we would set our prices to make vanilla more sustainable for our customers.

I am very glad that I met him, as I had heard very good things about him. I also felt that I had touched the heart of Vanilla Central!

After the final safari it was time for Olly and I to head for home. One interaction was on my mind, however, and that was when we visited the Masai tribe and looked at the wares in their shop. A young chap came over to help me. 'I am looking for a figurine for my partner', I said. (David collects little figures as mementoes and has a glass wall full of little people from places around the globe.) 'What I would like is one that looks like you. What is your name?' I asked. 'My name is Frank', he said. 'Frank – why that's an English name.' 'My name means "free man,"' he said. 'And my father's name is Emmanuel, which means God, so you see I am a free man of God.' 'Why are you so different from the Masai?' I asked. 'That is because in Africa we have lots of different tribes and I am from the Mbugwe tribe. We are the smallest tribe in Africa. There are just 60,000 of us left and we live on the perimeter of the National Park.' The Masai are a very organised group of people, so I think they may employ Frank because he is from the neighbouring tribe. Looking at him I could see his different features. He is small in stature and has very long earlobes with a hole in them. I think they look attractive. Frank asked my name. 'I am called Janet', I said. Frank stared at me. 'Why, that is an African name', he said. 'I don't think so,' I said, 'it's more likely Scottish. Apparently, a nurse at the hospital where I was born gave me my name as I did not see my mother for the first month of my life.' 'Well, in Tanzania, the tribes adopt a name for the tribe according to the meaning. The Chagga Chagga tribe in Kilimanjaro who are now mainly clerks and teachers adopted the name Janet for their tribe.' 'No!' I said, and I called Juan over. 'Did you know this?' I asked him. 'No', Juan smiled. 'I am so thrilled with the connection. I guess it's because Janet means "grace of God".' Frank gave me the figurine and said to me quietly, 'You are very brave.' I wondered about that statement on the way back to the hotel.

One morning I realised how much Juan had to contend with. We were having a presentation in the hall when not one, but two bombs went off in the distance. I saw Juan raise his eyebrows as if to say, 'Not again'. (As a teacher I recognised that sign. Some naughty boys had promised to behave and were not to be trusted.) Two people from the Philippines attending the course told us later that they knew what type of explosion it was because they get them regularly in the Philippines. I was so grateful that Olly had stayed in the hotel that morning to prepare his poster presentation.

At Kilimanjaro airport as we were about to embark, I wanted to share my newfound knowledge. My name was called out, 'Janet Sawyer'. I looked proudly at the cabin staff and said, 'African Janet'.

The interns are now hunting around in the orchard forest. They are looking up at some swifts flying past, possibly going to the rice fields on the other side of the forest where Made is with Paul and David. They are linchi swiftlets. There are swallows too, who swoop around the rice paddies. On the two previous occasions when I visited Bali, I cannot remember seeing bird life apart from birds in cages.

'Have you been to Bali before?' Syiraz asks.

'Yes', I say. 'I have visited twice before. Once in 1999 and another time in 2001. Back then things were very different. Your fantastic modern airport did not exist.' 'That was built in 2016', Syiraz advises me. 'Both times I stayed in Canggu

Permai. It was a village at that time.' 'Now it is a big village', says Syiraz. 'When I visited there were lots of rice paddies. I stayed in a desa (village) which was quite poor at the time and very rural.' 'Now it is the best place to live', the students tell me.

I remember that we camped in a rice field in a room on stilts. Our son Dan was with us, and David was afraid that the snakes would be able to climb up the stilts. Dan woke up one morning to find a young cobra curled up at the end of his bed! He found it very funny when the friend we were staying with attacked the snake with a stick and flung it out of the window.

I was taken by the women of the village into the paddy fields with bare feet wearing a coolie hat made from bamboo. They taught me how to walk through the rice plants quietly without frightening the snakes. I still have that hat hanging in my office. I forgot how the Indonesians had mastered the skill of irrigation; I was reminded by Dr Made that Indonesia is famous for its irrigation prowess. Those paddy fields were created, not natural, and that is why they could be re-sited to allow the town that is there today. It is not like building on a flood plain as we do in the UK.

The first time I visited in 1999, Bali suffered very badly from dreadful flooding and an apocalyptic storm. The villagers were terrified. Their homes were one-room concrete buildings directly on the ground, so the rain just poured in. The sky opened like a light box, bright white in the dead of night. Frogs croaked; geckos came inside. The sound of the sea, the rain and the thunder had an eerie feel, especially when the Christian community started singing hymns and the Muslim community sounded their call to prayer. The rest of the evangelical community started clapping. I have never heard anything like that since.

I had arrived from London a day earlier. I should have been more prepared, since there were only six people on the flight. The pilot told us that he would have to switch off the lights. We had already had a very dodgy two-and-a-half-hour flight with the plane barrelling around. After we arrived at the airport I sat next to the pilot on the bus. He told me that we had been caught all the way in the tumult of air between two other planes, one directly above us and one below, and there was nothing he could do.

It was New Year's Eve, known as Ogoh-Ogoh. The following day, New Year's Day, is known as Nyepi. In Bali people observe a day of silence and reflection; they stay in, there are no lights, no music, no noise. People make papier-mâché effigies, really tall, and burn them to cleanse the village of evil spirits. They also meditate and pray and have a period of self-reflection. It all sounded pretty healthy to me. I have been to Stonehenge with the druids performing their cleansing rituals on the summer and winter solstices. It is like an outpouring, ridding the old, ready for the new, a rejuvenation. A bit like our annual New Year resolutions but acted out and writ large!

I suppose that after such an unusual arrival I was inured to what was to come.

What was so amazing was that the day after the flooding people had been out and about clearing all the mess, throwing dead chickens and other casualties into the paddy fields for the snakes. By the afternoon all was shipshape and back to normal. People were dressed in their Sunday best (where, I wondered, did they find those clean and tidy clothes?), giving thanks that word had gone out that there were no deaths, apart from a dog who had eaten a frog. (The frogs are poisonous even to touch.) It was a reminder that life here is about constant renewal. I felt in need of some education.

The last project I had carried out with a group of primary children was on the weather. When reflecting on our work at the end of that term the children were asked what they had learnt from the weather project, and they in turn asked me, 'What have you learnt, Miss?' I replied,

'I have learnt about El Niño, and I think I need to learn more about this. It is going to be very important.'

As a child growing up by the sea, I used to listen to the Shipping Forecast on the BBC and loved the sound of the words – Cromarty, Forth, Dogger. They sounded like faraway familiar places. I don't recall thinking that sailors depended on those words. However, years later my life took me to Hull, where I had a post as a trainee statistician with the British Trawlers' Federation.

That followed Lloyds Bank, that I had joined straight from school, post A-levels. There I experienced the old school banking life. We still wrote in ledgers in pounds, shillings and pence. I was favoured as the first person to be trained on how to use the 'Terminal'. This was a computer which was connected to a centre miles away. It was the dawn of the revolution in banking.

In Hull I was working in Trinity House (it now opens for tour groups). The girls in the tickertape rooms produced spreadsheets of fish catch numbers for me to enter to a huge Anita calculator which looked like something abandoned on the Russian plain eons ago. I was also responsible for the accident reports. They presented grim reading. Definitely one of the most dangerous jobs going, being a trawlerman. I witnessed the end of the fishing industry during my time there. It was the second Cod War. The government let the people down by not negotiating harder. Families suffered, and

Top: Meeting Dr Made for the very first time
Bottom: Still cherished, a precious gift from Nobu

76   Real Vanilla: Nature's Unsung Hero

a way of life was lost. I knew, years later, when our government held a referendum on whether to stay in the EU, that those communities would have their say. The lesson I learnt from them is never to hold grudges. The best way to get revenge is to thrive and be successful. That is what I have taught my children.

My reverie is broken again by a quiet voice. 'How did you and Made first meet?' asks Syiraz. 'Oh gosh, that is a long story', I say. It is not Made 2 that he's referring to. Made 2 is guiding me around this wonderful garden paradise showing me his healthy trees and fertile soil and the mycorrhizal fungi that are keeping it healthy. He and I are comfortable in our silence. It feels as if we breathe together. Syiraz is talking about their mentor, Dr Made, for whom he and the other young men gathered here have such respect. 'He has taught us so much', Syiraz tells me. I look at the animated faces of the interns.

I can imagine the messages that Dr Made would send to Syiraz and this captive audience of young men. His quiet but cheerful demeanour belies his courage and tenacity. He is most suited to an academic environment, and yet he is hands on at Cultivate Oxford, teaching people to grow vegetables in a UK soil. He is not daunted by any practical task despite his intellectual leanings. He has a natural Buddhist philosophy of life. The spirit of his upbringing in this village, the son of a vanilla farmer, has never left him.

He reminds me of Nobu. One year when I was teaching a class of junior children I was asked to cover Buddhism in the curriculum. By chance a Japanese Buddhist monk was staying with a friend who had a language school. I asked him if he would be good enough to come to this class of little girls and tell them about a day in the life of a Buddhist monk. Like Dr Made he was gently spoken with a clarity of thought and the girls were transfixed. After the session Nobu wrote to his order to ask them to send him some bark of the Sen tree. He then painstakingly in beautiful calligraphy wrote on the pieces of bark in Japanese, one for each girl and one for me. The words translate as 'The mountain stream cares nothing for profit or loss, only people do.'

I framed this precious gift. It hangs on the wall of my office to remind me of what is most important in life. It echoes the words in the Bible, 'What doth it profit a man to gain the whole world and suffer the loss of one's soul?' *(Mark 8:36).*

The bark of the Sen tree is given to people who are starting out on their journey to enlightenment. This thought, insignificant at the time, was to become realised later in my LittlePod journey.

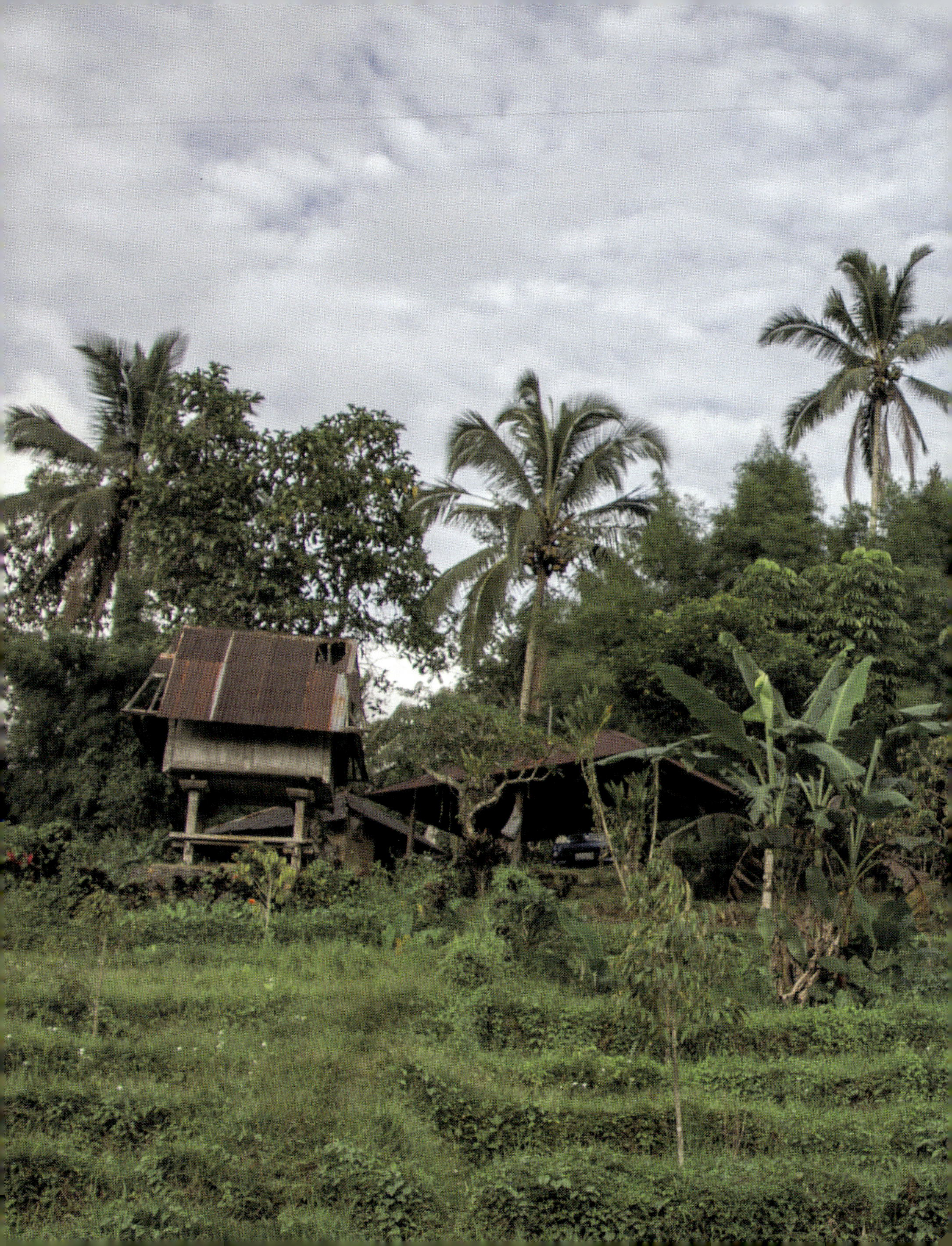

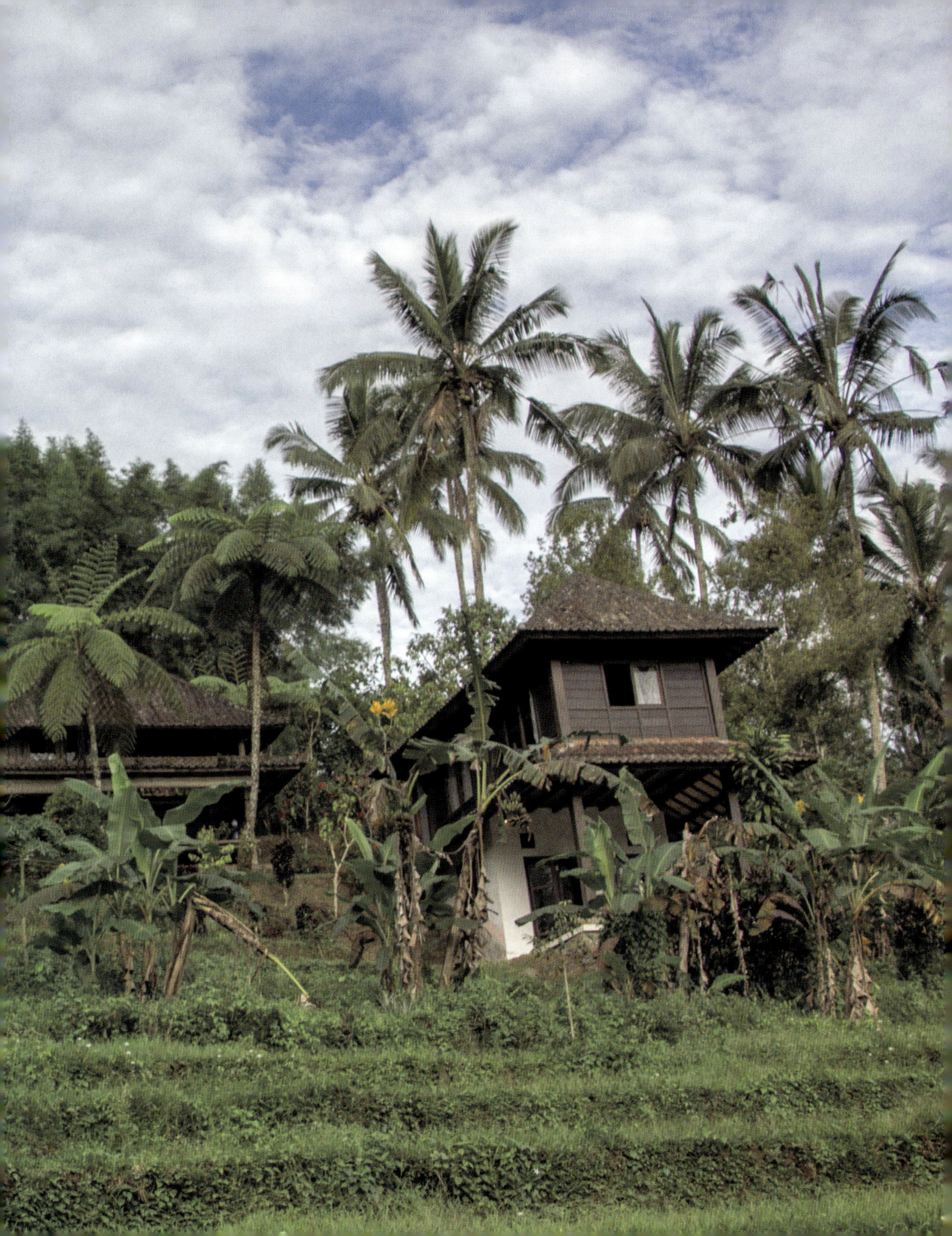

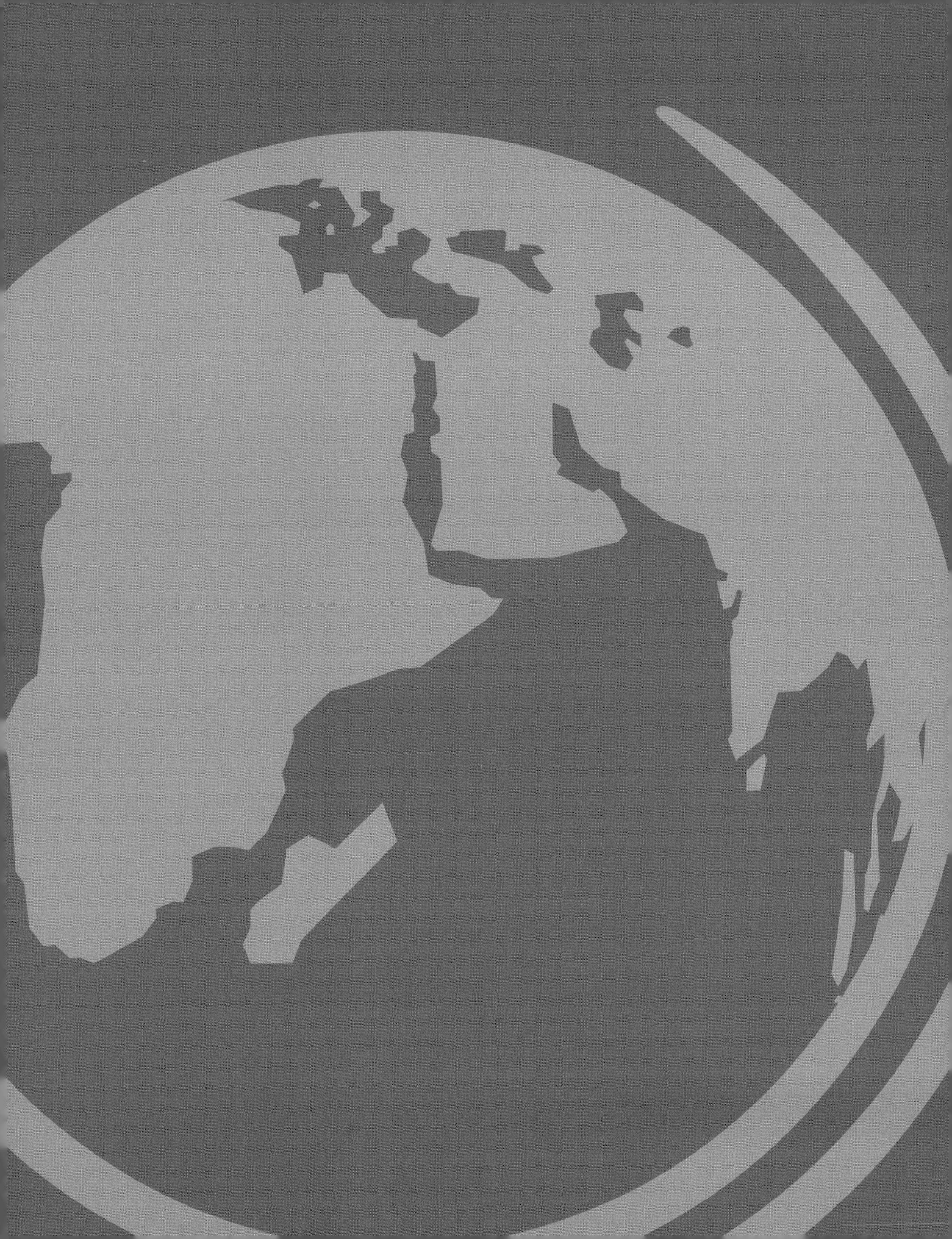

06
Our Doctor in Madagascar

82　Real Vanilla: Nature's Unsung Hero

I founded the LittlePod company in 2010 to campaign for REAL vanilla, to tell its story to a new generation, many of whom did not know that the ingredients they were purchasing were not real.

Left: A day trip to Madagascar – the Kew Gardens Orchid Festival in 2024

It is easy to think that vanillin bought in the supermarket is real, but that is far from the case. When I give talks I always say, 'Please do not be embarrassed to say you have not seen a vanilla pod before.' Samantha Cameron, wife of the former Prime Minister, famously pronounced on a Mary Berry TV show, 'Oh so that is what a vanilla pod looks like. I have never seen one before.'

I became aware that many of the top chefs did not know that vanilla came from an orchid and was the chef's secret ingredient! The story of REAL vanilla had been lost in time.

Most people had become used to the synthetic flavour of vanilla in their ice creams. Sadly, vanilla is a flavour that can be easily replicated in a lab. The fake version does not have the nutritional benefits of real vanilla: it only shares one compound with real vanilla, vanillin, which gives only the vanilla smell. Real vanilla is high in antioxidants, anti-inflammatories and other useful compounds. 'Vanillin' is so near to the word 'vanilla' that it is easy to see why people could assume that it was a real flavour. The artificial flavour can be the by-product of a petrochemical used in the wood pulp industry extracted from lignum. It can also come from other natural sources such as cloves, and in the past it was even associated with a hormone from a beaver's bottom!

There is also a vanilla on the shelves that is called natural but is a weak formulation or a mix of real and artificial vanillin. In any case the labelling of vanilla is very confusing.

Our Doctor in Madagascar

REAL vanilla must be extracted in 35 per cent alcohol. The vanilla pods must go through two further drying stages to have a moisture level of less than 10 per cent; they are then macerated in alcohol and water so the vanillin may be extracted. This first process is known as Fold 1.

Each further fold has less and less water. There are many different folds, but after Fold 4 the product becomes more unstable. Manufacturers engaged in New Product Development will experiment with different folds to get the perfect blend. Blending expertise is also very important.

Following the vanilla crisis in 2017 the price doubled. Many companies were forced to reformulate, and many did not recover. The crisis occurred because a cyclone called Enawo hit north-eastern Madagascar, wiping out 80 per cent of the vanilla harvest. LittlePod had to double its prices overnight. I am thankful to Sam who was with me at the time. It was his last day at LittlePod, having been with us for four years. He knew all the pricing and stayed late into the night to get things sorted before he left.

Madagascar, whose infrastructure is still very rural, did not have the capacity to cope when 350,000 people were displaced. It was devastating. Hunger and disease were rife. Madagascar has an annual outbreak of the plague that usually affects around 100 people. After the disaster many people moved to the cities, followed by rats who carry the fleas that cause the disease. That year the number of plague victims rose to 1,000.

It must have been a very difficult time for our friend Vik Mohan, a doctor in Exeter, to visit Madagascar. We are very proud to sponsor Vik on his excursions to the vanilla-growing regions. He enlightened us about Madagascar and gave us reports so we could follow his journeys. Tennyson, the Lincolnshire poet I am always quoting, wrote a poem called 'Ulysses', and there is a line there that I love. After a lifetime of travel he concludes, 'I am a part of all that I have met.' I feel that regarding LittlePod. All the people I have met on the long journey to this point have become attached to me rather like the attachment the farmers have to the little flower.

Vik told us about his time in the vanilla region. 'My first trip up into the north-east of Madagascar was maybe ten or twelve years ago.

I was excited to go there. I knew it was a vanilla-growing region and a beautiful place to explore in Madagascar. I knew about this fantastic conservation programme and this amazing hero of mine, a guy called Eric Patel, was leading that. I was hoping I would get to meet him.

'I bumped into him the day before I was going trekking. We had been looking forward to meeting each other, but we hadn't known it was going to happen.

'After my trip I spent a few days with Eric travelling through the vanilla-growing region, meeting vanilla farmers and looking at the work they're doing, looking at how they and the people who are the stewards of that biodiversity are being supported to live sustainably, and to have alternative livelihoods, so they're not exclusively relying on vanilla, not exclusively relying on logging. It was really exciting to see.

'People think of Madagascar as being an unspoilt paradise, with lemurs and chameleons, and that is true to a degree. It is also the fifth poorest country in the world; it has some of the world's weakest healthcare infrastructure, and some of the world's poorest healthcare provision. There are challenges when it comes to governance and corruption and infrastructure. These things are what communities experience on a day-to-day basis. People living in Madagascar aren't celebrating the country's amazing biodiversity. They're there and trying to survive.

'When I've been to Madagascar, I've always noticed how difficult it is to travel there. It's a hard country to travel around. At a minimum, as well as flying internally, I'll be on an overland 4x4 vehicle for nine to ten hours, travelling across dirt tracks to get to our programme sites.

'The infrastructure is poor, and travel is difficult. The poverty is grinding. These are some of the poorest people that you'll see anywhere in the world. Lack of support, lack of infrastructure is really, really apparent.

'And yet what I see is communities doing their best to live sustainably. Communities with a real sense of identity, togetherness and belonging; a real sense of equality and fairness within communities, despite all the difficulties. I've developed a real fondness for the country.

'I have friendships with people I have worked alongside for two decades. It's in stark contrast to what I see here in the UK. It is such a poor country. And yet some of the places you go to are spectacularly beautiful and the people are the same.

'Madagascar isn't really on our radar in the UK. It's a francophone country; it never had British colonial rule, although Queen Victoria did try to build bridges. It's not particularly important geopolitically, so people in the UK are not that aware of it, sadly.

'The people in Madagascar are a diverse mix. The first people to settle on this Indian Ocean island were from Indonesia. They sailed the rim of the ocean and eventually settled on Madagascar. Other people had travelled, but no-one had settled there. Arabs had travelled there, and in the north there's still a strong Arab influence. But the Indonesians were the first to settle. They brought rice and they brought their language and culture, and the fishing boats that they sailed in are the ones that are still used today, all this time later. The same boats, the same design, these Iron Age boats.

Left: Dr Vik Mohan
Right: Vik always sends us photographs from his trips

'Then people from mainland Africa started to come and settle. It's a real mixture. There's Arab influence, French influence, Indian influence, it's a real cultural melting pot with a variety of different ethnic groups, fifteen or so, each with its own distinct identity, language, culture, lifestyle and livelihood. From the Vezo, the people of the sea living along the west coast, who I know best, to the people living in the highlands, agriculturalists who are the best connected and most wealthy, there's a huge diversity. The language is a mixture – Bahasa from Indonesia, African dialects, with a bit of French and Arabic mixed in.'

This personal account from the ground by Vik Mohan has always been important to all the teams at LittlePod because of the trust we have in Vik and the work that he does. He is leaving a legacy to Blue Ventures, having achieved far more than he had hoped for.

Vik told Paul recently when we had a catch up, 'We had a founding team at the beginning, and I was part of that team. I look back on the work I did at Blue Ventures with great pride.

'I started offering community health services to one community in one village, with fewer than 2,000 people. By the time I left Blue Ventures, the model that I helped to pioneer was serving one million people across five or six countries. It wasn't just that. It was also helping to build a movement around thinking holistically in support of communities and in support of biodiversity and in support of conservation. I do feel proud of that.

'When my colleague first said to me that we should go from 2,000 people to 10,000 people, the colour drained from my face. I thought there was no way we could reach 10,000 people. By the end there was almost one million, so yes, it grew beyond all expectations.'

Paul intervened and said to Vik, 'Janet remembers you saying to her "Just keep focused on vanilla. There is much to do, and it is worthwhile enough if you can do that one thing." She has always been very uplifted by that comment you made to her because she says it can feel a bit lonely sometimes running a company and wondering if our voice is getting through. We are such a small company at LittlePod and the message is so important.'

'Yes,' replied Vik, 'Blue Ventures was just getting started as I joined. Blue Ventures had already established an expedition site in south-west Madagascar. The reason is that along that coast there is a huge barrier reef system. At the point when we first arrived there was relatively little human pressure on that. And yet we knew that lots of people relied on it for fishing. It seemed like a great place to go to study and to see if we could develop a marine conservation and marine management practice. I'm proud of two main things. One is working at a systems level and thinking and acting holistically to meet community needs and address the threats facing ecosystems. That holistic system level approach to biodiversity conservation was pretty unusual at the time. The other one is trying to foster a culture within the organisation that puts communities first and that values the Blue Ventures team.

'What really, really struck me on that trip was that if you engage communities sincerely and effectively you are building an allegiance for your mission, which is biodiversity and conservation and the stewardship of natural resources. In areas where communities don't buy into conservation, you see biodiversity degradation. In areas where communities buy in, they become the champions. They become the stewards, they become the protectors. They see the value. That's what I saw Eric Patel doing so well, so inspiringly.

It's about creating the enabling conditions. I think that's what we need to be doing. Supporting and inspiring people to do the things that they know are the right things and the things that are going to serve their needs in the long term.'

'Did you know much about vanilla?' Paul asked him.

'I didn't know much about vanilla before that trip,' Vik replied. 'I'd eaten it, but other than that, no. It was wonderful to see it being grown, wonderful to see it being harvested, wonderful to have a chance to see it in the markets and to meet the communities who are so engaged in vanilla growing.

'What we've seen in Madagascar is that the value of vanilla can distort local markets, can distort farming practices. In addition to creating the enabling environments for people to live sustainably, it's also important that we think about the value chain, we think about fair prices for farmers, we think about the impact that an industry, that vanilla production, can have on a wider ecosystem. During my time at Blue Ventures I saw that vanilla was considered to be so lucrative that people stopped growing everything else. When you go to markets in the most fertile part of Madagascar you can't buy food, because all they've grown is vanilla. It's complex.'

Paul asked Vik to tell him why he was now moving to offer his support to Planet Indonesia. 'You know that LittlePod has been supporting Made in his pioneering polyculture method of growing vanilla to aid forest regeneration. You have met him at our International Real Vanilla Day at Bickleigh Castle. Obviously moving towards Indonesia is coming even closer to the LittlePod farmers' forest orchard. It would be great if you could visit the project in Bali one day.'

'Well, I would love Made to show me around the LittlePod forest project and see the wonderful results', Vik said.

'As Blue Ventures narrows its focus, it's moving away from that holistic approach more and more, and focusing more on fisheries and a strong focus on data.'

'Ah, like the advice you gave Janet. Concentrate on one thing!' Paul continued. 'I suppose as charities scale up and employ more NGOs the dynamic changes and the needs change?'

'Well, yes. There was less room for me within the organisation. At the same time, I had known and supported Planet Indonesia for a long time. I was planning to integrate healthcare into their programme of activities about a decade ago, sharing what I'd learnt at Blue Ventures. They loved the idea, loved the model, and were keen to learn more. I went out to Indonesia to support them and to replicate the approach that I pioneered at Blue Ventures.

'Over time, I could see that Planet Indonesia was modelling many of the values and approaches that I had cherished at Blue Ventures. I saw them taking these ideas and modelling them. Human rights-based, holistic community-led conservation. They loved it and have taken it up and run with it. That's something that I feel very excited about. I have a real fondness for the founder and CEO, Adam Miller, and have a friendship with him. I could see there was a point when they were going to grow quickly, a bit like Blue Ventures had done a decade earlier.

'Having learnt much at Blue Ventures about how to do growth well, how to not make mistakes when you're at that reflection point, I was desperately keen to share what I had learnt. I wanted this precious organisation to continue to thrive and grow. I was keen to share what I had learnt. At the same time, they reached out to me and said, "We're looking to grow, we're looking to professionalise, we recognise that we'd benefit from your expertise." They said they'd love for me to become a board member, and having that relationship already, knowing them, I was delighted to be asked, and delighted to be able to provide Adam with a bit of informal guidance, mentorship, whatever he needs to steer Planet Indonesia along a path that's right. Blue Ventures grew at a dizzying rate and perhaps not hazard-free. There are challenges and costs associated with growth. There are pitfalls, and I was keen to help Planet Indonesia avoid those. That's my mission. To support Planet Indonesia to stay true to the beautiful organisation that it currently is.'

'Janet has grown LittlePod organically,' Paul said, 'and put systems and processes in place to future-proof LittlePod. There have been so many challenges. She started the company when the country was reeling from a deep recession, and there have been lots of ups and downs economically since; the terrible vanilla crisis of 2017 plus the Covid pandemic, the energy crisis and the cost-of-living crisis. Over the fifteen years since she started the company there has not really been a good time politically and economically, but LittlePod has weathered the storms, and the LittlePod forest orchard project is a shining example of the rewards of patience and commitment.'

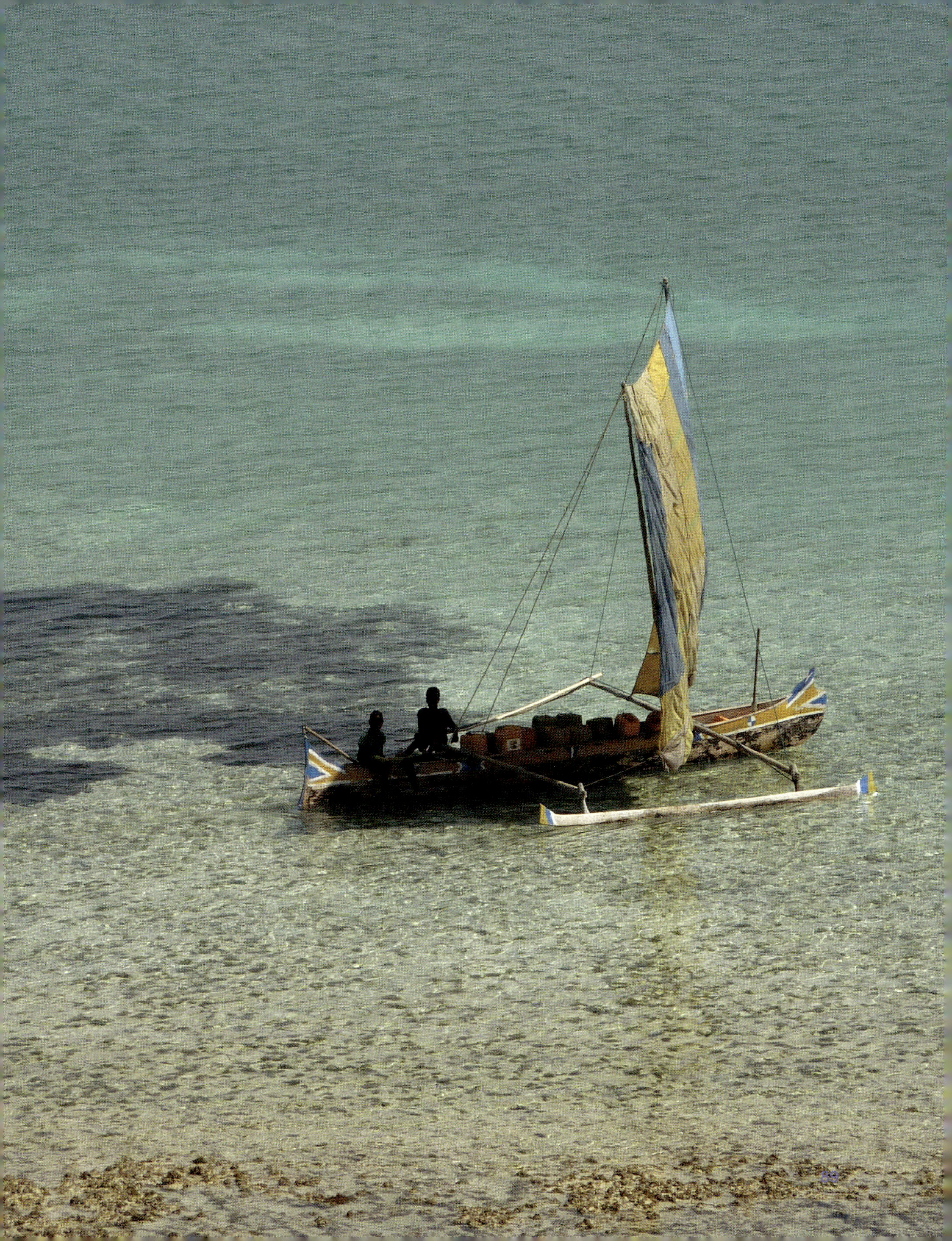

'It feels like we're well matched', replied Vik. 'Planet Indonesia is aligned with LittlePod also. There's a really clear alignment of values and vision. That's why I'm still such a proud member of the LittlePod team.

'That's why I'm excited to be moving to Planet Indonesia and taking LittlePod's support with me.

'I supported the replication of our model at Blue Ventures, our holistic approach to conservation, in the vanilla-growing region [in Madagascar]. One of the things that Planet Indonesia does particularly well is that it measures its impact.

'It's harder than it sounds. They are ahead of the curve when it comes to measuring impact. They're great at that and this matters to me because I'm not doing this for the ride, I'm doing this because I want Planet Indonesia to have a meaningful impact.

'My friendship with Janet is important to me. I've known Janet since almost the beginning. Janet was one of our first supporters. Back in the day when we didn't have big grants to run the programme and I was spending my own money to run the healthcare programme in Madagascar, I organised a fundraising auction and Janet kindly donated a beautiful hamper of LittlePod goodies. I was very grateful, and we got some money.

'Ever since then I've had a fondness for LittlePod as an organisation. There has been a clear alignment of values. It's about championing real vanilla, it's about sustainability, and it's about nurturing and supporting the LittlePod team. These are all values that really align with the initial values of Blue Ventures and with me. I've been grateful for all the support that LittlePod have offered over the years.

'Unrestricted money is hard to come by. To have a constant stream of unrestricted funding has meant that we could do the things that we really wanted to do. That has been really valuable. It has also felt like an endorsement of what we do. It's almost more important than the money that LittlePod is an organisation that really values what we do, it sees the value. That seemed very important too.

'The key message for me is that I've learnt an awful lot working at Blue Ventures over twenty years. I'm really keen to support Planet Indonesia to benefit from what I've learnt, the good and the bad, the successes and the mistakes. I'm keen to share that learning. LittlePod is, in a way, enabling me to do that, so I'm grateful.'

I am deep in thought remembering the words that Paul had scribbled down from his meeting with Vik. In Vik I had found someone I could trust to 'go along' with!

> **Vanilla's true value is not just in its uses to the pharmaceutical industry, the cosmetics industry and the food industry: it is also such a perfect plant to aid forest regeneration and biodiversity.**

People are perhaps not aware of how special the island is and how important it is to save it. David Attenborough wrote, 'Madagascar is an unrepeatable experiment: a set of animals and plants evolving in isolation for over 60 million years. We're still trying to unravel its mysteries. How tragic it would be if we lost it before we even understand it.'

Vanilla's true value is not just in its uses to the pharmaceutical industry, the cosmetics industry and the food industry: it is also such a perfect plant to aid forest regeneration and biodiversity.

The problem is that many companies do not recognise the difference between real and artificial vanillin so they go for the cheapest ingredient, little knowing what a catastrophe this is for the vanilla farmers, the environment, and ultimately all of us. Unless we support the indigenous farmers, who are the only people who can regenerate the rainforest, and make it worthwhile for them, we shall all suffer. We all benefit from the trees in the rainforest and the farmers who labour in looking after them. The rainforests are the lungs of the earth and the air we all breathe.

If we do not wake up to artificial flavours and insist on purchasing the real thing, the farmers will be tempted to chop down the trees and plant palm oil or sugarcane which offer a more consistent income. This is not good news for the environment. Palm oil needs lots of water

Our Doctor in Madagascar

If we do not wake up to artificial flavours and insist on purchasing the real thing, the farmers will be tempted to chop down the trees and plant palm oil or sugarcane which offer a more consistent income. This is not good news for the environment.

and takes all the nutrients from the soil. It does not give back. Yet palm oil is in so many of our products on the shelf. We need a lot of it. Slashing and burning is a way of managing the palm oil plantations. It adds nitrogen to the ground and clears the edges for planting. This was fine when there was a water table, but now with global warming when the process takes place there is no water to absorb the heat, and the embers from the burning can carry on scorching and polluting the atmosphere for twenty years, leading to soil degradation.

In 2024 I visited Madagascar for one day. There is an annual orchid exhibition held at Kew Gardens and this time it was all about the orchids of Madagascar. There was of course a vanilla vine involved. It was magical. It had the atmosphere, scents and sounds of the rainforest, and so many orchid species. I only wished I had a group of eager children with me to share my enthusiasm. I did find myself surrounded by a group of adults as I was telling a lady about the vanilla orchid. (My daughter took a photograph of me among the orchids when she organised for us to go to the Chelsea Flower Show one year. I looked like St Janet of the Orchids, in the centre of an arch festooned with orchids of all colours!).

I am fully aware of the impression I give people when I get so enthusiastically involved in telling them about LittlePod and what we are about. I know that it makes them smile. One day I had a visit from the Environmental Health Officer, who had received notification in Wales that he was to go to LittlePod at Farringdon, my village in East Devon. Our second year had passed setting up a little production site in the village hall, which had to be signed off by the Environmental Health Officer. The EHO allowed me to see the note he had been given: 'You are going to see a woman who is in love with a flower.' I laughed. 'Well, come and see something', I said to him. We walked around the corner, passed the ancient hedge (recorded in the Domesday Book), and there for him to see was a brand-new office and manufacturing facility. He looked and smiled at me. 'I see,' he said, 'you have been very hard at work!'

To tell the setting up of a company needs a whole book to itself: how to get funding, how to train up, all the courses that my office administrator Clara and I did together in the early years – VAT courses, manufacturing courses in HACCP (Hazard Analysis and Critical Control Points), and risk assessments for food programmes, health and safety; I even have a Level 3 supervision for manufacturing certificate; learning acronyms like RIDDOR (Reporting of Injuries, Diseases and Dangerous Occurrences Regulations) and EORI (Economic Operators Registration and Identification); even simple things like how to set up on Companies House and what that required to run a business. It becomes apparent really after a short while that starting a business is 'at your risk'. So I am very proud of our Queen's Award and King's Award and other accreditations and our kitemark as a 'Made in Devon Trading Standards-approved company'.

However, I can never know enough about orchids.

07
Saving the Orchid

Orchids are one of the oldest plants on earth. Orchid fossils can be traced back to 90 million years ago. The word agape comes to me again at the thought that orchids bloomed when the dinosaurs were about.

The first fossil orchid was discovered in Dominican amber. It is such a wonder. There are very few places in the UK that are nurturing a vanilla vine, but two of them are quite close to me. One is the Eden Project in Cornwall, where they grow it in a tropical biome and have developed educational films about vanilla. The other is Burnham Nurseries at Newton Abbot in Devon, where Sara Rittershausen is the third-generation family member who is guardian of their orchid business. Sara is known worldwide for her extensive knowledge of orchids. There was a monumental vanilla orchid which was about 30 metres in length and which did flower. Sadly, during the Covid pandemic the plant died; the polytunnel could not be kept at the temperature it needed. I felt sad because on several occasions Sara had invited me to stand by this plant on a weekend in its hot, humid polytunnel to tell her customers about vanilla planifolia. I even opened the Vanilla Café. There was another occasion when Sara asked me to give a talk to the National Orchid Society, and that really did have my heart thumping. I asked the chairwoman to stand next to me so that I could appeal to her for technical terms about orchid maintenance. I found out, as I seemed always to find out when I gave these talks, that very few of the people in the audience knew about the vanilla orchid or that it had been declared an endangered species by the IUCN (International Union for Conservation of Nature).

The third place to see vanilla planifolia up close and personal, and in my view the best, is in the new glasshouses at the Chelsea Physic Garden in London. There is now an audio guide to tour the garden with and I am thrilled to say that it is my voice you can hear when you press the button to hear about vanilla!

Many orchid species are under threat of extinction as they are destroyed in the felling of trees in the rainforest. Orchids need the canopy of trees to exist. They are not parasites but epiphytes. They cling to trees for support, but whether their roots are terrestrial or simply aerial they find their nourishment from the air.

Orchid collectors are not only enjoying a wonderful hobby for their own wellbeing: they are also archivists and protectors of what may be the last species of the orchid they own. One day it may be these collectors who will be able to rewild the orchids once we all with one voice call for forest regeneration across the globe. It cannot be that the guardianship of such a resource as the quality of the air we breathe is to be the responsibility of the poorest nations who scratch a living on the equatorial belt. It must be the responsibility of us all.

The UK is one of the most nature-depleted countries in the world. As a teacher, whether working in the East End of London or in villages in Devon I have found that more and more children do not relate the food they are eating to something natural that is grown in soil. The crisis we are facing in nature is mainly due to ignorance and the high-rise living that people must endure in the cities. It saddens me that a child could possibly live and die without smelling the earth or having planted a seed and watched it grow.

In 2017 I decided that I would take a course at the Open University: I signed up for a foundation year in Environmental Science. May I warn all new business owners that running a business is itself a degree course. It is time-consuming, and there is a lot to learn. I had supported so many

Above: There are estimated to be around 35,000 species of orchids – these ones were photographed at Kew Gardens in 2024

graduates to do apprenticeships by that time that I thought I could find the time to study. I made a valiant attempt. I passed my modules on Global Warming and Climate Change. I passed the modules in maths, geology and physics. However when it came to chemistry I found that the periodic table had changed in the decades since I had studied the subject. The pass mark was 40 per cent, which I managed, but I cannot be very proud of myself apart from having given it a go.

I mention it for one reason. In that year I discovered that geologists could see from rock formations what was happening during the fall of civilisations. It was always assumed from the patterns and the history that the fall of a civilisation because of climate changes happened very slowly over hundreds if not thousands of years. However that is now thought not to be true. Some civilisations came to a rapid end because they did not have time to adapt to climate change. This small piece of knowledge should alert us to get ready and start adapting now. I believe that we can do this.

We live on a beautiful planet amongst some of the most educated people around the world. If we listen to the wisdom of the indigenous people and marry this with modern technology, I am certain there is an answer that we can all be part of.

Our children will not think much of us for leading hedonistic lives focused on the getting and spending of money, but they will think very highly of us if we can leave them a healing planet.

There is a call for the government to introduce a new GCSE in Natural History, which I hope would involve a hands-on approach. How can the next generation be asked to conserve nature of which it has no experience? In Japan the government pay for young people to go to the mountains to connect with nature. The current UK government have apparently thought to shelve the idea because it was not born from their own party; they propose to fold the idea into a review, which means that it may become embedded in part of a wider initiative. It should be an urgent mission. It is this kind of inaction that inhibits all sorts of growth. Carl Jung, the founder of Jungian psychology, would describe this as an idea born out of the 'collective unconscious'.

We are deeply concerned about our planet. We know that it is calling us to do something. Remember that when the ozone layer was at risk the primary schools were the harbingers of change: the children educated the parents about the perils of CFCs. The success is evident. We all heard the children and now there is evidence that the hole in the ozone layer is healing.

In my own primary school days in rural Lincolnshire in the 1950s nature was all around us. At the entrance to the school on either side of the path Mr Laing would grow vegetables. A lady in the village called Ruth would make the school dinners using Mr Laing's vegetables. We would take regular nature walks with our teacher, listen to nature programmes on the radio. I am sure that I prefer project method teaching because of the teaching I had at my primary school. It was very similar to the teaching methods in Finland today, thought to be one of the best educational systems in the world. Back in my day we would study the history of the North American Indians and build teepees in the school grounds. Our toilets were outside. They were compost toilets known as the 'outhouse'. Very sustainable and useful compost.

'What are you thinking about now, Janet?' Syiraz enquires.

'Oh, I am just musing on my own past and how I grew up, Syiraz. I grew up in a little village not unlike the one I live in now. It has all changed. It is a bit like Kuta. I grew up on the beach, a free-range childhood. Look at Kuta now. I am sorry to say but its environment has been destroyed by the growth of tourism.' When David came to Bali in 1976 he had to cut his way onto Kuta beach. It was completely empty, just pure sand and sea. He spent two years travelling around the world after university. He rode his bike through Afghanistan. How the world has changed.

The rot started to set in to my childhood village when I was about sixteen years old. Until then I had a very satisfactory life. I had a pony called Lady who was my confidante, and I replaced her with a boyfriend. On reflection that is something I wish was my sliding door moment that I could change.

Right: The vanilla vines are laden with pods at the LittlePod orchard in Bali

Saving the Orchid   101

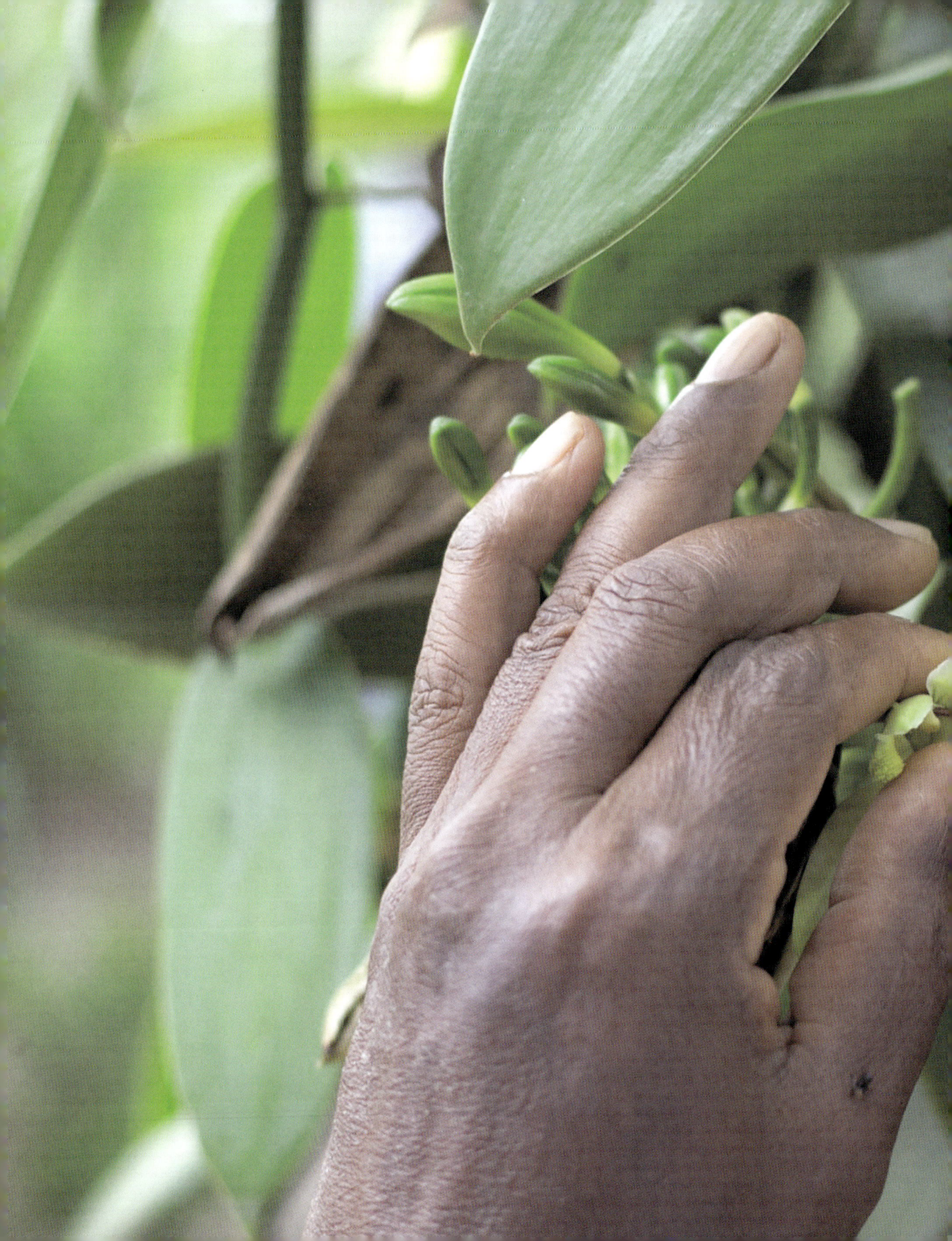

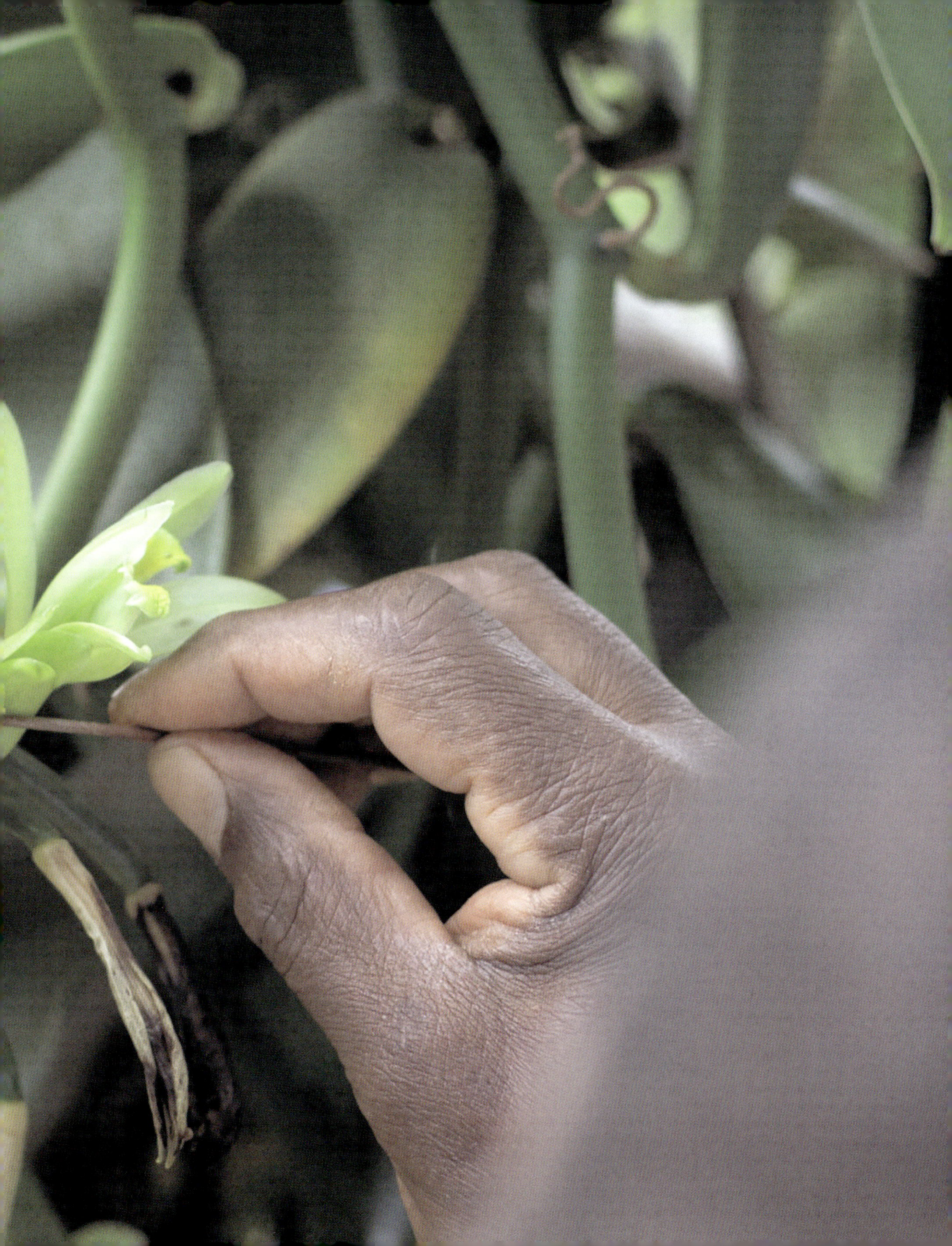

08
Memories of a Lost Village

During the Covid pandemic I managed to call up my father's RAF records. While scrolling the internet for any obscure mention of my dad, tracing his footsteps in Lincolnshire, I came across a book called Deadlines.

It is a story inspired by a photograph kept on a desk of a man in RAF uniform. His nephew never knew him but had an interest in aircraft, as he had grown up in Lincolnshire, known as Bomber County. He researched his uncle's life and wrote a book about his escapades. The book caught my attention because I was tracing my father's footsteps. I then looked to see who the author was. 'No, surely', I thought to myself, 'It can't be.' It was. The author was called Mike Curtis. He was the son of the rector of the village in rural Lincolnshire where I attended a little primary school as a child.

I made contact. We remembered our teachers and Mr Gill, the headmaster, who we discovered was now a hundred years old. We thought it might be possible to get in touch, but sadly he passed away shortly after. Mike validated something that I had felt about my childhood but had never understood from the perspective of other children who knew me. He told Paul in an interview: 'I lost touch with Janet for a long time. We moved to Filey in 1967. Janet came across something online to do with my book, Deadlines. This email came out of the blue. That was during Covid, 2020, I think.

'From the mid-sixties through to 2020 we had no contact at all. I had no idea where she'd gone or what she'd done. It's true of everyone else I was at school with in the 1960s, of course.

'I was there when I was six until nine years old. The overriding thing that I remember about Janet and Ann, her sister, from that period is that they never came to the school morning meetings, prayers and such like. I could never really understand this. I was the son of the Church of England Anglican rector of the parish and yet these two friends of mine were excluded from this meeting because they were Catholic. They were the only Catholics in the village. I must have asked my dad why that was, and the answer probably was "because they're a different religion, we're Anglicans and they're Catholics."

'Being at the centre of things my dad knew everyone. He particularly liked Paddy, Janet's dad. Her dad had been in the RAF. He was a great character. I remember that. He was the Donkey Man. The overriding memory that I have of him is that in the summer if you were out and about near the rectory you would hear this jingling of bells and, sure enough, this little herd of donkeys would come down Sea Lane with Paddy on his bike behind them. None of them was on reins or anything like that: they were just trotting along freestyle, and he was taking them to the beach. There wasn't so much traffic, even in the summer, and everyone just made way for this herd of donkeys and Paddy on his bike. You couldn't imagine anything like that today.

'It was an enjoyable period. Dad was at the centre of village life. He organised garden fêtes on our fields in summer that would end with a firework display. It was exciting. He'd get in celebrities to open the day. There was an illusionist who would catch bullets in his teeth. Those sorts of things stick in your head, fancy dress competitions and stuff like that. I'd get inveigled into taking part in these things. Janet and Ann would have almost certainly come to the fêtes, which were quite big affairs. There were meetings to discuss what would happen if the weather was bad. We could move it into the village hall – although not the fireworks (obviously). There was one local farmer whose name was Sam Whaler, sitting there puffing on his pipe and listening to this. Someone turned to him and said, "Sam, what do you reckon?" He slowly took his pipe out of his mouth and said, "It won't rain, rector." And it didn't. I only had three years there and I was bumped off to boarding school, although I was back for holidays. I liked Janet and Ann a lot, I remember that. I liked her dad. I can't remember her mum. The abiding memory was of the school, that there were these people who were friends of mine and they were excluded from the morning prayers.

'Janet once told me that she was sometimes given some sandwiches and told to take the donkeys down to the beach if Paddy was occupied elsewhere.

'I returned to Lincolnshire to work. That was before I joined the BBC. I got a job at Radio Lincolnshire, which meant that occasionally I was able to go back to see how the village had changed over the years. In my view, not for the better. Worse and worse, commercial and overcrowded. It just wasn't the place where we had those formative years in the early 1960s.

'Janet and Ann were what I would call outliers, because they were the only Catholics in the village.

'It has been great to reconnect. I was so interested to hear about what she has done, the awards she has won and the accolades she has received.

'I think the early years gave her a determination to stand up for herself and succeed. In that respect, looking at it with hindsight, I'm not surprised that she has gone on to do such great things. What she has achieved is fantastic, the awards she has received are well deserved, and she continues to go on and do these things. She's not letting go of the reins or easing up. I'm very impressed. It's a great story.

'One of the things that had an impact on me that she would have been aware of was that her dad was in the RAF during the war. He never went back to Ireland. Lincolnshire, of course, is called the home of the RAF. One of the recurring noises and sights in the village at that time was the Vulcans, which were based at RAF Coningsby, about 25 miles from the village. If you take a line from the runway out to the North Sea it goes directly over the village.

'Nearly every weekday, the Vulcans returning to Coningsby would fly over quite low. It's what they called the letdown, 25 miles direct into the navigation aid at the airfield. These Vulcans would go over the village day and night. Janet would certainly have been aware of that and had that constant reminder of what her dad came over from Ireland to do.

'I don't know if Janet ever went into the Anglican village church, but it famously had a palm tree next to the entrance, which was regarded as quite exotic. Janet and Ann would have seen that palm tree many times. We were only aware of palm trees on the Devon coast, around Paignton. But for as long as I was there, that palm tree was outside the church. I don't know the background or the story. But it was part of the village. You associated palm trees with what you read in books or saw on television, waving in the sun, not stuck outside a church on the Lincolnshire coast. I wonder if Janet thought about this when she saw the palm trees out in the orchard in Bali!

'One of my passions in life has always been music. In 1962 when Janet and I were first knocking about together at the school, that was the start of the big musical revolution. The first single I was given was Cliff Richard's *The Young Ones*, which came out in January 1962. That year, in October, the Beatles' first single was released, *Love Me Do*. That set me off on a great musical journey. We would have talked about it, as friends do. Have you heard *Love Me Do*? Pestering our parents to buy singles, even at that young age.

'It was the age of Teddy Boys. You'd see gangs of lads around the village with their winklepickers and Brylcreem. These are the things you remember about the early '60s. You looked in awe and slight fear at these older boys.

'There was a little cinema down at the beach end of Sea Lane. It's now a Spar shop. I do recall going in there with my dad for shows. There were always things going on. They raised funds to build a village hall. There was a real sense of community. Being the rector, dad was at the centre of things and knew everybody. He liked Paddy a great deal. There was a stream near the rectory, we would go fishing for minnows and sticklebacks and newts and set up a little zoo. It was a happy time.'

It was very poignant reading Mike's recollections of our village as a child, and I certainly remember it with the same fondness as he did. We were lucky growing up after the 1948 Education Act and lucky growing up in the 'country by the sea', even though the flat landscape made me feel melancholy at times. I think that influenced my dad at times too. Sometimes, maybe once a year, he would go to the sitting room and stay there all day playing songs by the Irish tenor John McCormack, who was born not far from where my dad came from. He also played ballads by his favourite singer, Joan Baez. His favourite song was *What a Wonderful World*, sung by Louis Armstrong.

I grew up as the Donkey Man's daughter. He had a horse called Silver and we would ride on the beach in the wintertime. My dad was very different from the other dads. He taught me to box. He had been a featherweight boxer in the RAF. Those skills came in useful when I went to secondary school.

After his death at the age of fifty I remember going into the local pub and the landlady said to me, 'You would never see your dad in here. Those men would be jealous of your dad. He never spent a day indoors and they would have loved to have been like him.' It was true. I must have tramped miles as a child with my dad. For almost a year after his death I would listen to a song by Gordon Lightfoot called *The Pony Man* over and over again to remind me of those lost times.

Our summer days would be spent on the beach, my father giving donkey rides. I would oversee one of the deck chair huts. From the age of eight I was meeting and greeting and totally in charge of my domain, making sure that the deck chairs came back in good order.

I spent days watching families on the beach, wondering what their city lives must be like. We were definitely 'outliers' It was a weird experience being left in the classroom while the rest of the school (there were only fifty children in the whole school) went to assembly. I am glad that Mike observed that, as I do feel that it was an unusual experience for all of us. Meeting Mike again I realised that of course my father had come to that village because he had been rejected by his country and rejected for being Irish in London and the RAF was the place that had welcomed him, 'Bomber County' was where he felt safe.

Reading Mike's book *Deadlines* revealed more to me about the landscape of my youth. Interestingly, Mike became a BBC radio journalist and set up the first Asian radio station. He wrote about that time in his book *Asian Auntie*. Imagine that today. A rector's son from a nowheresville village where you must wrap up from the Siberian winds in winter had the presence to think about those who came from the hot countries.

We had a menagerie of animals. There were goats and horses, donkeys, ducks, hens, some from time to time that needed repairing. My dad would wake me up in the middle of the night to go to West's farm to see the lambs being born or the chickens. One Christmas around midnight we walked a few miles in the dark to go to a hall. I remember walking in the cold and seeing a light ahead of me. We went into a hall where the Salvation Army were meeting. They had been out carol singing. Then they switched off all the lights and brought into the hall this pure white foal that had just been born. It was so magical that I cried.

My sister and I would walk to and from school, always past the rectory where Mike lived. In the summer we would stop and play with the minnows in the stream or lie in the wildflower meadows by the rectory. One day we arrived home to hear a barking noise coming from the bathroom. We very cautiously opened the door. On the side of the bath was a 1940s type baby's feeding bottle shaped like a banana. In the bath was a seal pup. It had been stranded on the beach and its mother had died. My dad looked after it until he could set it free into the sea.

So many stories I can tell of the Donkey Man's daughter's experiences. They were happy days. At the end of the summer my dad would have two weeks when he would invite the disabled children's society to come for free donkey rides on the beach. Life was short for my dad, and he lived every day as if it were his last. He was half man, half bicycle, whistling in the morning and laughing in the evening. I do think that after all the horrors he had endured he was primarily a happy man.

I feel very sad now that I became embarrassed when he would drive the donkeys by the school gates in the morning and all the children would run to the railings shouting, 'Paddy, Paddy'. I would run into the washrooms and offer to wash the art equipment to hide my embarrassment. There was one occasion when my father became obsessed with a tree that was earmarked to be felled. He wove a story about a fairy ring that appeared at a certain time of the evening, and warned people that it would be detrimental to their health if this tree was chopped down. The whole story was reported in the local press. The tree remained.

Looking back, it was foolish to be embarrassed. I think it all stemmed from my first arrival at school. My mother was an Irish-speaker and taught me lots of songs in Gaeilge. My first day at school with my Irish tongue did not go down well: the other children laughed so loud. I was mortified. I decided to learn English pronunciation from then on. I told my mother, but in her Irish way she would say to me, 'Janet, be thankful they are doing it to you because that means they are leaving some other poor sod alone.' I never quite got the logic of that.

My mother was an O'Leary. She came from Wexford, a Republican town. My grandfather had been the black sheep of the family for joining the IRA in 1916. My mother benefitted by having her mother to herself until the age of five. She attended a Loretto convent school from two to eighteen years of age, and passed her leaving certificate. This was not easy, as all her lessons were in the Irish language then not spoken at home. This was the effect of President Eamon De Valera's attempt to convert Ireland back to an Irish-speaking nation. You had to pass Gaeilge and mathematics to get the leaving certificate.

I mastered my new English accent by imitating the Queen's English with a radio programme called 'Listen with Mother'. I was very pleased with myself, but when I went back to school the children laughed even louder at my new strange tongue. I suppose after that I learnt to just be myself and I learnt to love my peers. It was always a challenge. When I was ten years old we were studying Oliver Cromwell at school. My mother took me straight out of school and on the ferry from Fishguard to Wexford. There she

> **But when people ask me 'Why are you doing that, Janet?' or 'Who gave you permission to do that, Janet?' or more so, 'Where do you get your natural sense of authority from?', I have to say, 'My dad.'**

walked me up and down the high street telling stories of the gruesome things Oliver Cromwell did to the babies and children. I could imagine their heads on pikes. I suspect I didn't sleep for weeks. My mother then deposited me back at the school gates and said, 'You go on in there and tell them what Oliver Cromwell did to Ireland.' She was well-meaning, but her greatest complaint about me was that I was just too much like my father.

When someone so charismatic in one's life dies and their philosophy of life is so different from the prevailing tune of the day it is bound to change one's life forever. But when people ask me 'Why are you doing that, Janet?' or 'Who gave you permission to do that, Janet?' or more so, 'Where do you get your natural sense of authority from?', I have to say, 'My dad.'

When I moved to the big school my father

never once stepped through the gate. My teachers thought my mother was a single mum. I had been given the title of Catholic (although my parents were lapsed), so I had the choice at eleven to go to morning assembly or to go around the corner to the Catholic church. I elected to go to the church, all in Latin and full of Hell, fire and damnation.

However there was one time when I did go to assembly. My class were a bit riotous. I used to teach the naughty boys to read at lunchtime. (My father had set the pattern for that. He was friendly with a man called Mr Gray, whose wife had died; he was Romani, and lived in a beautiful colourful vardo or carriage. My dad would sit outside by the fire with him, having pulled down the steps of the vardo and sent me inside with notebooks and pencils to teach Naomi and Silus, aged sixteen and fourteen, to read and write). The time came for our class to produce our own assembly. No-one wanted to do it. They were truculent teenagers and en masse resolutely refused. After so many arguments with my peers I offered to do it by myself, to represent our class and get the coveted points. At thirteen I stood on the stage in the assembly hall where I was very rarely seen and proceeded to give my thoughts to the school about revolution and change. I played Bob Dylan's song *The Times They Are A-Changin'* and argued for incremental change as opposed to revolution.

My family lived near the beach. In winter the times were hard. When the summers were good, we made enough money to get us through the winter.

In 1950s Britain there were still food ration books. I think people forget that after the war families had to work together to earn enough to get by. People had to be resourceful. We grew our own vegetables, and my dad would come home with a rabbit, hare or deer to eat. In the autumn I would be out of school from time to time picking potatoes and riddling them until late at night. We would have to wear plastic covers early in the morning to pull up Brussel sprouts: they would be wet by mid-morning, and had to be picked crisp. Lots of my friends at primary school worked on the land with their families or on other farms. In the spring we would be up early to pick mushrooms.

My mother would say, 'Well, one thing you can always say, Janet, that you ate well.' I can just close my eyes and smell the unforgettable scent of soil.

There is an urgent need for soil. It is thought that we have around sixty years of topsoil left. Here is an article from the Guardian newspaper by Susan Coster of 30 May 2019:

The world needs topsoil to grow 95% of its food – but it's rapidly disappearing.

Without efforts to rebuild soil health, we could lose our ability to grow enough nutritious food to feed the planet's population.

The world grows 95% of its food in the uppermost layer of soil, making topsoil one of the most important components of our food system. But thanks to conventional farming practices, nearly half of the most productive soil has disappeared in the last 150 years threatening crop yields and contributing to nutrient pollution, dead zones and erosion. In the US alone, soil on cropland is eroding 10 times faster than it can be replenished.

If we continue to degrade the soil at the rate we are now, the world could run out of topsoil in about 60 years, according to Maria-Helena Semedo of the UN's Food and Agriculture Organization. Without topsoil, the earth's ability to filter water, absorb carbon, and feed people plunges. Not only that, but the food we do grow will probably be lower in vital nutrients.

The modern combination of intensive tilling, lack of cover crops, synthetic fertilisers and pesticide has left farmland stripped of the nutrients, minerals and microbes that support healthy plant life. But some farmers are attempting to buck the trend and save their lands along with their livelihoods.

There is a need to start composting now, collectively. It is the one thing that everyone can share in. The daily food waste of vegetables should be composted, if it is not being turned into soup for people who need nutritious food.

We need to help the farmers on the equatorial belt, and then they in turn can help us – purchase their real products and not spend endless time and vast amounts of money trying to imitate the real thing just to save a few pennies. The real thing will last longer too. LittlePod's vanilla paste in a tube lasts for two years once opened and kept in a cool cupboard.

At the heart of Ukraine's agriculture is its highly fertile soil. Nearly 25 per cent of the world's most fertile soil, known as chernozem, is in Ukraine. It is full of the nutrients we need. And it takes five hundred years to produce one inch of soil. It is imperative that we all start to love what is under our feet! This is why we urgently need to start teaching our children to embrace and love the environment and look after it.

Fortunately, there is a new science that children will be learning that will help them to see the relevance of the forest floor. It is termed the Woodwide Web. Albert Bernhard Frank, born in 1839, was a German botanist and biologist. He was the first scientist to use the word 'mycorrhiza'. His observations and hypotheses in 1885 flew in the face of conventional thinking. He hypothesised that mycorrhiza and its host rely on each other for nutritional support. In other words, the fungus extracts nutrients from mineral soil and humus and passes them to the tree. The tree in turn nourishes the fungus. It was revolutionary thinking.

Fast forward 140 years and there are scientists who are still arguing about this find. However, at the University of British Columbia is a professor of forest ecology aged sixty who has dedicated thirty years of her working life so far to research into forest ecosystems and mycorrhizal networks (connections between plants and fungi). What is going on under our feet is extraordinary. What we can't see as we pass through a wood are the threadlike fungi that mix with the roots of the trees, helping them extract water and nutrients in a process of exchange made through photosynthesis. The network in the soil is a neural network, and the chemicals that move through it are the same as our neural transmitters.

Because of this Suzanne Simard, a Canadian forestry scientist and conservationist, believes that trees recognise us. I believe this too. A tree is not silent. It is full of noise and busyness. It's just that we cannot hear it. As J. G. Frazer shows in his book *The Golden Bough: A Study of Magic and Religion*, tree worship and tree lore and legends are ancient in cultural histories around the world. We do not have to believe that a broken twig is some harbinger of darkness, but we do have to have more respect for trees and their place in the ecosystem.

Suzanne is currently collaborating on research to see if trees can recognise us as human beings. We as a society today have separated ourselves from nature and are unaware of the mysteries around us. Suzanne says, 'Some trees have lived for thousands of years. They get along, developing sophisticated relationships and listen. They are attuned. Attunement is something we all need.' Her new book, available as an audio book and video, is called *Finding the Mother Tree.*

There is another book I would recommend. It is *Entangled Life* by Merlin Sheldrake (what a wonderful name). It is about the hidden life of fungi. In his book Merlin says that thinking there is a network of fungi that spreads across the forest floor might be somewhat problematic because 'fungi make entangled webs whether or not they link plants together'. He writes, 'Today, even with their own root systems almost all plants still depend on mycorrhizal fungi to manage their underground lives. Mycorrhizal fungi are not built into plant seeds. Plants and fungi must constantly form and reform their relationships. Faced with catastrophic environmental change much of life depends on the ability of plants and fungi to adapt to new conditions whether in polluted or deforested landscapes or in newly created environments such as urban green roofs.'

There are scientists now mapping this web,

and it is very exciting to know what they are going to find – a whole new science for the next generation of primary school children, who I guess will come to love trees.

This is why I believe, turning to Syiraz, that he and his team can believe that their environment can be restored. It needs education. It needs people to be awake to the world beneath their feet.

An understanding of soil properties is fundamental to assessing the character of vegetation that soil will support.

New technologies are going to help collect field data, and from that information scientists are going to be able to measure the extent of soil erosion. LiDAR or Light Detection And Ranging (active laser scanning) is a remote sensing method that can be used to map structure. It directly measures the height and density of vegetation on the ground, making it an ideal tool for scientists studying vegetation over large areas. Light is emitted from a rapidly firing laser. Think of light strobing or pulsing from a laser light source. This light travels to the ground and reflects off things like buildings and tree branches. The reflected light energy then returns to the LiDAR sensor where it is recorded. Imagine the data that can be collected quickly, as opposed to conventional on the ground methods.

As I think about all this, I look around me now at this extensive forest orchard in Bali, appreciating the work of the farmers. I can see that they are happy to show me around. Dr Made told me that when they started the polyculture project the LittlePod Orchard was barren, without much biodiversity. He told me that there were times when they felt that they had bitten off more than they could chew; LittlePod's support and patience and understanding when things went wrong was consistent and faithful. The process has involved lots of different risks, but here we are now with an abundance of healthy, fine quality vanilla and lots of mycorrhizal fungi keeping the forest nourished with increased biodiversity.

Moreover, the farmers do not have to rely on vanilla as a cash crop. They have other crops to sell when the weather is too wet. They can take their time with vanilla, not force the growth, and allow the full term for ripening, because they are LittlePod's pods, and we are not in a hurry for them. We can wait.

It makes me tearful to think that in 1962 Rachel Carson published her seminal work, *Silent Spring*. Her book changed the attitudes of a generation when she exposed the reasons why using fertilisers and pesticides on crops would damage not just the earth but also us. Here we are more than sixty years later going around in circles having the same conversation.

There is no question that in the coming decades we are going to need to adapt both in agriculture and in everyday life. We must support the farmers and incentivise them to find ways of reducing environmental harm. The effects of the climate emergency are all around us – floods, droughts, increased rainfall, famine – all of which affect crop yield and change crop seasons.

Mycorrhizal fungi exist nearly everywhere in the world, but they have been depleted by modern agriculture practices. By introducing them there is a chance of restoring the natural balance of the soil. Farmers will have higher yields and save on water and fertiliser costs.

We must heed the message. This is nature's siren call to us.

09
A Promise to Dr Made

> **'Have you travelled much, Syiraz?' I ask. I find that he has. He has studied in England, the US, Vietnam and elsewhere.**

I tell him that I seem to travel to places at the most unusual times when there are not many visitors around. I remember a trip to China in January 2002.

I went with David, who had been invited to teach at a university. While he was busy in Shenzhen I decided to go to Guilin, the place that every poet and artistic soul wants to visit at least once in a lifetime. It is home to incredible natural scenery – the karst limestone mountains that stretch over 2,000 kilometres. It was a definite agape moment for me. I remember exclaiming 'Oh WOW' very loudly in the car as we approached. When I arrived at the hotel I discovered that there were only five international guests: three people from Chile, one from the USA, and myself. They were concerned for me as a woman of a certain age on my own. Visitor numbers were down because of 9/11. People were not travelling. The hotel staff decided to call me Braveheart. They gave me a translator called Ginger and a very lovely chauffeur whom I referred to as Parker. They asked me if I would like to do something special. I said 'Yes please. I would like to go to the theatre, to an art exhibition and I would like to visit a mountain school.' They were true to their word and arranged everything, including a five-hour trip along the River Lee and an amazing cave tour.

When I started LittlePod I felt connected to Frances Ma, who I met at the Restaurant Show at Earl's Court in 2013. She was living in Hong Kong. I told her about my visit to China and my memorable journey to Guilin. Frances had grown up in St Albans near London and had attended a small primary school where she was the only Chinese child in the class. The bond was made. I told her of my experience of my own rural primary school days. Frances has been our LittlePodder in Hong Kong for nearly thirteen years. We met recently in Japan when I attended the Foodex show with Yumi and Otayo, LittlePod's representatives in Japan. I was able to tell her that the Barakura English Garden in Japan came to our stand, and that I shall be going there in 2025 as a guest for their harvest festival event. We agreed to meet up again when I am there. Meanwhile Frances, having gained the certification and permissions, is about to launch LittlePod in China. Another circle completed.

The students are urging me on impatiently: 'You were going to tell us how you met Dr Made.'

'Ah yes', I say while musing. It feels as if we have been here for days. It has a magical sense of extended time. When my daughter was twelve years old she asked me to make a clock cake and to put on it the words 'Time no longer'. I often wondered if it was her unconscious telling her that times were changing, and she was about to leave childhood behind. Either way there was something rather mystical about the phrase and I am lulled here into that same feeling of an altered state.

'Well,' I begin, 'it all happened because I had started my own company called LittlePod. My company was almost two years old when one day I received an email, which I still have, from a man who said that he was reaching out to ask if we needed someone to source our vanilla. When people ask Made 'How did you meet Janet?' this is what he says.

'I was born in Bali and raised on a smallholding farm. I'm a son of a spice grower – my father farmed vanilla and cloves – and I always wanted to return and establish my own orchard. I sent emails to all the vanilla distributors

Top: Frances Ma, LittlePod's long-time representative in Hong Kong
Bottom: Celebrating LittlePod's first anniversary with Patricia Rain, the Vanilla Queen, in 2011

Left: LittlePod HQ in Farringdon, East Devon
Right: Receiving the Queen's Award for Enterprise (Sustainable Development) in 2018

in the UK and EU enquiring about supplying them with Indonesian vanilla. Only LittlePod came back with a serious reply. LittlePod sparked my environmental spirit and inspired me to use vanilla for ecological conservation and restoration. I wouldn't be here without the encouragement of LittlePod.'

Made's dream to resurrect his father's long abandoned vanilla farm struck a chord with me. The consensus at that time was that vanilla could be lost in a generation if we didn't act now! I had been warned by Patricia Rain, a sustainability expert known as the Vanilla Queen. In 2005 I had held a special LittlePod day in our village of Farringdon in East Devon, that we called 'Vanilla Spice and All Things Nice'. I had invited my friend Nash over from the US to give a talk about vanilla farmers and how they scratch a living producing vanilla pods, and he had told Patricia about the day. She sent her regards from California and copies of her book, *Vanilla: The Cultural History of the World's Favorite Flavor and Fragrance*, and wrote to me, saying,

'If we could encourage one per cent of consumers to purchase REAL vanilla, we could double the cultivation of the crop to the benefit of us all. We will lose REAL vanilla within a generation if we don't act NOW.'

I was stirred by her passion. *(For the 2005 event see p136.)*

Dr Made's plan to establish a community-owned forest orchard that would benefit the farmers and the environment was just what was needed to save vanilla for the next generation. I read in the Vanilla Queen's book that 'the potential for vanilla growing in Indonesia is tremendous. The climate is consistent enough in many of the islands to allow for greater production, cheap labour is readily available, and the people are accustomed to selling their vanilla collectively. It remains to be seen if this potential will be realised in the coming years.' To me it was like a call to arms when I received the message from Dr Made. Was he the man to spearhead the resurrection of vanilla to be grown in a sustainable way in Indonesia?

Farringdon, where the headquarters of LittlePod are nestled, is a farming hamlet of around a hundred and fifty houses fairly spread out from Exeter airport to the road that takes the summer visitor east to the beautiful Jurassic coast. There its eco build sits happily beside the seventeenth-century cottages and the ancient church. We were selected to be part of a new kitemark called 'Made in Devon', Trading Standards Approved. Our reputation as a company with integrity is very precious to us. It is also important to our customers, suppliers, and the farmers we work with.

We proudly display a photograph of David Fursdon, the Lord Lieutenant of Devon, who presented us with our Queen's Award for Enterprise in Sustainable Development in 2018. When we won the King's Award for Enterprise in Sustainable Development in 2023, David came to a gathering at my house, and we held a presentation ceremony; Dr Made and Ketut, his cousin, joined us by video link from Bali.

The Lord Lieutenant said: 'It is always a pleasure to celebrate success and LittlePod is the perfect example. The King's Award is designed to celebrate and reward very special businesses, and LittlePod is one.

'I'm well aware of how difficult it is to win one of these awards. Storytelling is very important, and LittlePod always does that well, but you also have to deliver against various specific criteria, which isn't easy.

'King Charles is particularly interested in the sustainability side of the awards programme and that is very much on show here. I want you all to realise what a big deal it is to win this award.

'For me, what LittlePod is able to do that a lot of other businesses aren't is to have an impact that goes so far beyond the UK. So many businesses and initiatives focus just on what they're able to do in this country, but LittlePod is the opposite. LittlePod is making a difference in countries such as Indonesia and as we've heard from Made, they're able to aid reforestation and make a difference to communities there as well as here at home. That's a big deal.

'There is a symbiotic relationship between growing vanilla and protecting the rainforests and LittlePod is making a difference in countries across the world.'

Since the Lord Lieutenant represents the King, the farmers have invited him to visit whenever he can. When we won the King's Award in 2023, Councillor Rufus Gilbert, Cabinet Minister for Economic Recovery and Skills, Salcombe Division, said: 'The fact that LittlePod has remained true to its roots here in Devon makes this award even more special. This success belongs to the local community almost as much as it does to LittlePod and that's a very special thing.'

'What are LittlePodders?' asks one of the students. 'People who love vanilla', I tell him. 'People who are passionate about their food source. People who care for their environment. People who like to keep things real. People who support our Campaign for Real Vanilla.'

'What kind of people do you employ

at LittlePod?' asks Syiraz. 'People who are inquisitive', I tell him. 'This is what I look for when I take on an apprentice. At LittlePod I have mentored every apprenticeship standard from level 1 to level 7 including an MBA. Not a year has passed in the fifteen years of LittlePod when I have not had a student or intern or apprentice striving to achieve their own ambitions in their working life. Various people – advisers, business owners, people curious about startups – have all asked me, "where do you find the time?" It comes naturally to me because I was a teacher.'

My mind begins to wander again.

It was a vocation that drew me into teaching, and I loved my job until the government decided to implement a national curriculum. I was there in the early days when it was being implemented. However I was teaching in a private school at that time. I was teaching the chief education officer's daughter, the area education officer's daughter, and many lovely daughters who were too precious for the state system. We did not have to adhere to government policy. It was abundantly obvious that there were far too many attainment goals and that they would eventually have to be watered down. And they were, pretty quickly. There was no common sense.

The problem was that subject area specialists were in a war zone for space and time in the curriculum. Had the system been introduced incrementally, weighing up the benefits and loss to children's education, I think it might have, yes, it could have been beneficial. Instead it created an atmosphere of fear and loathing, and I believe that the young people of today are probably the most examined and stressed of all children that I've ever known.

There was a terrible loss of experienced teachers and many casualties during the implementation of this system, even suicides. One lady I met in hospital, who was dying, begged me to tell people that it was the system that was killing her. People do not realise that children notice these things. The number of times I have heard the phrase, 'Oh, children get over things. Just a matter of time.' Education is a political football. My advice to parents, for what it is worth, is not to sacrifice your child on the altar of ideology. You want your child to grow and to be individuated, so think only of the needs of your child and do the best you can despite your political leanings.

My father tried to persuade me against becoming a teacher. My mother even cried, saying, 'You never look so nice as when you worked in the bank', and perhaps more prophetically, 'Oh, and nobody respects a teacher.' My father said he had met more educated people outside the system than in it. Nevertheless, I had a desire and followed my heart. I am always curious to understand how other cultures educate their young. This curiosity has led me to have lots of enriching experiences. My interest in different systems of educational practice led me astray sometimes, especially when I've been visiting a country with David.

I was once invited as a guest to accompany him to Cuba, where he was to give a presentation on health practices at work. We were walking in one of the main squares in Havana when I spotted some primary school children doing their morning exercises in the street. There was a little girl about four years old standing in the line with her hands placed resolutely on her hips,

Opposite: Receiving the Queen's Award for Enterprise (Sustainable Development) from David Fursdon, the Lord Lieutenant of Devon, in 2018

A Promise to Dr Made

tapping the ground. She was looking around and behaving in a very anarchic fashion, clearly bored by the whole experience. The other children, ignoring her, finished their morning routine by punching the air and shouting 'Fidel, Fidel, Fidel' as a tribute to their leader. The little girl looked at them with a wholly comical expression of contempt and just sighed. I could not contain myself. It was so funny. What was so interesting was that nobody tried to reprimand her for her behaviour; they all just turned and walked into class. Mesmerised, I walked in after them. The teacher was welcoming and allowed me to say something to the children while she busily scrawled her contact details on a piece of paper. 'Keep contact', she whispered as she handed me her details. David was wondering where on earth I'd disappeared to when he heard a voice saying, 'Good morning, children', and realised what must have happened.

In 1999 I came to Bali and spent five weeks there. Two years later I returned for another five weeks. It was not surprising for my friends there when I announced that I had been asked to teach in the local village school. I'd wandered off to find the nearest primary school, where to my delight a Balinese dance session was happening. I introduced myself to the head teacher, who on hearing that I was a teacher myself immediately said, 'You will come? You will teach English, maths and the four seasons.'

The children were fascinated to hear about spring, summer, autumn and winter. They wanted me to describe what snow is like. They have just two seasons, wet and dry. This school was in a poor desa, a rural village. The class, a mix of Christian, Muslim and Hindu children, all lived there. They had no pencils or paper. Their head teacher (well, their only teacher) held my hand. As I spoke, he smiled at the children and smiled at me. 'How old are you?' I said, 'I am forty-six.' 'Ah,' he retorted in a deliberate fashion, 'I am fifty-five.'

In Bali the older you get, the wiser you get, the more intelligent, more capable you become. Of course. It was necessary to survive in a system that has no safety net. I realised the handholding was a gesture to show the children that I was not to be feared, but to be trusted. School was from the early mornings until about midday, after which it got too hot and the smell of the pig farm just behind the school became unbearable. There was no public schooling after twelve years of age. The children here were sitting upright in white blouses or shirts with grey skirts or trousers, all equal in the eyes of their teacher. They had limited chances of education when they left this school. I asked them what their ambitions were for the future, and I was startled to hear them say, 'Oh, I hope I grow up with more confidence so that I will not be fearful about what people say about me.' 'I hope I will grow up strong so that I can help my parents.' They had such different priorities from the children I was used to teaching. Their responses had a great impact on me.

In 2001 I returned with my son Dan, then aged thirteen. I introduced him to Nnga, the teacher, and he was asked to teach mathematics to the students. He could not believe their level of mental arithmetic, which was a consequence of having only four walls and a good teacher. But their ambitions were changing. They talked with a new perspective: one would like to become an engineer, one would like to be a teacher, one would like to be a doctor. Others said that they would like to own a scooter. That had definitely changed since my last visit: the place was festooned with scooters.

I was very proud of Dan when we returned home to Devon. At school he wrote about his experiences of meeting those impressive young people. His letter about the injustices of their educational opportunities, how ambitious the students in Bali were, was sent to the local press and printed in full. He also wrote to Gordon Brown, at that time Chancellor of the Exchequer, who was about to embark on a journey to Bali himself to take part in a conference on equality in education. In response his department sent Dan three sets of reports on the government policy for International Education. Did they realise that the letter was from a thirteen-year-old? His father and I thought it would have been much more appropriate for them to offer him the opportunity to tour the hallowed halls of Westminster.

'Oh!' I suddenly stumble, coming out of my rumination. One of the interns caught me. 'Thank you. I was getting lost in my memories of times past here in Bali. Have you all been to university?' I ask them. 'Yes', they reply, with assorted degrees

Thinking of the empty nest and missing the fun times with my own children I am glad that I have a purpose with LittlePod.

in history, economics, chemical engineering and business.

Here we are more than twenty years since I taught in that little primary school, looking at state education in Bali today. Education is compulsory and provided free of charge at public schools from grades one to nine, but money is needed for uniform, pens and equipment. There are scholarships for university and government sponsorship for postgraduate education in universities abroad. I am so impressed with how things have developed. 'What are your ambitions today, then?' I ask them. I was so uplifted with their replies. 'We need to restore our natural world, regenerate our forests for the next generation', they say. 'It is our most important task for our children to come.' They are all full of admiration for Made and what he is achieving in the forest experiment. Over half of Indonesia's population are young people. There is hope for the environmental future if all the young think like this.

I note that in the UK we are an aging population, and many young people feel that the older generation have let them down. There is a generational divide that is not to be seen in Bali. There is no hint of self-pity in these young people, but rather a desire that their own children will look to them as they do to Made and their environment will be restored. There is something of a legacy in the thinking of these people that reminded me of those young people I first met in Bali.

'What does your son do? Syiraz asks. 'He is a doctor', I answer – and then I qualify my answer: 'he is also an actor and a musician.' 'Oh, my wife is a doctor', he replies. Syiraz looks young for his age, but then all Asian people defy their age, I think. 'Dan will be pleased to hear this,' I say, 'especially having met the children in Bali when he came here, and they had such ambitions.' 'Has Dan been back to Bali?' Syiraz asks. 'Well, he is a surfer so that has drawn him back. When he came with us the first time and met the children in the school, the headmaster invited us to his house one evening. We arrived with biscuits, and he provided the tea. He then sat cross-legged on his patio near his papaya tree and proceeded to entertain us with a gamelan recital. It was so special. We sat for around two hours in the cool of the evening air listening to him playing. Every now and then he would lift a leg and let off a fart. It was so natural. I thought Dan would laugh, being thirteen and normally seeing the funny side of things, but he was mesmerised by the playing. As we left Dan said to me, 'The music made you feel so full, don't you think.'

Thinking of the empty nest and missing the fun times with my own children I am glad that I have a purpose with LittlePod. There was a period that nearly changed Dan's life forever, a sliding doors moment when the turning could have been very different. When people ask me what my motivation is for pursuing LittlePod I say my children. They work so hard and play hard too. I don't think they would appreciate a mother who sat pining for them. I am sure all mothers feel the same way, but I truly have been inspired by my own children. I have been so impressed by their fortitude and resilience at various points in their lives. In many ways it is because of them that I have been so resolved to do something to help the planet, to be useful in some way.

'Syiraz, is the story of Harry Potter well known in Indonesia?' 'Yes. In Indonesia everyone wants an owl. There is a demand for wild owls in the market because of the book.' 'Real owls?' 'Yes', says Syiraz. The emergence of Harry Potter on the scene is one of those nodal times when people want to know Where were you? When?

'Well, Dan was selected at an audition to play the part of Harry Potter.' 'Really, how did that happen?' asks Syiraz. There is silence from the others as I tell the story. 'When he was ten years old he was watching a programme on TV called 'Blue Peter'. It said that a film company were looking for a boy to play the role of Harry Potter, and a competition had been announced to find an English boy. Dan had read the book, and was quick to get some paper to write a letter. As you know, he is a good letter-writer. He pestered his father to take him to have his photograph taken wearing round glasses. They went to a photo booth to do the deed and posted the letter.

We moved house shortly afterwards and forgot all about it. One day several months later while Dan was at school I received a phone call. The woman said that her name was Susie Figgis, and that she was the casting director for

Time Warner. I said 'Oh, but that was a long time ago. Why are you getting in touch now?' She said that it had taken so long because they had had 50,000 letters and felt obliged to read them all. I asked her if it was difficult. She said no, just long to read, and that Dan's letter stood out. She asked to speak with Dan. I said that he was at school, and asked what she wanted him for. She said that they had really loved his letter and that they would like to offer him an audition for the Harry Potter role.

When he arrived home I gave Dan Susie's number, and he phoned her. There began a journey never to be forgotten. Dan's school asked if he would be prepared to give a report in assembly about his progress. He obliged.

As the mother I was relegated to sit in a corner and watch as these strangers began to question Dan about his background. They noted that he sang with the National Children's Choir and that he played chess for Devon, they quizzed him on his interests and asked what he wanted to be when he grew up. 'A doctor', he replied.

Throughout all of this he kept very calm. When we left he said to me, 'They want me to come back next week.' This happened several times, and each time in assembly Dan would report how he got on, until he was called for the final interview and screening in Covent Garden in London. I remember the day so vividly. Ten little Harry Potters sitting in a row, all in their blazers, waiting to go in for their screen tests. I was sidled up to by an actor called Richard Briars (who sadly passed away a few years ago), and he asked me 'Which one is yours?' I pointed to Dan. 'He seems very calm', he said. 'Yes, that's because he plays chess', I replied, and then checked myself for being so silly.

Each child was in the audition room for around ten minutes. Then it was Dan's turn. He was in the room for twenty-five minutes. Susie Figgis came out with her hands in the air, saying, 'Where's your mother, Dan?' I rushed down, wondering what had happened. She put her hand on Dan's shoulder and said, 'Well, it's Dan. We are sending your film off to the bigwigs in America tomorrow and will be in touch.' That was that.

'What happened?' All the students wanted to know.

We heard nothing for ages and then Susie phoned to say that they were having trouble because Steven Spielberg, who was going to direct the film, initially wanted to work with an American boy; J. K. Rowling, the author, wanted a British boy, so Spielberg pulled out. They would have to wait until they knew who the next choice of director would be.

By this time the whole school wanted to know how Dan was going to fare. In their eyes he was Harry Potter. When Dan took part in a two-week festival of acting and singing at the time he was judged to be the most promising all-round performer and won a cup.

Time passed, and we went on holiday to Naples. That was another occasion when I experienced being in a place where there was no one around. Dan and I went to visit Herculaneum in the early morning and found ourselves wandering around that ancient site all by ourselves. As we walked up the lonely street to catch the train we met a terrified American who asked us if it was safe in these parts.

On arriving home Dan received another phone call from Susie. This time it was not good news. She told us that the new director was not a choice that she or other casting directors would recommend, and that she had pulled out of the casting. It remains to be seen if Tim Burton had got the role of director would Dan have then been Harry Potter?

Of course the worry was how was he going to deal with this? The whole school had followed his progress and had been waiting for the outcome. One of his teachers had said to me, 'I would worry about some children but not Dan. He is his own man.' We should never have worried. The summer was coming and the cricket season. That year the local Sidmouth team were at the top of the league. Dan was a spin bowler, and he was selected for the team. All thoughts of Harry Potter disappeared, as if by magic!

'What a story to tell his children', said Syiraz. 'Perhaps if Dan had been Harry Potter he might have raised awareness of the need for rainforest regeneration and then everyone would have listened to him.' 'Perhaps,' I said, 'but we can't leave things to the desires of an actor, can we? We all must play our own part and hope it's enough, though I do get your drift about publicity.' In fact, there is a fictional film that has been released about the idea of the boy who came second and the dream of what might have been.

10
Arts and Culture

'Janet, how did you get into the vanilla industry in the first place?' was the next question from Syiraz. Well, the answer to that goes back to the village where I live.

When I had settled in Farringdon and had got to know a few people I went one evening to a committee meeting in the village hall. The people were thinking of selling the hall. There were repairs needed, and some debts, and they didn't know what to do. I suggested that they should put on some fund-raising events. No one raised their hand, so I offered.

That is how I set up the Farringdon Society of Arts. I gathered some talented people from the village and we formed a committee; we met once a month in my house and created a series of talks, plays, art events and dinners.

Once I wrote to a famous chef called Yotam Ottolenghi and told him about our village and a food event we were having; he sent us some recipe suggestions and said how much he loved the idea of 'art, music and food all in a living village'. It was a memorable evening, and I used his recipes to cook nine large platters for sixty people. Later he was to be important because when I set up LittlePod he sold our vanilla paste on his online shop!

Our very first event was 'a fairy harp recital and fairy tea' in the village hall in May 2004. Two friends of mine, Sofia and Elizabeth Jane, one a talented artist and the other a world-renowned harpist, offered to be involved. Elizabeth Jane had found fairy music written in Victorian times in the Bodleian Library in Oxford and thought our little church would be perfect for a recital. Sofia made fairy costumes and a fairy chair. Alex, a neighbour, made fairy cakes for the tea.

I invited a local doctor to come to the event. I thought it might be wise to have someone who knew the community as a seal of trust. I was rather surprised and shocked by his response. He said, 'You have not been long in this village, have you?' I replied 'No.' He continued, 'You are setting yourself up for rejection big time, aren't you?' I had not thought about this. It had not occurred to me that anyone would reject this offering. I was to be proved right: seventy-two people turned out with magic wands and gossamer wings, and our society began. Three hundred events later and a celebration of twenty years and we are still here. In 2012 when I was awarded the British Empire Medal the doctor came to an event and gave me a hug. I was called a pioneer of social prescribing before it became a real job!

In 2005 Live 8 was happening in London, raising awareness of starvation in Africa. I suggested to everyone that we should have our own Live 8 event in the village, and that it would be interesting to know about the vanilla farmers that my friend Nash works with. I invited him to come over from America to give us a talk about the vanilla farmers on the equatorial belt and how they tend their vanilla.

Top: LittlePod has become part of the landscape in our corner of East Devon

Bottom: A community celebration – toasting LittlePod's King's Award for Enterprise success at the village hall in Farringdon

Arts and Culture   137

Left: Naushad Lalani
Right: Sharing our Queen's Award success with Dr Made
Opposite: Vanilla, Spice and All Things Nice – where it all began!

Nash – Naushad Lalani – is an old friend of mine from university days. I had encouraged him to become a barrister, but that did not interest him enough and he chose accountancy and business. His family were Ugandan Asians. He had come to the UK in 1967 to reside with his uncle. Nash was eleven years old and came with his two older brothers, as they all had UK passports. His mother also had a UK passport, but his father had chosen to have a Ugandan passport, and it was to be five years before they were reunited as a family. When the new dictator Idi Amin took over the country in 1972 Ugandan Asians were given 90 days to get out. Nash eventually moved from the UK to America and found a calling in the vanilla industry.

It was an excellent day and presentation. Nash had prepared me by sending vanilla pods from across the globe and other products like vanilla powder and vanilla sugar. The house was filled with the aroma of vanilla. Roskilly's came from Cornwall to give everyone vanilla ice cream. (I decided against telling people that there is a compound in vanilla that is the nearest taste and smell to mother's milk, and that is why it is the world's favourite flavour in all cultures. In third world countries mothers use vanilla to tempt their babies to their milk.) We also had a local chef who came to demonstrate the culinary uses of vanilla.

Everyone went home with a goody bag of vanilla gifts and with the promise that Nash would return one day and tell them the story of his life.

Paul interviewed Nash recently to find his recollections of the day.

'What do you remember of your visit to Farringdon, Naushad?' he asked.

'I remember that talk in the village hall in Farringdon. I've known Janet since I was eighteen or nineteen years old. I went to Hull University, and we met there and became friends. Janet is an old soul. Our friendship continued after we left

Hull. We have always looked out for each other. We have always been there for each other. Life is unpredictable. You need friends like this in your life.

'I'd always visit her in Devon. On my way back to London from Madagascar I would always stop by to see her. Once I brought a hand-carved chess set made in Madagascar for her son Dan, who was a good chess player. One day she asked if I would give a presentation on vanilla. I agreed.

'I was living in Pennsylvania, and I came specifically to give that talk.

'I gave a rather long-winded presentation. I really wasn't sure why she wanted me to do it, to be honest. It's such a niche, esoteric business. Vanilla, at a village hall near Exeter? You'd think they'd want something more exciting – the arts, music, or something like that.'

'Did Janet tell you that it was their version of the Live 8 charity concerts at the time?' Paul asked.

'I didn't know that then, but Janet is a very creative person. I was surprised at the turnout of people, and they all seemed very interested. I suppose it is exotic.

'Once vanilla gets under your skin, it's very, very hard to get it out. Once you get involved in this industry, it's difficult to get out of it. It's a very special product, I think. It's a beautiful product.

'The product is excellent. There's a lot of romance and mystery to it. I remember going to Madagascar, to Papua New Guinea, to Indonesia, all these places, visiting the farms. Sometimes to look at the crop. You'd take that crop, and you'd bring it back home, you'd manufacture and extract it and then you're applying it in all its various ways. How many products can you do that with? It's really magical, a magical product.

'Once vanilla gets under your skin, it's very, very hard to get it out. Once you get involved in this industry, it's difficult to get out of it. It's a very special product, I think.'

'It's going to be magical forever. It's not going to go away. There are two important products in this world, the two most expensive spices. One is saffron, the other is vanilla. Saffron can be very expensive. I've dabbled with saffron a little bit, but vanilla takes the cake. It's special.'

Paul said, 'Janet was inspired by your talk, as was everyone in the audience. How did you respond to Janet's suggestion about making a vanilla paste using all of the farmers' pods?'

'The presentation I gave was not a manufacturing presentation. It was more about the growing cycles.

'Janet has taken this to a completely different level. She has just blown me away. She came to the business with a completely fresh perspective. She has basically reinvented the way vanilla is marketed, the way it is sourced, that kind of thing. I'm proud, absolutely. Proud to see what she has done and all she has achieved. I'm watching from afar and Janet keeps me updated. It's unbelievable what she has done. I gave her that help and support. It was our friendship that nurtured it.'

'Janet said it took quite a while to develop the paste', Paul observed. 'How was that?'

'Janet came over [to New York] to visit. It was a social visit. She saw the facility being built. I don't know what sparked her interest. We didn't really know what we were doing. We were idiots, trying to build a manufacturing facility. It worked out in the end.'

'What do you think of the polyculture project in Bali?'

'The model at the LittlePod Orchard in Bali? That's the model, yes. It provides a level of stability and education. In Madagascar you just don't have it. People have started growing rice and staple crops. Just to give an example, when I was in Madagascar what shocked me was that they were importing rice. It's a staple product. Such a fertile country. They were not growing it at the time, but people have started growing rice now. Education is so important.

'In vanilla it is a matter of boom and bust, every six years or eight years or twelve years. You go from a price as low as $10 or $15 a kilo, then suddenly there's a shortage and it's $600 a kilo. The fluctuations are wild. A lot of it is to do with the life cycle of the crop. It regenerates itself, after six or seven years. When you put the vine in it doesn't start to produce fruit for another year or two. Then it's good for another five years, and then boom, it's gone. There were a lot of price fluctuations. It was very, very hard. Very hard.

'People used vanilla, pure vanilla, natural vanilla, and all that kind of thing. But it was very speculative. Very cyclical. In Madagascar you have the issue that there is no sustainability.'

It was interesting for Paul to meet Nash and hear about Madagascar from him.

When the Vanilla Queen came to stay with me for three weeks in 2014 I learnt from her that Nash was known as 'the master'. I told him that; he raised his eyes in a dismissive way, and I giggled.

My suggestion to Nash was that we had to find a product that would make it easy and affordable to use REAL vanilla in everyday cooking – an essential everyday ingredient. I asked about the leavings, pods that are not long and straight as chefs like them to be. He said that they were of little value. I suggested that we should use all the pods and add value by turning them into a paste. That way it would be possible to use real vanilla without having to slit and deseed the pods, and so have less wastage. It would make vanilla more versatile and creative to use. It could be like the champagne industry. Keep some good pods back each year in case of a bad harvest, to make sure that the quality remained the same. Put the paste in a tube and keep a stable price. That way it would cut through the boom and bust of the market, and it would be cost effective to choose real vanilla.

Three years later Nash popped in to see me with the trial paste. It happened that I had been invited to an Elizabeth Finn Foundation luncheon in the nearby village of Talaton. I was told that a retired cookery author would be there, so I divided up my tub of vanilla paste and took half with me. This lovely lady talked very eloquently about her store-cupboard and said, 'I only keep real vanilla extract and real almond extract in my cupboard.' I approached her with my half tub of paste and explained that I intended to bring this innovation to market so that home cooks and chefs could manage the costs and do more with real vanilla. I told her that it was the simple way to use a vanilla pod: no more slitting and scraping – it's all done for you. The paste is more intense than vanilla extract because it has less bake-off. It's more versatile too: you can put it in your porridge, yoghurt, coffee, rub it into meats, make a vanillaigrette, use it in fish dishes, and it is fantastic in buttercream for cakes.

There are more than 250 complex compounds in vanilla, and they work with compounds in other foods to round out those flavours. Most of all it is REAL.

Use it in all your baking. The great thing is it lasts for two years in a cool cupboard once opened! The lady called her husband over and said, 'Do you know that Janet is going to put this paste in a tube and bring it to market?' I gave her my half tub of paste and a recipe for celeriac pancakes and left.

Six months later I switched on my television and there was that lady. Her name is Mary Berry. She is perhaps the most loved baker in the UK.

One year later and the Great British Bake Off was a resounding success, so I sent Mary a gift pack of all our products; she responded with a testimonial for our website. On another occasion I got caught out by Mary. It was the launch of my book *Vanilla: Cooking with One of the World's Finest Ingredients* at the BBC Good Food Show. I was invited to be interviewed and found myself in a room with a vast audience. I was very pleased that they had all turned up to hear me read from the book. As I left I realised that no-one was moving. They had all come early to be ready for Mary Berry. I was simply the warm up act!

Opposite: LittlePod's natural vanilla paste – no more slitting and scraping pods!

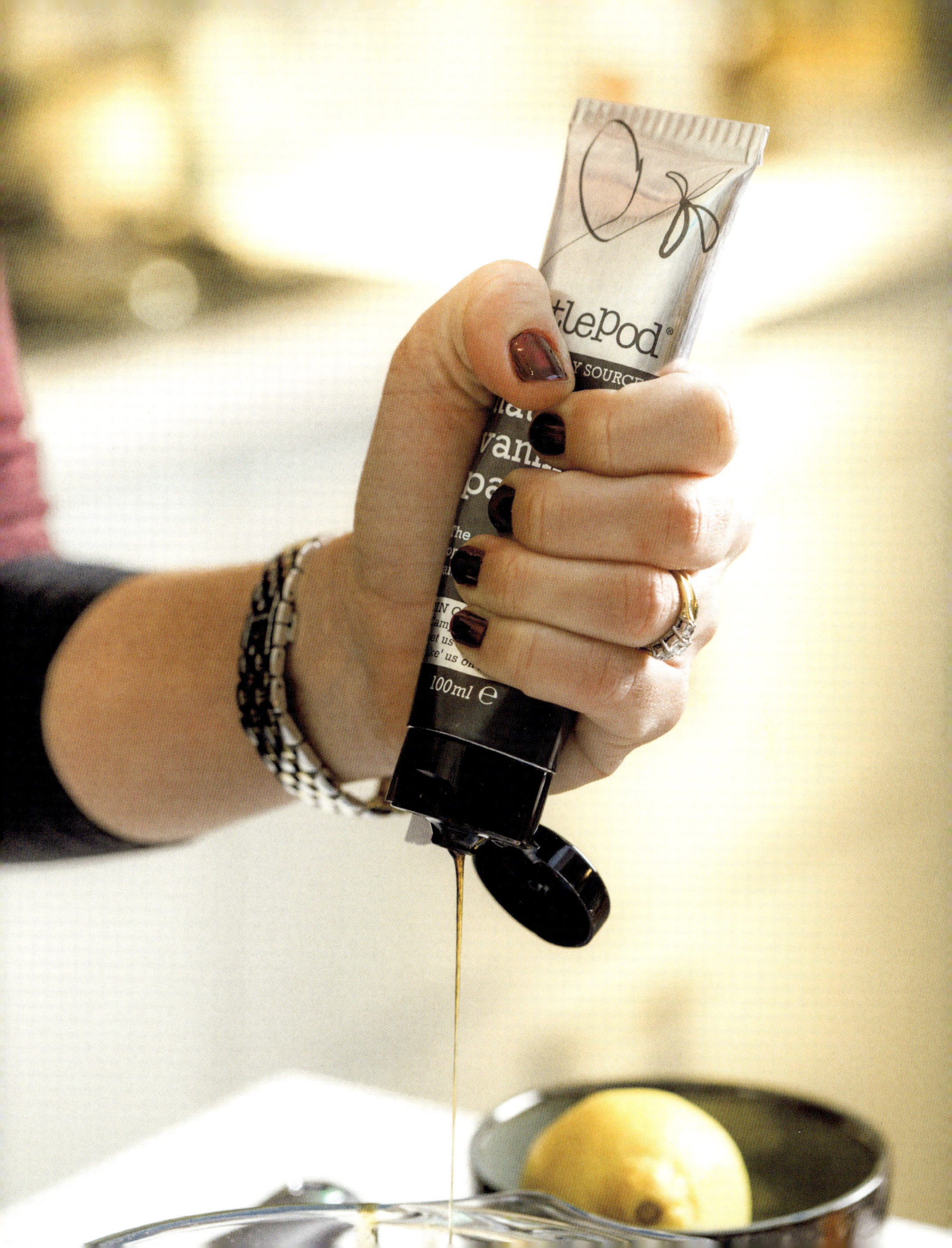
tlePod
100ml ℮

11
A Tribute to Trust

'Where is Made?' I ask. The interns tell me that he has gone with David and Paul to visit some of the farmers in the villages on the opposite side of the orchard.

I am glad to be here with Made 2. It was he who understood the logic of Dr Made returning to Bali, because he wanted to revive vanilla growing at home. Made 2 never lost faith in the project, while other farmers laughed at Dr Made and his ambition to resurrect his father's old vanilla farm. He was teased and mocked: he had left Bali for Oxford, only now to return regularly and talk about planting vanilla, a crop that everyone had dismissed long ago.

There were so many hurdles to overcome at the beginning of the project. The location had to be kept a secret for many, many years for fear of theft. Dr Made had to earn the trust of the farmers in his own home. They were very sceptical. So many earlier initiatives had come to a disappointing end when growing vanilla, including a lack of a decent curing facility.

Madagascar is regarded as the prime place for vanilla, with its soil conditions, very poor workers, and companies who over a hundred years had invested in the best curing practices. However Madagascar has its own problems of child labour and poor infrastructure and the boom and bust character of the vanilla industry. It has many environmental problems that need to be supported by the rest of the world. Madagascar is a special island that we must all care for.

When I first started LittlePod I attended one of the last courses offered to start-up businesses from a local organisation called Business Link in Devon. The theme was Leadership. The woman running the course said that to start a business it would be helpful to have some psychotherapy background. Tick, I thought. I had completed a pre-clinical course in child psychotherapy at the Tavistock Clinic in London. Our Freud lectures were even held in Freud's house! Freud is regarded as the founder of psychology, although many theories have developed since his time. Even so, work on emotional literacy is still in its infancy, especially in the workplace.

The course involved following the life of a baby before birth until the age of two (with the

Opposite: A memorable meeting at Made 2's home in Indonesia

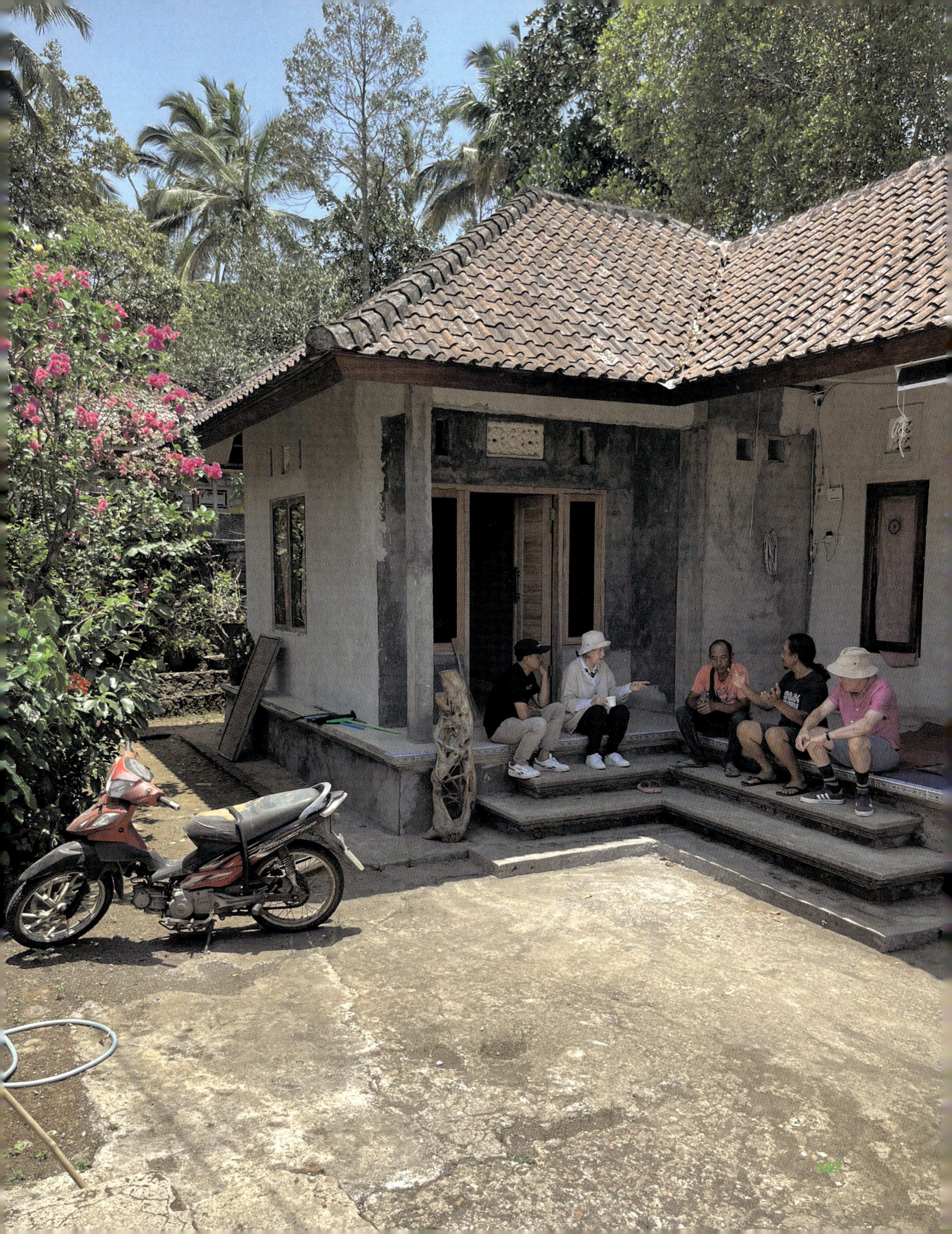

parents' permission). During this time I came across the work of a paediatrician called Donald Winnicott. To anyone setting up a business I strongly recommend an introduction to his work, *Boundary and Space*. It was my go-to book, along with *The Art of War* by Sun Tzu and *Meditations* by Marcus Aurelius.

The building up of trust can be very hard. There is more debate about trust than there is about love. Trust is fundamental to any relationship. Sadly, in our litigious society community trust has been replaced by institutional oversight committees and belief in contracts. Gone are my father's days when a spit on the palm and a handshake was regarded as the bond of an honest man.

A lovely headmistress from Billericay once said to me, 'I am not a leader, but I like to be a goer-alonger. I need to choose who I go along with very carefully. Someone I can trust. I would go along with you, Janet.' It must be the greatest compliment one can receive. It is this that I see in Dr Made. I trusted him implicitly from the start, and I was prepared to go along with him even though I was ignorant of the landscape of vanilla and its history for the farmers. I know that today I will meet farmers confident in the knowledge that they trust Dr Made.

Perhaps the development of the internet and the new AI is a reason why we are not able to trust the opinion or expertise of the other anymore. We can go and check things out for ourselves. However there is no cross-checking.

Top: David and Syiraz enjoying coconuts at the LittlePod orchard
Middle: Dr Made and Nyoman, one of the elders in the village, who believed in the LittlePod orchard from the very beginning
Bottom: Thumbs up for REAL vanilla!

At school I remember learning how to cross-check references in the Bible from the Old Testament to the New Testament. Now Google seems to be the reservoir of cross-referencing, and we have no idea whether what we are reading is correct. Even if we do not have a clue about astrophysics, we look to distil that knowledge and believe whatever we want to believe.

During the Covid pandemic lots of people looked outside science for succour. In the early 1900s Carl Jung, psychologist, friend and collaborator of Freud, would say to his patients in time of stress and difficulties, 'Go back to the church of your youth.' Where is that church today? Many people are growing up without a background of religious belief. So where do they go? In his brilliant play *The Cure at Troy*, Seamus Heaney looks at this from the perspective of the ancient world:

'Believe that a further shore
Is reachable from here.
Believe in miracles
And cures and healing wells.'

The two dictionary definitions of trust that I looked up (on the internet!) are from the Cambridge and Webster dictionaries. Cambridge says it is 'to believe that someone is good and honest and will not harm you, or that something is safe and reliable'; for Webster it is 'assured reliance on the character, ability, strength, or truth of someone or something'.

Eric Erikson, another psychologist, wrote about the 'Eight Ages of Man' in his book *Childhood and Society*: he outlines the development of a life from birth to death; he proposes that there are opposites in growth of the person, and that a person can get stuck at any stage. For example, when I arrived in the village of Farringdon and found myself without a purpose my life could have become stagnant had I not found a way to become generative, especially at that stage of life. Erikson proposes that if all development is finally to meet old age with integrity, not despair, then we must look to the integration of our whole life. However, the first stage depends on the first building block: to trust or mistrust. He says,

'Trust is the first of our ego values. Integrity is the last. Healthy children will not fear life if their elders have integrity enough to not fear death.'

We learn this first from our relationship within the family. Many people who have lost much have great difficulty regaining trust. This is how it was with Made and his village. The farmers had lost trust in planting vanilla. They had lost many savings. One farmer told us that he had lost £10,000 of an investment in vanilla: some plants died of fusarium, and those that were fine he could not sell as a continuous crop. Buyers would come and purchase a one-off, but they didn't come back. There was no reliability of sales.

Dr Made put the case for polyculture planting – vanilla to be grown among other crops; the tutor trees, varied in the forest orchard, encouraged the mycorrhizal fungi to aid soil health. The farmers were unsure and suspicious of Dr Made at first. They knew the risks, and were reluctant to have a go. Who would purchase their vanilla? Dr Made told them that LittlePod would purchase it, and provide the money for the saplings. There was a lot of soul-searching; younger farmers had to go to

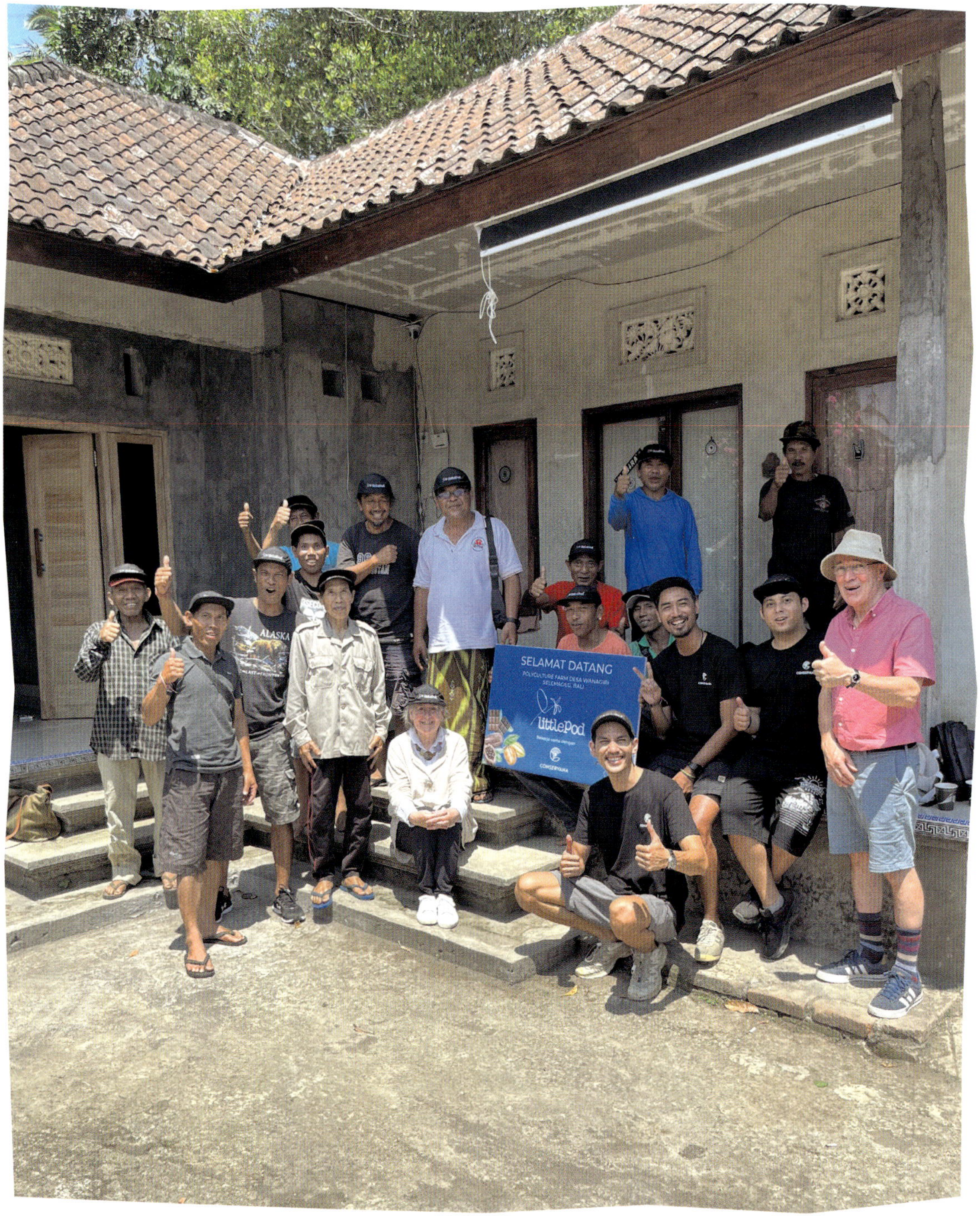
SELAMAT DATANG
littlePod
CONSERVANA

their elders to seek their knowledge of planting vanilla.

Nyoman, one of the elders in the village, understood what Made was suggesting – that vanilla could become an important crop again if LittlePod and the farmers could agree on a fair pricing structure. He had long hoped for a scenario such as this. It was a risk, but Made 2 was keen to try. It was he who kept belief in the project alive. The other farmers needed to be convinced that all the time and effort needed in producing vanilla would be worthwhile. Could it become another crop among many in their forest orchards? Could they produce a high quality? Dr Made explained that it all depended on quality. They would sacrifice quantity for quality. By having a mixed crop they would not have to depend on vanilla for their livelihoods. If one year the weather was not suitable, they would have other crops to sell.

LittlePod would wait. There were many years when frustration set in. After the first five years the harvest was only 50 kilos. It was not until after the tenth year that things started to look good.

Dr Made went back to Bali a couple of times a year to keep the spirits up and used his persuasion to encourage the farmers to keep going. He had to be very resilient and determined to show the possibilities. He enlisted the help of his cousin Ketut to help him. Ketut is an architect by training, but had grown up on the vanilla farm with Dr Made. They have a close bond. When I eventually met Ketut he had the air of an older brother concerned with the wellbeing of the community. He also designed the new curing facility. This is very important, because it is the curing of the beans that offers the quality assurance.

Dr Made and I had our own conflicts. Building a manufacturing business in the West requires a lot of legislation and compliance. It was important to LittlePod that we fulfil all the requirements that our customers needed to see. We understood each other's constraints and knew that we would have to be patient with each other.

Noises are in the air. The gathering of the farmers is happening now below us. I look over to the landscape on the other side of the farm, where I can imagine Dr Made enthusiastically showing off the farmers' dedicated work to David and Paul. This visit is full of awe and is the culmination of nearly thirteen years of trials and tribulations, something I describe as the 'knaw' – wanting to work at something for it to be successful. It is something that I tried to do when I was a primary school teacher – to develop the awe and the knaw to help children see their vision and work to achieve it.

Working with Dr Made is an extension of the project methods I used as a teacher. It is not always the results that we remember from our education. It is the feeling of satisfaction when we finally understand things – that heuristic moment when everything falls into place, and we understand that place for the first time. And it is a desire to resurrect that feeling that makes us do it again and again. Many of the graduates who have come to LittlePod and skilled themselves on apprenticeship courses have told me that being at LittlePod has switched them into the learning mode again. It is a sad fact that much education, as my father saw it, dulls the senses.

Opposite: Our first face-to-face meeting with the LittlePod farmers in Bali

At one time I was a school's experience tutor. When the student teachers came to me I almost felt subversive when I told them that I believed that to be a good teacher you must have two attributes: transferable enthusiasm for your subject, and affective attunement with your pupils. I am certain that the teachers in Finland where the project method is core to the curriculum would understand my philosophy.

These qualities are also very useful when starting a company. I often quote from T. S. Eliot: 'We shall not cease from exploration, and the end of all our exploring will be to arrive where we started and know the place for the first time.' I'm feeling that now, here in this little paradise built on hope, desire, dedication and toil.

My role in this success story started before I met Dr Made. Fifteen years ago, my son Dan was leaving home to become a medical student. I knew it would be six years' study, and given his fearless, curious, determined character I knew the world would take him and he would only look back occasionally. I tried to persuade him to think of something other than medicine and he asked me why. I said, 'I fear medicine will gobble you up.' He laughed, put his arm around me, and said, 'Something will gobble me up, mother.' I'd had a similar feeling when his sister Clare graduated from university. I asked her, 'What now then, Clare?' She stood confidently looking at me, 'Oh, complete independence, mother.'

Of course parents hope for their children to fly the nest with confidence. It is their reward as they go through the stages of parenting. However, when the nest is finally empty there is a sombre moment. Life comes full circle, concertinaed into one painful realisation. They are off. The future is theirs. What of the parent now as the child looks with a questioning glance at the person they called mother? I felt as if I was having to ask myself, 'Who are you now, Janet?' How to respond? An answer was required. It is one of those fight or flight moments. I clung to a poignant poem by William Blake called *Eternity*:

> 'He who binds to himself a joy
> Does the winged life destroy.
> He who kisses the joy as it flies
> Lives in eternity's sunrise.'

So I kissed the joy! I feel connected to any parent in the world who felt that pang at the parting of their grown child, feeling a little part of themselves dissolve.

Fortunately for me this moment of pain was short. David and I had moved to the village of Farringdon at the turn of the twenty-first century. A five-acre wood came with the little cottage we purchased. It was full of ancient trees, and my first project was to become a tree warden. I arrived at the local agricultural college to learn about tree health and the law relating to trees very soon after arriving. I wanted to share the woods. We held a special environmental walk in the woods, inviting Kate Tobin, who was the Great Trees of East Devon Project Officer.

We walked the bounds, pointing out remnants of the Old Stone Age. Neolithic flint tools have been found, and there is evidence of continuous occupation. There is a map of a Romano-British farmstead, and it is believed that there was a Romano-British villa near the woods. Kate wrote a piece about the day. Here is an excerpt:

'The trees give a few clues to the way Farringdon's landscape has developed over time. By looking at the few remaining very old English Oaks, and comparing with old maps, it appears that the slopes above the church would have been pasture with a lot of mature trees standing amongst them. The mature trees would have been felled occasionally for timber or sometimes 'pollarded', which means that the top would be cut off and allowed to regrow above grazing height, providing lots of poles for firewood, tool handles or turning.'

This highly prized native parkland landscape was then added to by the landowners with some exotic planting – probably in the eighteenth century. This is very obvious in the wood at the top of the slope, where there are Sweet Chestnuts, Lime and one or two Lucombe Oaks. In 1790, there is a record made of how the village looked by Rev. John Swete, who says '...the view when the Dogstar rages a Zephyr is to be found and where the beauty of the Prospect is without a rival in the neighbourhood.'

I would walk in Ivy Woods every day. The woods are on the top of a hill. This was once the parkland of Farringdon House. It has an icehouse where game and ice were once kept.

The landowners added some exotic planting, probably in the eighteenth century – a Scots pine, the highest tree, and some rhododendron (managed, to stop it being invasive). A lime tree (possibly used for making rope) has a girth of 9.2 metres, probably one of the oldest in the country as there are not many limes left. Limes are associated with fertility and liberty and are often planted near battlefields.

There are eight handsome sweet chestnuts, which are around three hundred years old; the Romans always planted sweet chestnuts when they settled. There is also a yew tree, which is reputed to be a thousand years old; pagans used to plant yews to ward off evil spirits. There are three buzzards constantly flying about. Pipistrel bats hide in the icehouse. On one side of the woods are a few sycamore trees, home to a rookery.

There is an abundance of ruscus, commonly known as butcher's broom because of its sharp leaves which butchers used to clean their wooden chopping boards; it is also an indicator of ancient woodland. There is a badger sett; I have seen young foxes playing in the shafts of light on a summer eve; and deer have their den and give birth in the wood. One morning Dan was up early. Hiding in the trunk of a vast lime tree he heard something scuffing the ground; he cautiously raised himself and came eye to eye with a stag. What a magical moment. Thankfully he was safe in the tree. He ran home with stars in his eyes.

Around that time, in 2000, I received an

exciting invitation to dinner in London at the Irish Literary Society, to inaugurate the nature poet Seamus Heaney as their first president. I had attended his poetry evening in Oxford many years ago, a memorable occasion. I had been very excited travelling up on the train clutching a copy of his poems. I was appalled that evening when Seamus opened his reading saying that it was his first poetry evening in Oxford and that people had teased him about his English degree. I was perhaps too sensitive. But that night he gave his redress. The talk was on the theme of 'What does it mean to be Irish in an English tongue?' The title pierced my soul. I was living in London, the daughter of Irish parents speaking in an English tongue and leaving my past behind, a little out of fear and a little out of shame. That evening the road to healing this conflict began. Seamus spoke to the intimate group of around fifteen listeners and traced how the Irish lost their language. He read his own poems and interspersed his talk with titles of literature and poems he had read for his English degree. In summary he said, 'Yes, it is true I have an English degree, but as you can see all the authors of the literature and poems I read for my English degree are Irish.' He concluded that the Irish had indeed found a new language, and it was called English! I travelled home that night feeling whole and proud of my heritage. I had a renewed self-confidence, born out of the knowledge that if Seamus Heaney could be teased and mocked and could deal with it so eloquently, then so could I.

This new invitation to meet him was very timely. I had moved to a rural, farming village very similar to the one I had known as a child. I knew no-one there. I had to give up my position as a teacher so I could drive my son to his new school. I was feeling rather irrelevant and menopausal. There were no phone calls or demands being made on me. It felt strange. I was living a simple life.

That evening of the dinner was very special. There were about sixty people there. I renewed my acquaintance with the poet. He asked me what I was doing with my life now. I shared my thoughts about finding myself with space in my life and wondering what to do next. When Seamus gave his inaugural speech his first words were: 'There is nothing more worthwhile than the simple life, simply led.' It was the inspiration I needed. The following day I wrote a letter to all the families with children in the village, inviting them to meet my son (aged twelve) and me in the village hall for tea and cake. Thirty children turned out, mostly boys aged twelve to eighteen; only eight of the children were under ten. I listened to their needs and organised a gathering once a week for the older boys and a gardening club for the younger ones. I was about to embrace village life!

My Irish parents moved to a remote English seaside village after the Second World War. Before the war my father had deserted the Irish Army to join the RAF. I remember him telling how he was arrested and taken to Fermanagh to be charged;

there he went to the toilet, left his boots under the door, and escaped through the window. His father was a tailor, who had gained his apprenticeship in London's Savile Row; like others of his generation, he had been swept up in the enthusiasm of the war in 1914, and as a result suffered from shrapnel wounds all his life. When I was studying A-level economic history I first spoke to my father about his decision to join the RAF, given that Ireland was neutral in the Second World War. In his soft southern Irish voice he said to me: 'It was not like my father. It was a conscience call for me. At that time what was I to do? Was I to sit on the side of good or evil?' He was nineteen. Those Irishmen who joined the war effort were given one month's training and then sent to a squadron. My father's papers show a little of where he went for training; his record says 'good', so he clearly abided by the rules. On one occasion when he was parachuted into enemy territory at night he was shot. The bullet severed his big toe. It is very important to have a big toe when you are trying to escape. He found his toe and managed to find something to act as a splint to tie it to his foot. That was the reason for his strange toe. I wish he had lived long enough to tell me how he did that. His mother, my grandmother, had been born in India, where her father was an army captain, from Yorkshire. He sent her to Ireland when she was eight years old to live with her grandmother, because her Irish mother had died. My grandmother was skilled in herbal medicine. I often wondered if it was something she learnt in India and that she passed on to my dad.

Long after my father's death, when I became interested in psychology, I made an important connection. I had grown up surrounded by animals. My father collected animals and birds in disarray. They might have broken wings, or torn limbs, or a displaced eye. He would bring them home, put them in cages, nurse them back to health, and then release them. He was a true Dr Dolittle. It was my job before school to feed them, using a pipette each day. I realised late in life that my father was repairing the trauma of his severed toe. It was his therapy, repairing injured animals. He was never sentimental about them. Just their doctor.

My father was demobbed after the war at Dunster Beach in Somerset and described that place to me vividly in story time at the fireside. I had a traditional Irish oral upbringing: songs and stories of Tir na nóg, of fairies, and people long ago. When I finally visited Dunster I recognised it instantly. It was as if I had been there many times.

My father did not return to a hero's welcome. After spending some time sleeping in the woods above Dunster Castle he eventually tramped the roads of England and finally reached London. London was rebuilding after the war, and the air was toxic. Everywhere he went signs said, 'No dogs No blacks No Irish'. He could not return home. He faced a court martial if he did. The Irish took a dim view of men like my dad: they did not give amnesty to men who fought in the war until 2013. He lived the rest of his life in exile but never rescinded his Irish citizenship.

Just before the UK finalised the Brexit agreement, I had a phone call from someone on behalf of the Irish government. He opened the conversation with the words 'Now we don't know who you know', to which I replied, 'That's very true.' 'But you are being talked about among the highest echelons.' I giggled, but he continued, 'and the Irish government would be prepared to offer you all the manufacturing facility you need and £60,000 for a salesperson if you would like to relocate LittlePod to Ireland.' What a turnaround, I thought. My father was not allowed back home, but LittlePod was being greeted with open arms.

In 2008 I wrote to Seamus Heaney asking permission to put on a production of his play *The Burial at Thebes* in our village. I told him about my dad and the nature of his exile. He gave his support and allowed me to put the play on. 'I am confident that you will rise to the occasion and fulfil Yeats's ambition for theatre; to embrace the present and dominate memory.' We certainly did achieve that. It was a huge success, and we were invited to put it on for one night in the Great Hall at Dartington. Thirty members of the Yeats Society came over from Ireland for the first night of the play in Farringdon. Our little village is very special for having had the opportunity to perform that play in front of our ancient church, with the chorus calling to Dionysius, the patron saint of trees. I had asked the Arts Council if they would contribute to the theatrical experience (it was a site-specific play), and they had replied saying, 'Who would want to see a Greek tragedy translated by an Irish poet in a tiny English village?' Well, 450 people did! And 300 more at Dartington. Will Halfacree, our filmmaker, recorded our performance at Dartington and I sent a copy to Seamus. He sent me a postcard. It was of a painting by Jack Yeats, *The Riverside*, depicting two people in 1922 obviously about to leave Ireland.

In 2012 I received the British Empire Medal, and I enrolled to take part in the Yeats Society summer school in Sligo. I had met the marvellous Stella Mew, who was their first CEO, and I wanted to invite her to come and talk to the Farringdon Society of Arts. Seamus Heaney was on the programme in Sligo. He was giving a recital and talk about his poetry preparations for the coming centenary of the First World War. He had been to 'Anthem for Doomed Youth', an exhibition of First World War poets at the Imperial War Museum in London, as had I. I had the chance to talk with him again just before the summer school event. Miss Mew had dined with him the night before and had told him about my British Empire Medal. When we met, he said, 'Ah, Janet, we were only talking about you over dinner last night.' I glowed with pride. He said he was pleased to hear that the Irish government were to give pardon to the men who had served in the Second World War, 'those men for whom Ireland does not have to hang its head in shame'.

Tears fell silently down my cheek. The BEM was for my dad.

Seamus died in 2013. It was a Friday, and I had a call from Stella Mew. She told me that she was with Seamus's wife, Marie; he had been taken to hospital and was to have an operation. I remember Stella's words. He had been in touch with his wife to thank her for all her love. He wrote in Latin, 'I am all prepared. Do not be afraid.'

I had always wondered how and why my parents had ended up in the remote flat landscape of rural Lincolnshire where I could trace a piece of paper tossing in the wind from east to west without interruption.

During Covid I finally found the answer to my question when I researched my father's RAF history. Then I wondered about Farringdon – was it fate that brought me to this feudal village at the dawn of the twenty-first century? I finally had the time to reflect on Carl Jung's theory of the unconscious. He believed that until you make the unconscious conscious it will control your life and you will call it fate. If the war was a defining moment for my dad and his generation, then Covid must surely be a defining moment for the generation leaving university in 2020. Certainly, it was the call-up moment for my son, who spent his days as a doctor treating patients in a Covid 19 intensive care ward. We all kept our distance. I did not see Dan for four years. A silence had descended on our lives that I had not known for such a long time.

Top: Enjoying open-air theatre in the LittlePod garden
Bottom: Receiving the MBE from LittlePod's postman Lee

A Tribute to Trust

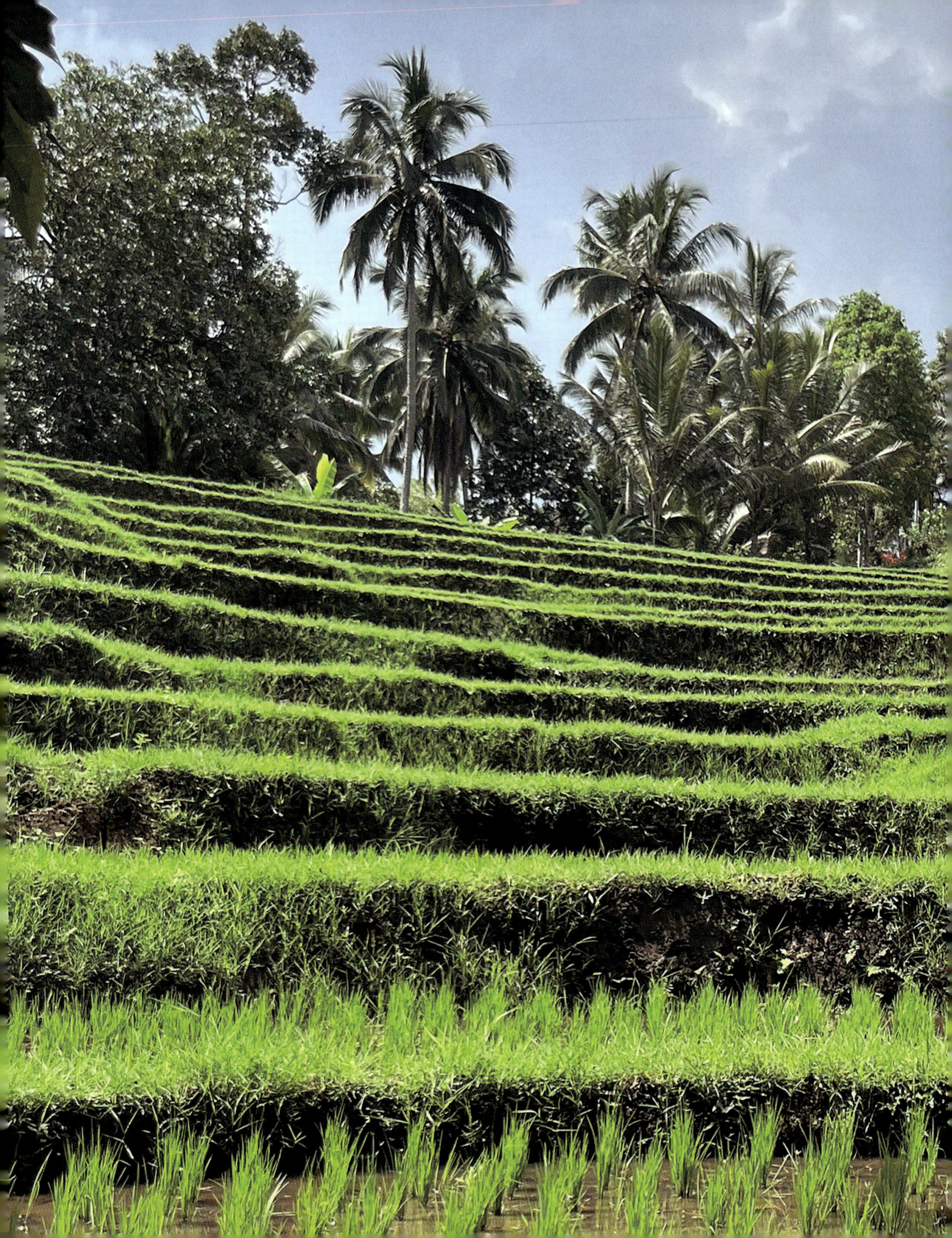

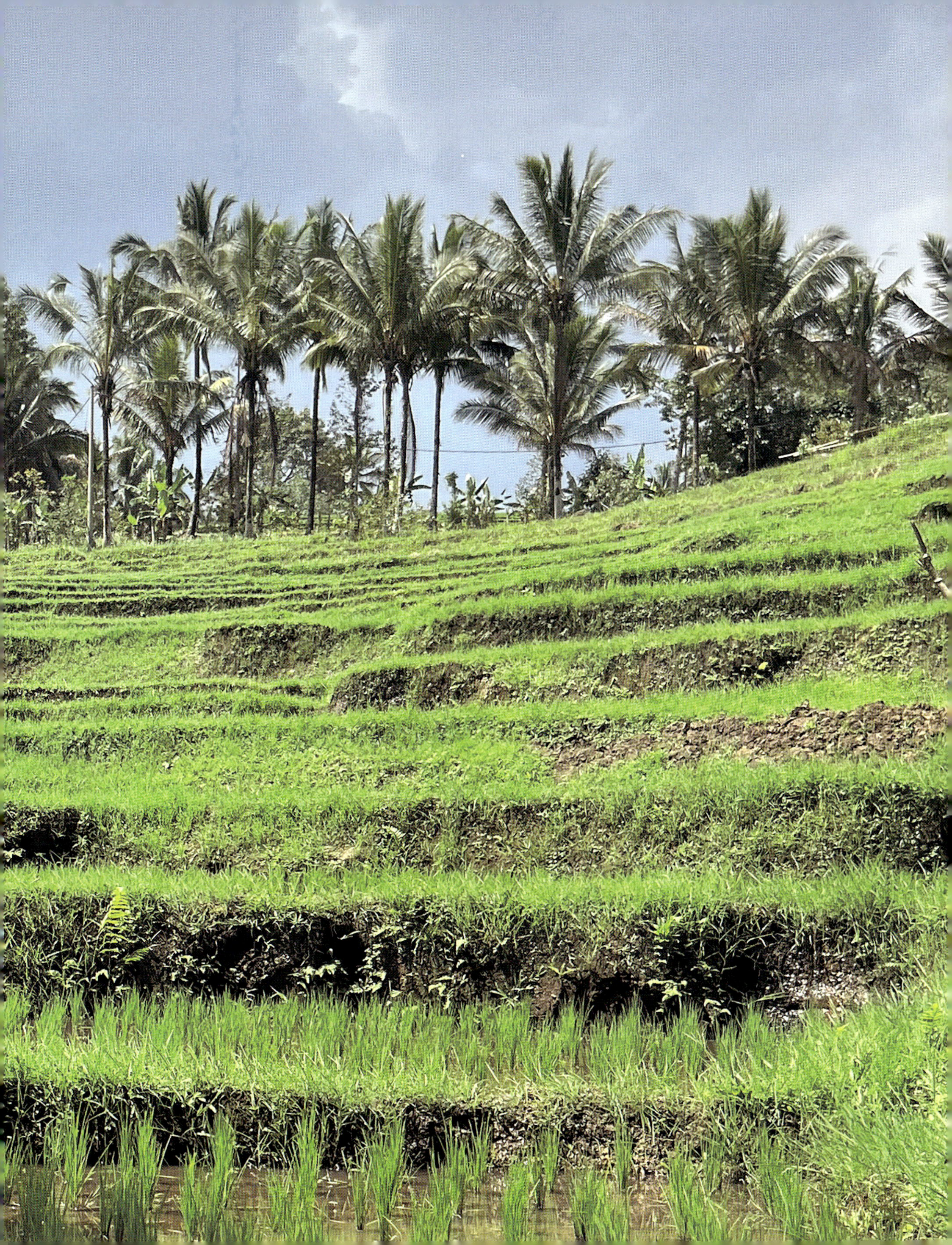

12
Vanilla and Wellbeing

Syiraz and the team in Bali are tending to some of the vines. 'Every time we come to the forest we look at the vines. It is important to catch the flowers as they arrive,' he says.

I tell him about Sarah Gillard, a LittlePod friend and artist.

An article in a paper had said that the vanilla vine was flowering at Kew Gardens, and she managed to get permission to paint it. She got there and set up her easel amidst the dripping foliage and caught the flower just as it was opening. She laughs at the memory of the school groups watching her, asking her questions as she was getting wet trying to capture the dripping flower in paint. We love the painting: it hangs on our office wall and we had it made into the LittlePod greeting card.

My recollections are interrupted once again.

'Do you see flowers, Janet?' I am back in the forest and one of Syiraz's students is pointing at an orange lily and questioning me. 'These were left by the Dutch colonialists. They are all over Bali', he tells me. 'It is good that they left some beauty behind', I say. I don't know the history of Indonesia as I should. Of course, the Dutch East India Company.

Suddenly the tranquillity of this luscious scene is broken by the sound of horns from the people who are gathering down below. Word had got out around the village that the visitors had arrived, and in the distance, I could see a congregation of scooters and mopeds. We needed to descend.

I am quite reluctant to leave the verdant natural habitat here in the forest. I am enjoying my musings. No pressure to talk – time to remember. There is a scent of freedom here. It made me think of what I value most, freedom. Freedom from what and freedom for what?

I began to ask myself, why am I so smitten by the story of this little vanilla flower?

Is it because it is threatened with extinction? Is it because it winds so naturally in the forest, taking nothing and always giving? It does not compete for nutrients: it gets its nutrients from the air and dust around its foot. It attracts insect life and protects the trees as it needs their canopy. It is the second most expensive spice in the world, after saffron.

Vanilla and Wellbeing

There are around 140 species of vanilla orchid, but only 3 are cultivated for trade.

The main species is vanilla planifolia, which originated in Mexico. It is extensively grown in countries about 23 degrees on either side of the equator. Madagascar is the main source (where it is known as Bourbon vanilla, because the Île de la Réunion whence it came was French), then Uganda, India, Papua New Guinea, the Comoros Islands, Tonga, Tanzania, and further places. More recently vanilla was introduced to Ecuador, Colombia, the Philippines, and even California.

In addition to vanilla planifolia, two other varieties are grown. Vanilla pompona originated in Guadeloupe and is indigenous around the Caribbean. It has less vanillin content and shorter bean length and is not grown commercially; one particular person buys all the pompona to make a special perfume. The other species is vanilla tahitensis. This is a hybrid, probably a cross between vanilla planifolia and vanilla pompona, both of which grew in Guatemala. Commonly referred to as Tahitian vanilla, it began its evolutionary journey as a pre-Columbian Maya cultivar in the tropical forests of Guatemala. It has less vanillin, but it has a beautiful aroma, delicate floral notes with a sweeter note as a result of the increased presence of floral heliotropin. Some chefs prefer this vanilla pod for their delicate dishes.

On the final day of our trip to Tanzania I met a geneticist called Alan Chambers, from California. He told us that he was working on the DNA of vanilla, because not many papers had been published on the subject. I noticed that he had the Vanilla Queen's book in his bag, and he told us that he had been in touch with Patricia Rain as they were experimenting with growing vanilla in California. I told him that Patricia and I call each other sister, and that she had been to stay with me for three weeks. 'There are so many compounds yet to be discovered', he said. The Sloan-Kettering Institute in the US have used vanilla to calm people down during MRI scanning. Studies have been done in the Netherlands looking at peoples' different perceptions of fruit yoghurts: when they reached vanilla it spiked as a preference, so they did blood tests and found that people had an increased amount of oxytocin levels when they ate the vanilla yoghurt. It led to the strapline 'Eat vanilla yoghurt and be happy!'

I suggested that he should look for a compound in vanilla that could cure sugar cravings. Scientists have long believed this to be the case, and anecdotal evidence does show that if you sniff vanilla it can help to reduce reaching for a chocolate bar at those low sugar moments.

In 1991 researchers at the Memorial Sloan Kettering Cancer Center in New York found that the smell of vanilla lasts for three minutes in the nasal cavity. As Alan had said, they found that vanilla can reduce anxiety and claustrophobia during MRI scans. Patch experiments have indicated that there may be something in this hypothesis. Whoever finds that compound will become very rich.

There is no doubt that vanilla with its over 250 known compounds has been found to promote wellbeing. The indigenous Totonac people used vanilla medicinally.

The first reference to vanilla, not known by that name, was found in the Badianus Manuscript of 1552 (formerly in the Vatican Library in Rome, now in the National Institute of Anthropology and History in Mexico City). It is an illustrated list of herbs used as medicines by the Aztecs, composed in Nahuatl and translated into Latin in Tlaltelulco in Mexico. It is used widely in aromatherapy practices today. It is also used in the cosmetics industry, and vanilla absolute is the core scent for most of the world's expensive perfumes. Vanilla has also been suggested as a mood enhancer, offering pain reduction and an increased sense of calm. Here, looking around me with Syiraz, I can definitely feel that sense of calm coming from the forest floor.

No wonder the Japanese say that the forest floor is good for mental health and rejuvenation. In 2020 David and I were in Hakone, high in the mountains in Japan, and we met lots of students who told us that the government had paid for them to have a holiday in the mountains. Students are apparently funded to experience the natural world for their mental wellbeing. What a great idea. Covid was very much present when we travelled to Japan, but the government had decided to go for herd immunity. Dan said that we might as well go because they would be taking precautions. This was very true. Japan had no tourists. I was due to go to a trade show, but it had been cancelled, and as we had invested so much time and money I thought we should go anyway. I had spoken to Andrea Speciale, a young Italian student who was putting the last note to his dissertation for his master's in Japanese language and culture; I had asked him if he would like an internship at LittlePod, and would he meet me in Japan. He said 'yes' immediately.

David had booked me into a cookery class. I arrived masked up and met the teacher, Yumi, also masked up. I was her only client. She would normally have had ten per session. I asked her what she would do if her classes had to close; she did not know. I asked what she did before she started her cookery school, and she said she had been head of sales and marketing for some prestigious hotels in Tokyo. I had my bag full of LittlePod products, and I arranged them on her

Top: Keeping it REAL in Tokyo – a cookery class with Yumi
Middle: Jamie Raftery, the Holistic Chef, during a visit to LittlePod HQ
Bottom: WIth Andrea at the British Embassy in Japan

table. I showed her the tube. I asked Andrea to translate. I told her that Jamie Raftery, known as The Holistic Chef, explained the product very clearly: 'Quality, convenience and affordability all in an easy-to-use tube'.

It was an innovative product. When I took it to the Speciality and Fine Food Fair in London in 2011 it was called 'an evolution for the kitchen'. We were the first to market it.

She said, 'Come back next Saturday.' The following week David and I returned. We had been to Kyoto to visit the Fushimi Inari shrine, which is known for its 10,000 torii gates and 12,000 steps. When you pass through the torii you enter the realm of the gods. It marks the transition from the everyday world to the sacred. This is the last journey on the way to enlightenment. A Buddhist monk in England had given me an inscribed piece of the bark of the Sen tree for my journey to enlightenment *(see p. 77)*, and now I wanted to complete this life work. It was another agape moment for me. It took three hours to walk the complete mountain. The gates seem to embrace you after a while. We were blessed, as there were very few people climbing that day.

Yumi and Otayo of the Kookai Cookery School were waiting for us. Andrea had left, so we thought we would have to use gestures to communicate. However we found that Yumi had an English degree and could speak the language very well. LittlePod had found our distributors in Japan!

We arrived home from Japan on the first day of lockdown in the UK. We managed the last flight out because a rock band needed to get back. There were only a dozen people on the plane. Heathrow was deserted. Once home I discovered that the whole country was locked down. However, being a food company, LittlePod could keep working. It was a saviour.

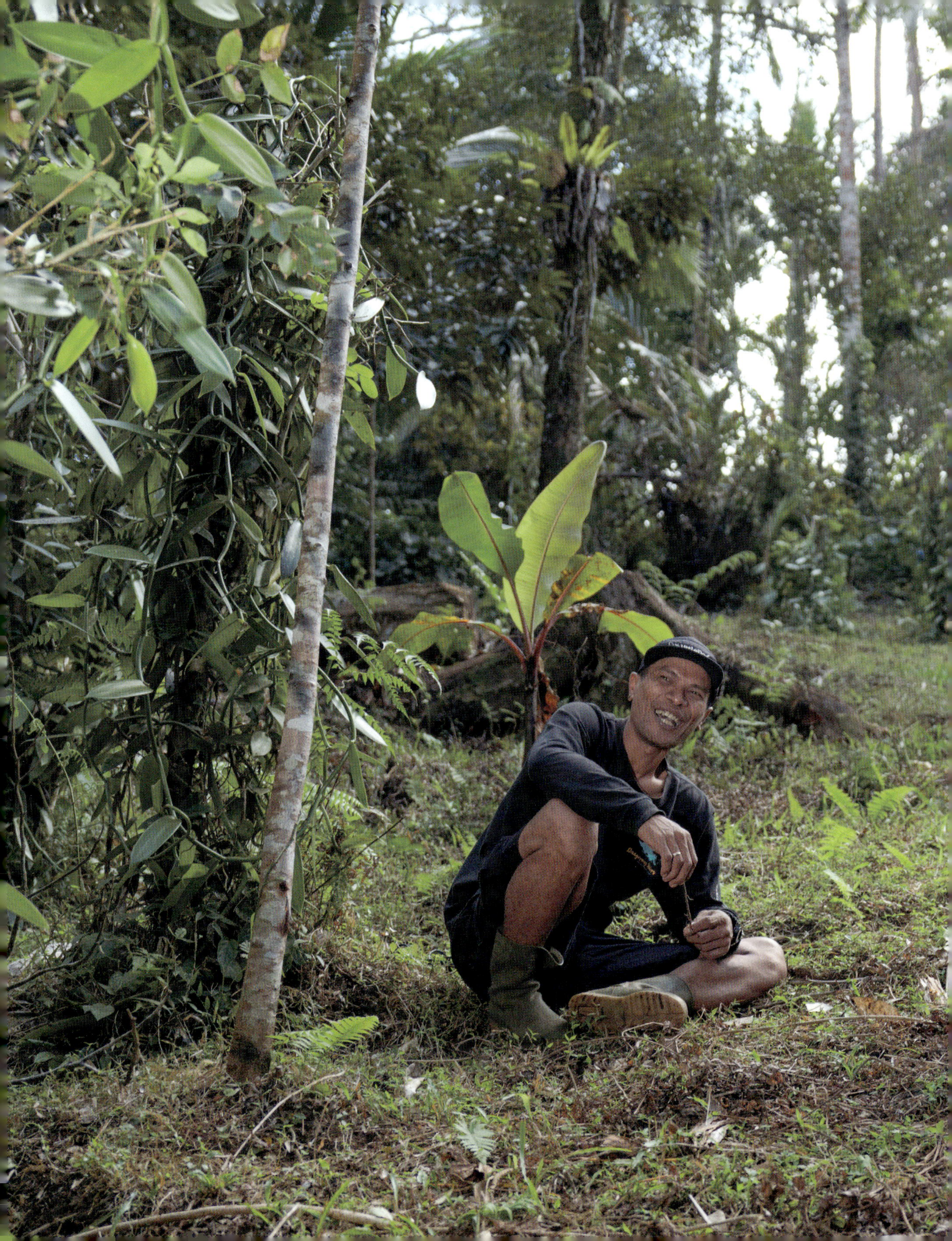

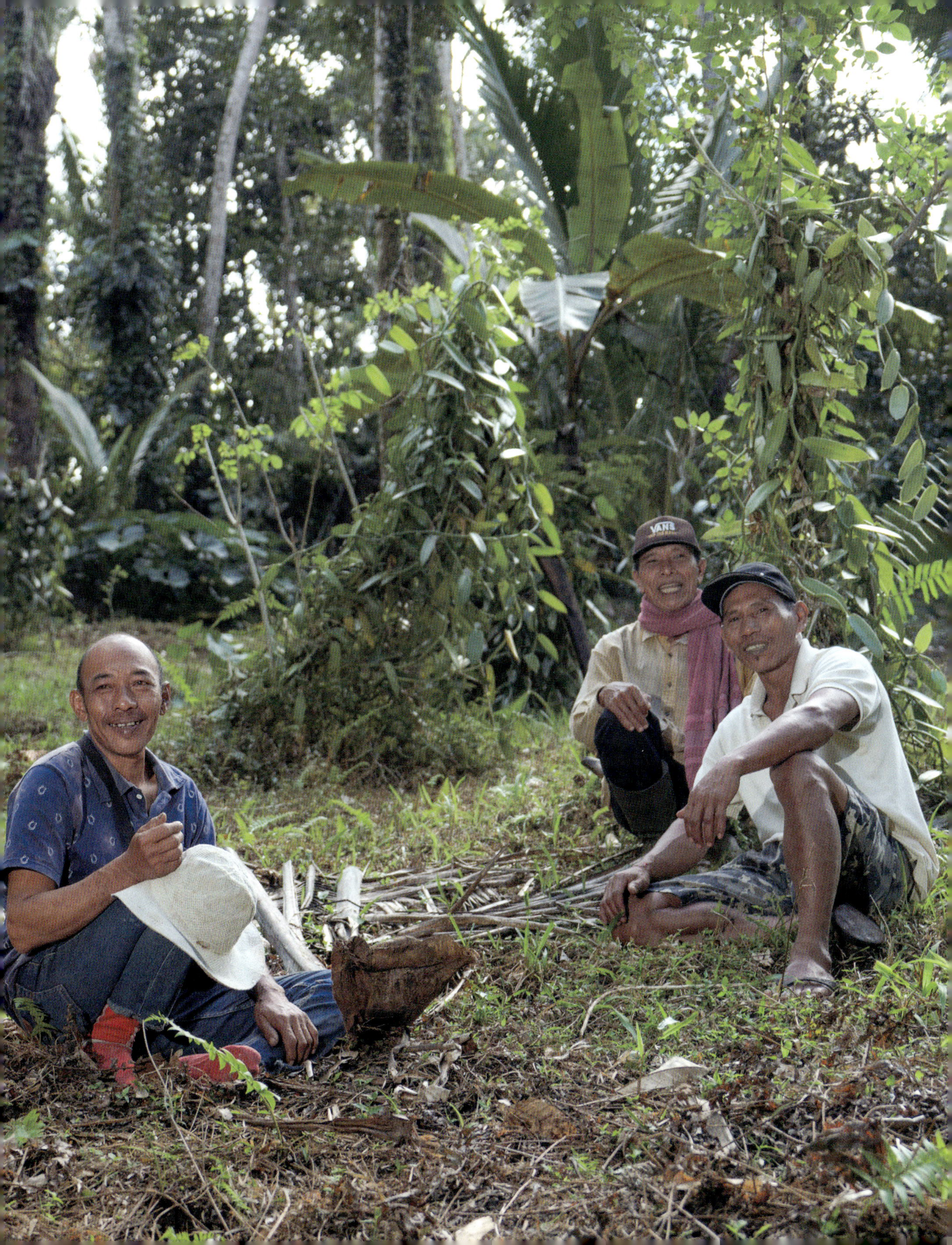
VANS

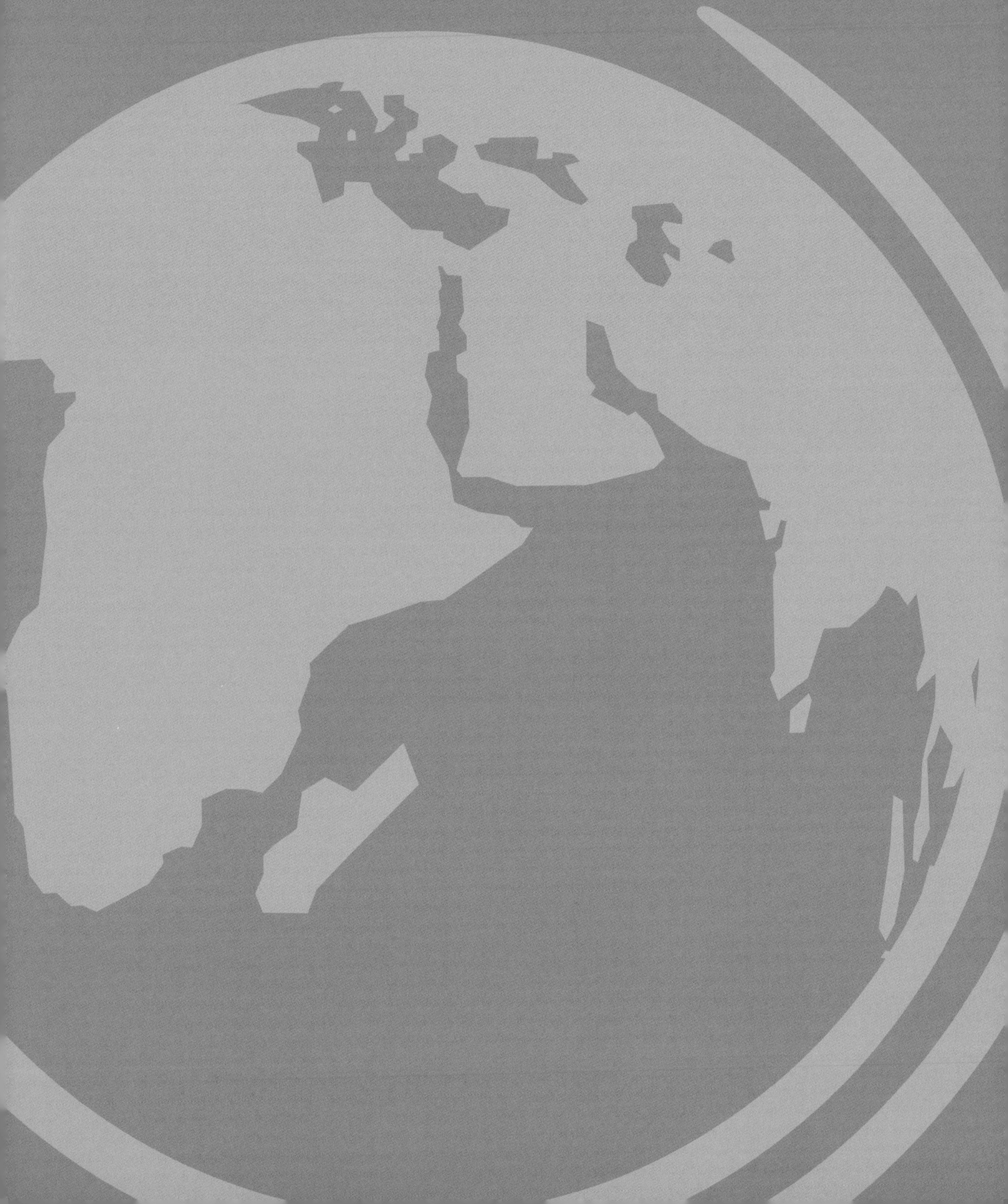

13
The Importance of an Education

When I met Dr Made in May 2012 and heard his story we connected immediately.

He had attended a primary school in Bali like the one where I had taught in 1999. I recalled magic memories of working in that little school. I told him of the children; when I took in some pens and paper and asked if they would draw pictures of their environment, they produced pictures of their houses and their gardens. I still have the drawings *(see pages 178-9).*

Made told me that he had been fortunate to be sponsored to go on to senior school. He had been to university in Denpasar, had taken a master's course in the Netherlands, and had a PhD from Chicago. He then found a position teaching at the university in Bali, before moving to the UK. I was so impressed. I knew the long journey he had travelled and knew I had to work with this man and help him to re-establish his father's vanilla farm. He explained that the children in Bali would hand pollinate the vanilla flowers on their way to school. However vanilla farming was precarious: over the years the fungus fusarium had damaged the crops, making vanilla an unstable product. Speculators were buying in early, and the harvest was being collected before the beans were ready. This led to a deterioration in quality. The farmers were told to burn their rootstocks because it became unviable.

I asked how Made had been able to fund his university education. He replied, 'My grandmother had a dream that one day one of her grandchildren would go to university. She saved and sacrificed to purchase one room in Denpasar to ensure that her grandchild would have a place to sleep and study if that happened. So it is thanks to my grandmother that I was able to go to university.' This confirmed my decision to do what I could to help this man's dream to re-start his father's vanilla farm.

In researching the political and historical background I found that Bali at that time had been under the dictatorship of Suharto. When

I went to Bali the first time in 1999 the military dictatorship was just over. It had been a turbulent thirty years for the Indonesians.

When I met Dr Made he had moved to Oxford. He had left with his wife and two children with the recognition from his community that he was a successful academic going to live in one of the most educated cities in the world. There was a sense of Great Expectations. The reality when he got to the UK was very similar to what my father, and Naushad (Nash) and his family, had found: things were far from favourable. But he managed to get his two sons into good schools in Oxford.

However, the economy was in a very bad way in the UK. The year 2008 saw the largest economic crash in living memory. Dr Made had hoped to get some research work at the university, but funds were tight. He had a momentary vision that he would be stacking shelves in Tesco if he did not find another way of settling his family into this new environment. He managed to get a job with Cultivate Oxford that he had offered to help, teaching people how to cultivate a smallholding producing vegetables. Not until 2013 did he lean on his vanilla farming background: he decided to put his credentials out on the internet and see if anyone would respond. I received an email from him.

I had launched LittlePod at the Foodies Festival at Hampton Court in May 2010. We were one of only a handful of start-ups that year. In the week of the launch the newspapers announced that the country was experiencing the worst recession in living memory. I had done my homework and knew that even top chefs were unaware that vanilla came from an orchid. I had telephoned Simon Hulstone, a renowned chef in Devon, and had asked him 'How do you use

> **Vanilla does not have a scent when it is growing. That comes during the curing process.**

vanilla?' His answer buoyed me up: 'If I had my way,' he said enthusiastically, 'I would use vanilla every day in absolutely everything.' It was enough to make me believe that I was doing the right thing.

Made and I met for the first time at a little fair that I was attending in a school in Oxford. The girl organising it had phoned to ask if I would take part; her father had just had a heart attack. I felt the need to support her and decided to go. I then invited Made. It was an appropriate place to meet up, in a school. When he arrived I felt that I knew him instantly. He was wearing a sort of donkey jacket and boots and a flat cap. My father always wore a flat cap. It may have been that boho look of familiarity with my dad that made me trust him instantly. He had long black hair in a ponytail, which in Bali signifies that you're married to a foreigner. He had a very big smile with perfect white teeth. I felt a kind of shy reserve. We shared a little bit about our backgrounds. I told him about my upbringing, about my father, and he understood and declared 'So, Janet, you have known social isolation like me.'

Made told me his story and his desire to renew his father's vanilla farm. He said that vanilla had been a constant in his life as a child until the government declared that it was no longer a commodity to trade unless you were licensed to do so. It seemed a daunting prospect for him to embark on restoring the farm, and equally it was a daunting prospect for me to offer any support.

I explained that LittlePod was very young. I was doing it alone. I had the support of Nash, but he later admitted to Paul, our media manager, that at the time he did not see the vision and wondered how I was going to market the tube of paste. I told Made that 98 per cent of start-ups in the UK fail by their fifth year. It takes five years to produce a vanilla pod. We had to create a bond of trust and have no expectations. I had already escaped making a promise to Juan on the same grounds when I started the company. I suggested that we meet properly and discuss things more.

Meanwhile I invited Made to London where LittlePod was holding its second anniversary. Leonel Gouveia, the head pastry chef at Patisserie Valerie, had arranged for LittlePod to hold an event in their Norman Foster-designed premises in Spitalfields. We were launching our new vanilla beer and hoping to establish the LittlePod brand in that trendy part of London. However, as luck would have it, there was a tube strike that day. It was swelteringly hot, and people were heading to the beaches and the countryside. My daughter Clare took four hours to get to the venue. I thank her to this day for her support.

Vanilla is used a lot in brewing. It has over 500 complex compounds, of which 250 are known to work with compounds in other foods to round out flavours. For example, we brought to market a vanilla shortbread biscuit because people loved the tasters I made for shows: the vanilla brought the buttery taste to the fore. Clara, our office administrator, was concerned that we did not have an NPD (New Product Development) policy drawn up, and it was a huge risk. I remember saying that if I were ever to write a book about starting a company it would be called *It's Your Risk!* Over fifteen years of running LittlePod I have been told numberless times 'It's your risk, Janet.' Fortunately on the day the biscuits were placed on the LittlePod online shop I had a phone call from a hamper company in Germany who ordered 15,000 packs.

Vanilla does not have a scent when it is growing. That comes during the curing process. However, the beautiful frangipani tree – the signature tree of Bali – has a most wonderful scent. The frangipani in Made 2's orchard is covered with vanilla vines, and the pods absorb the smells and scents around it. No two pods are alike, although there are similarities depending on the soil types. When Dr Made smells a vanilla pod he can trace its history in the forest. From the woody, or the fragrance, he can say which tree is most likely to have hosted the vine the pod comes from. It is like listening to a wine connoisseur. In areas where vanilla is worked as a cooperative each bundle of vanilla beans has one bean that is marked to show which village it comes from.

In the West a chef does not know that the vanilla pod comes from an orchid. However, the top chefs know that vanilla has natural calmatives and uplifters and special characteristics that blend beautifully with other foods. Used with hot spicy food made with chillies, for example, vanilla rounds out the heat. Used with things like bitter chocolate or bitter beer it rounds out the bitterness and makes the taste smooth. Creative chefs love vanilla. It is their secret ingredient for cakes, sauces, creams, fish dishes, desserts, all manner of things. If you look on our website, you will see many recipes using vanilla.

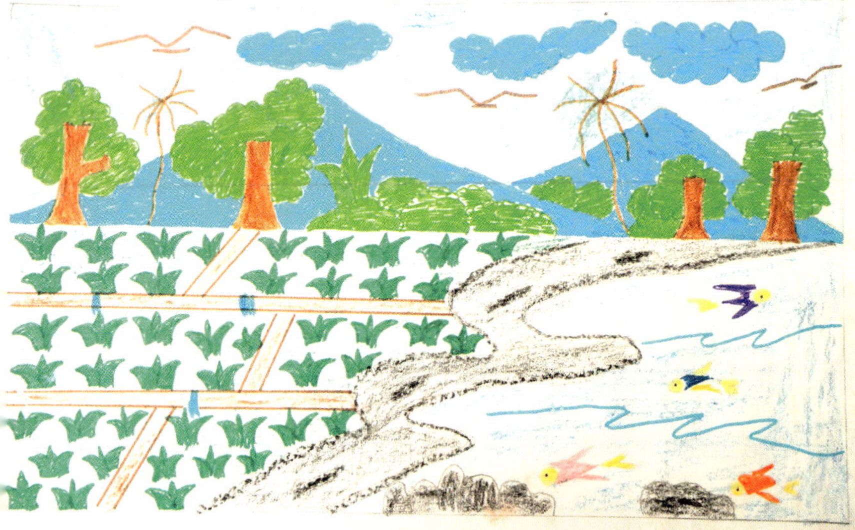
NAMA: Yusniati

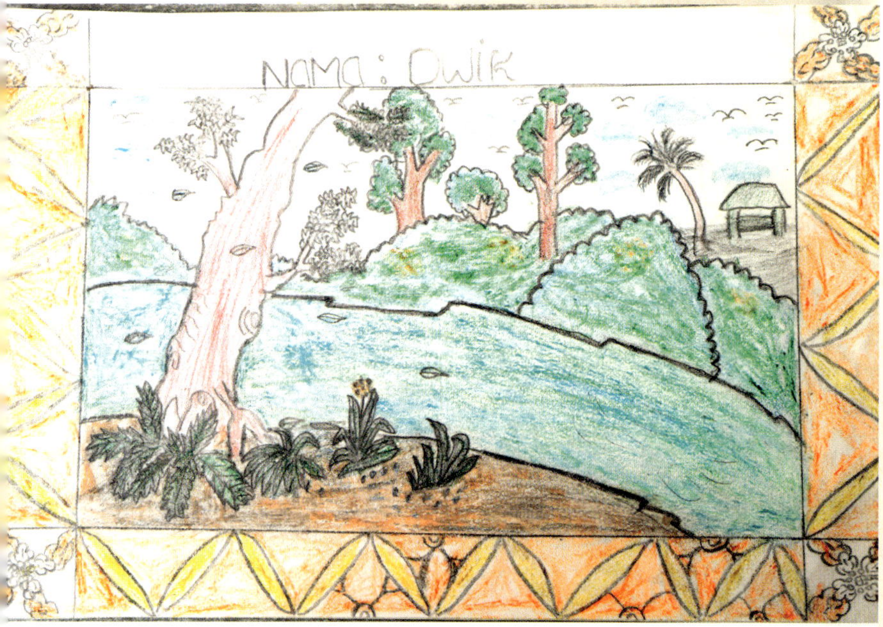
NAMA : DWIK

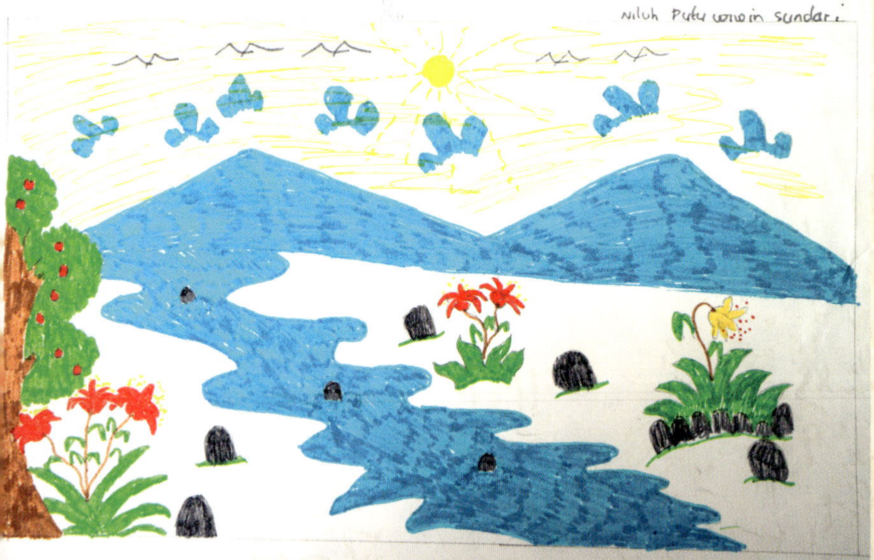
Niluh Putu
sundari

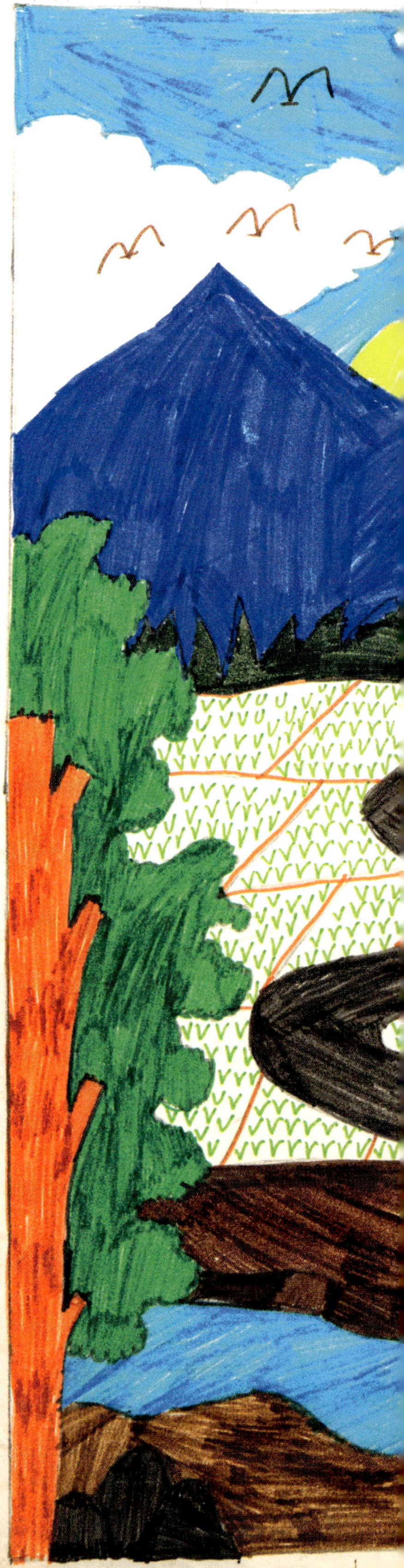

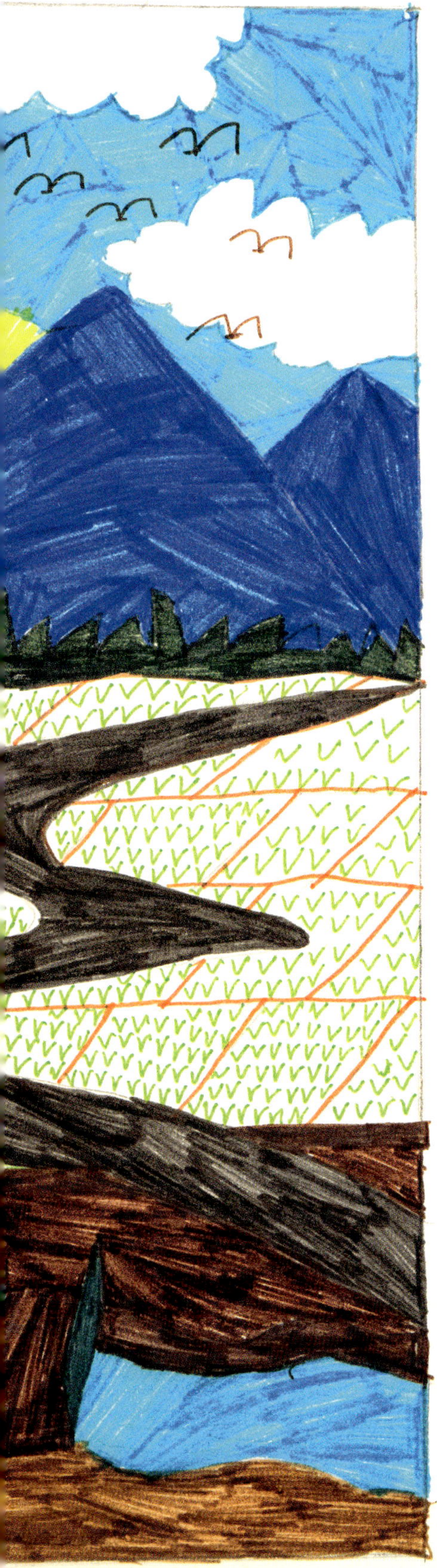

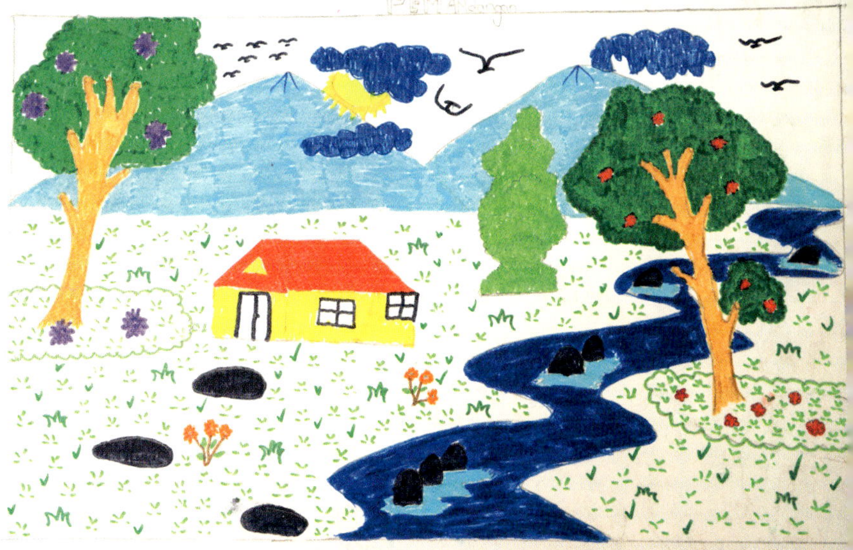

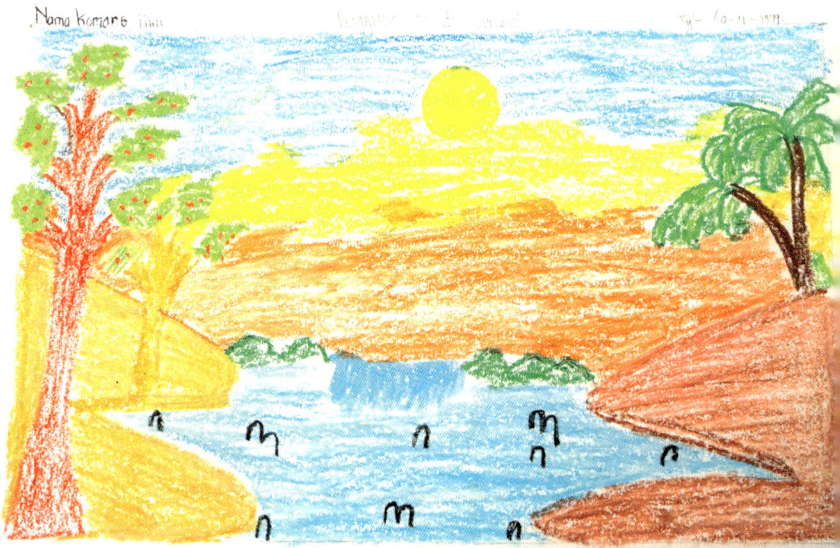
Nama Komara

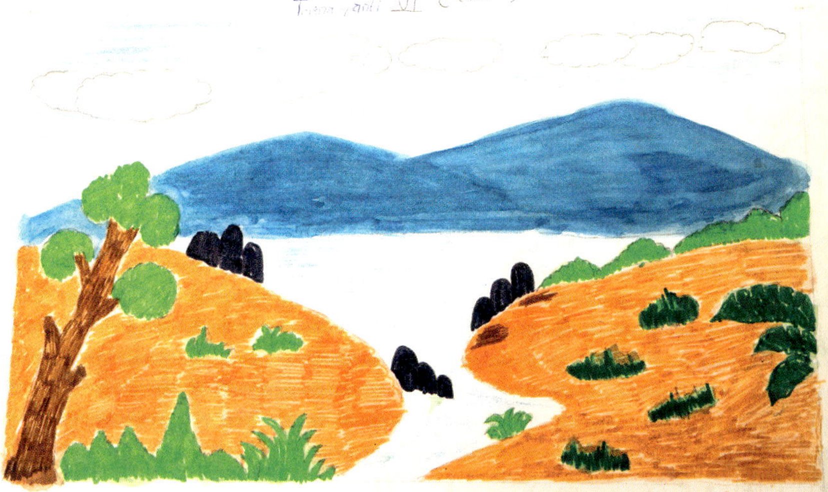

14
Keep it REAL

182   Real Vanilla: Nature's Unsung Hero

> **Our olfactory senses get used to fake vanilla too. The students in the forest in Bali have gathered around me to learn more about the use of vanilla in the UK.**

I tell them that in the West 97 per cent of vanillin is made synthetically, mainly from a by-product of a petrochemical used in the wood pulp industry. It has the smell of vanilla, and most people do not realise that what they are using in their baking is not real vanilla. They are missing out on all the flavour compounds that real vanilla provides. Fake vanilla is an easily replicated ingredient that is very cheap to sell in supermarkets. In some chefs' kitchens I have seen what looks like a bottle of white PVA glue used in primary schools, with a distinct artificial smell.

Consumers of the fake are missing out on the nutrients, the antioxidants and the anti-inflammatory character of real vanilla, and the knowledge that vanilla adds value to the forest floor. They do not know that scientists have discovered that where a vanilla orchard is planted in a hectare of forest there is more biodiversity than with any other plant. They do not know how the plant is tended, and its true properties.

This is what LittlePod does. We tell people about the importance of supporting the farmers of real vanilla, not just for the benefit of cooking but for their children's inheritance. We tell them that it is the indigenous farmers who know how and where to plant the trees that will regenerate the rainforest, that vanilla revitalises the soil, that by purchasing real vanilla they will be supporting the farmers who cultivate the vines, increasing the mycorrhizal fungi in the soil, so important for forest regeneration. Ultimately the air we all breathe is from the rainforest, the lungs of the earth.

Saving vanilla is to the benefit of us all. It creates a virtuous circle that binds the farmers on the equatorial belt, the providers, with the people in the temperate climates who are fortunate to go to some of the top restaurants and experience the delight of real vanilla, for breakfast in porridge or coffee, for lunch in creams, butter, fish dishes, for afternoon tea in cakes, for dinner desserts and even savoury dishes like steak or game with vanilla. I once made a huge cassoulet for a lot of people I invited to a gathering in our wood, and everyone wanted to know about the depth of flavour in it. I told them it was the addition of a spoonful of vanilla paste!

In 2018 Prince Charles came to visit LittlePod at the Honiton show in East Devon. LittlePod had won the Queen's Award for Sustainable

Opposite: LittlePod's natural vanilla paste is very versatile, with a huge variety of uses

Development, one of only eight companies to do so that year in the UK. Olly and I had been to Buckingham Palace just two days earlier, and the Prince asked if we had enjoyed the reception. 'Yes, thank-you', we answered. After introducing him to all the team I asked if he liked vanilla. He said that he adored it. I said 'That is not surprising, as it must be in your genes', and told him the story of Queen Elizabeth I. He said that he was partial to a real vanilla ice cream. He was very keen on our tube of paste and then eyed the vanilla extract. 'Oh, you do extract, too', he said, looking at a gift set on the table. I had been told not to give him anything as he would be given a selection of products later. However, he looked so longingly at the gift pack that I asked, 'Would you like to take one home?' 'May I?', he said. Of course he took one home! When the Prince left I turned to the team, who were all applauding me. Austin, our apprentice at that time, said, 'You are a good saleswoman, Janet.' I said, 'No, Austin, I gave it as a gift!'

The interns are getting very excited about the information I am giving them. 'We need to find out more about the chefs and how they use real vanilla', says the tallest of the students. He has a serious look on his face as if he had missed out on an important element for his dissertation. 'I wrote a book', I tell them. It is called *Vanilla: Cooking with One of the World's Finest Ingredients*. It has lots of recipes in it, introducing people to the ways in which vanilla is used in both sweet and savoury dishes.

'I launched the book at Bickleigh Castle in Devon – a beautiful romantic castle set in a glorious location. Dr Made came because we decided to make the event very special and called it National Real Vanilla Day. The Vanilla Queen came from California to be with us.

'It was such a special day. Every year on 17th October when the flowers are appearing here in Bali, we celebrate our harvest festival at home and include vanilla.

'In 2020 when I went to Japan we decided to rename it International Real Vanilla Day!'

'In a castle', said the youngest intern. He called to Made 2 and told the story to him in Balinese. Made 2 smiled. He said he remembered Dr Made telling him that he had visited a castle, and that Janet had been honoured by the Queen of England. The interns look at me as if to say, 'Well, tell us more.' I tell them the story, although I am unsure as to how much they understand. I start with beer, something that has a resonance everywhere, although some of these students are Muslims and will not drink alcohol.

'It is a long story, are you sure you want to know?'

'Yes, I will translate', said the older of the interns.

'Well, it starts in 2012. LittlePod was only two years old. One morning I received a very special letter in the post. The postman felt such a guardian of the letter that he knocked on the door to present it to me rather than putting it in the post box. He was from the Royal Mail, and this letter was from the royal palace.' I could see the interns intently looking at me. The orchard was silent apart from my voice. I explained that the letter was from the Queen of England. It said that the Queen was celebrating her Diamond Jubilee; it had been decided to reintroduce an award called the British Empire Medal (BEM), and she

Top: Introducing Prince Charles, now King Charles, to our Campaign for Real Vanilla in 2018
Bottom: Bickleigh Castle

Keep it REAL   185

Top: LittlePod's vanilla beer proved popular!
Bottom: Vanilla, coffee and chocolate are perfect partners in both the rainforest and the kitchen

wondered if I would be agreeable to receiving this award.

'Can you imagine receiving a letter from the Queen?' I asked the interns. It was a proposition too far as the concept of Queen was enough of a stretch, although a few of them had done their master's courses in England and of course knew of the Queen as a figurehead. I knew that Bali is made up of kingdoms, so the idea of a ruler was not unknown here. In fact, when I came to Bali the second time and visited the primary school again the children stood up and sang 'God save the Queen'. I felt like I was representing England that day.

'What did you say when you received the invitation?' enquired one of the students. 'Well to be honest I sat down for a few hours with several cups of coffee trying to assimilate this communication. Then I phoned David.' 'What did he say?' the students asked. 'I told him what I had received in the post, that the Queen wanted to know if I was agreeable to receiving the British Empire Medal. He was dumbfounded too. "Does it say what for?" he had asked. "Yes," I answered, "for my contribution to employment and culture in East Devon." "Wow," he responded. It also finishes with a line that says "I remain your obedient servant." "Yes, well, they use that kind of archaic language," he said.

'It was an overwhelming experience, and to this day I have no idea why I was selected to be one of the first 293 people to receive this award or what the selection process consisted of.

How, I wondered, did the Queen know about my work in the community, setting up a not-for-profit society called the Farringdon Society of Arts? How did she know about LittlePod and our work in promoting the farmers in the equatorial regions who produce vanilla?'

It was a landmark day for me personally. I had a naivety about my character that has been lost since, but then I was enthralled in a childlike experience, rather like the agape experience I was having that day in this forest – that fairytale feeling of something operating higher than us.

'Did you accept the invitation?' one of the students asked.

'Yes, I did, and that is why I brought out the vanilla beer.

'I wanted to thank the Queen for this recognition. I decided to put a basket of LittlePod products together to send to her. However, there was something lacking. I realised that it needed a celebration drink; her husband, Prince Philip, enjoyed a tipple. so I thought of a vanilla beer.

'I worked with a local brewer. The team at the time loved trialling the different bases for the beer. There was a clear winner.

'The beer went on to prove its worth. It received a gold at the Great Taste awards and was then selected to accompany the coffee panna cotta for the Chairman's dinner at the House of Commons in London. Top chefs know the value of vanilla when working with other flavours. You see the coffee in this orchard and the cacao? They grow together naturally in the forest, and they are natural flavour partners in the kitchen. It was a sure success, and I even got an invitation to the Christmas party at the House of Commons!'

The interns were laughing at the idea of me at a beer party. I can still remember that night looking out at the River Thames from Parliament thinking that I should savour the moment as it was a view I would not be privy to again. I had received a letter from the secretary of the All-Party Beer Committee. I remember being appalled that such a thing existed. I attended the party, however, which was wall to wall mostly men. There was some mention of the film *Skyfall* which had been released, and that a particular beer had managed to market itself in the film. I remember blurting out 'Oh, that's an idea. I think Miss Moneypenny should have her own beer and it should be called LittlePod.' Everyone laughed.

I say to the interns, 'LittlePod – that is every team that has been part of LittlePod – has taken us on some amazing journeys, and now we are here with you all having fulfilled our promise to Dr Made.' I tell Syiraz and his team that I am taking Dr Made out for a special meal this evening to celebrate the thirteen years we have worked on this project, and most especially his expertise in proving that the polyculture method is good both for the environment and for the people in the village. 'Syiraz, please can you tell Made 2 that I also appreciate his patience and endurance in keeping the project alive and positive when some of the farmers began to question the viability of rekindling the vanilla business.' Syiraz turns to Made 2 and translates what I have said. He nods his head nonchalantly in recognition of my appreciation.

'There is still such a lot to do, Syiraz,' I say. 'We need to support and encourage the young people to realise what has been achieved here and show them how they can be involved, particularly in telling the story. Stories are the best way of communicating.'

'Yes,' says Syiraz, 'we are so interested in your stories today, Janet. We get to know you, how you think.' 'I know that it is important. That is why I had to come.

'The only thing I wish is that I could smile a big smile and show you how happy I am to be here.' 'Why do you say that?' asks Syiraz. 'I had an operation on my nose a few months ago and I am still healing from it. Unfortunately, the pain is worse when I smile. The people at the Pita Maha Hotel where you came to visit have been fantastic. They noticed that I was not eating my food and asked if I needed anything. I explained about my condition, and they brought me soft things to eat. I am so grateful.' 'Ah, that explains how carefully you have been treading the forest floor', Syiraz says. 'We noticed how you walk.' 'I will be better, but it will take a bit longer because of my age. My consultant, Mr Khatwa, was so positive when I said I wanted to go to Bali. I just feel a bit sad that I cannot jump up and down and laugh in my usual way.' 'Nevertheless, you are so positive', says Syiraz.

'There is one thing I would like to do for the people at the hotel, Syiraz. When I told them that I was here to meet the vanilla farmers they looked amazed and asked where the vanilla farmers are. Paul and I had a cookery demonstration with the head chef at the hotel and I gave him some LittlePod vanilla paste. I asked if he used vanilla in his cooking, and he said that vanilla was far too expensive for the hotel kitchen. The other members of staff had told me that they had grown up with vanilla and had hand-pollinated the flowers on the way to school, then one morning they woke up and the vanilla was gone. Some were children of vanilla farmers, and their livelihoods had just disappeared. I want to remedy that, Syiraz. I have told them that they can grow

their own vanilla in the hotel. The wonderful trees they have are like a small rainforest. I told them that I would ask the vanilla farmers if we could plant some vanilla under the trees.
I suggested to the hotel manager that it could be a great marketing story to see the vanilla growing at the Pita Maha and then taste it in the food. When I told the head chef he said, "We can be the restaurant in Bali that has vanilla in our Nasi Goreng!" Can we do this Syiraz?' I ask. 'Well, if Ketut and Dr Made agree, it is possible.' 'I will ask them tonight', I say.

Syiraz and I begin to discuss the broader picture of climate change and the political and social will to adapt to the new environments that global warming is causing. I tell Syiraz the story of the safari that Olly and I enjoyed on our last day in Tanzania – how all the animals came out as if to say goodbye to the wildebeest who had gathered at the water's edge before making their long journey to the Serengeti. Syiraz says he would like to take his daughter there one day.

The rest of the team want to know about the safari. 'We saw everything that day, including a leopard. It was the first one the guide had seen all year. He told us that the weather patterns are changing so much that the people who had paid a lot of money two weeks earlier to see this sight had missed out. It was a beautiful day, and so joyful to see the elephants and giraffes, warthogs, the zebra, the lionesses, the cheeky meercats, and the African baobab trees! These trees can live up to five thousand years.

Top: The Mexican Tree of Life embroidery, a cherished gift from the Vanilla Queen
Bottom: Planting vanilla vines at the Pita Maha hotel in Ubud

Keep it REAL

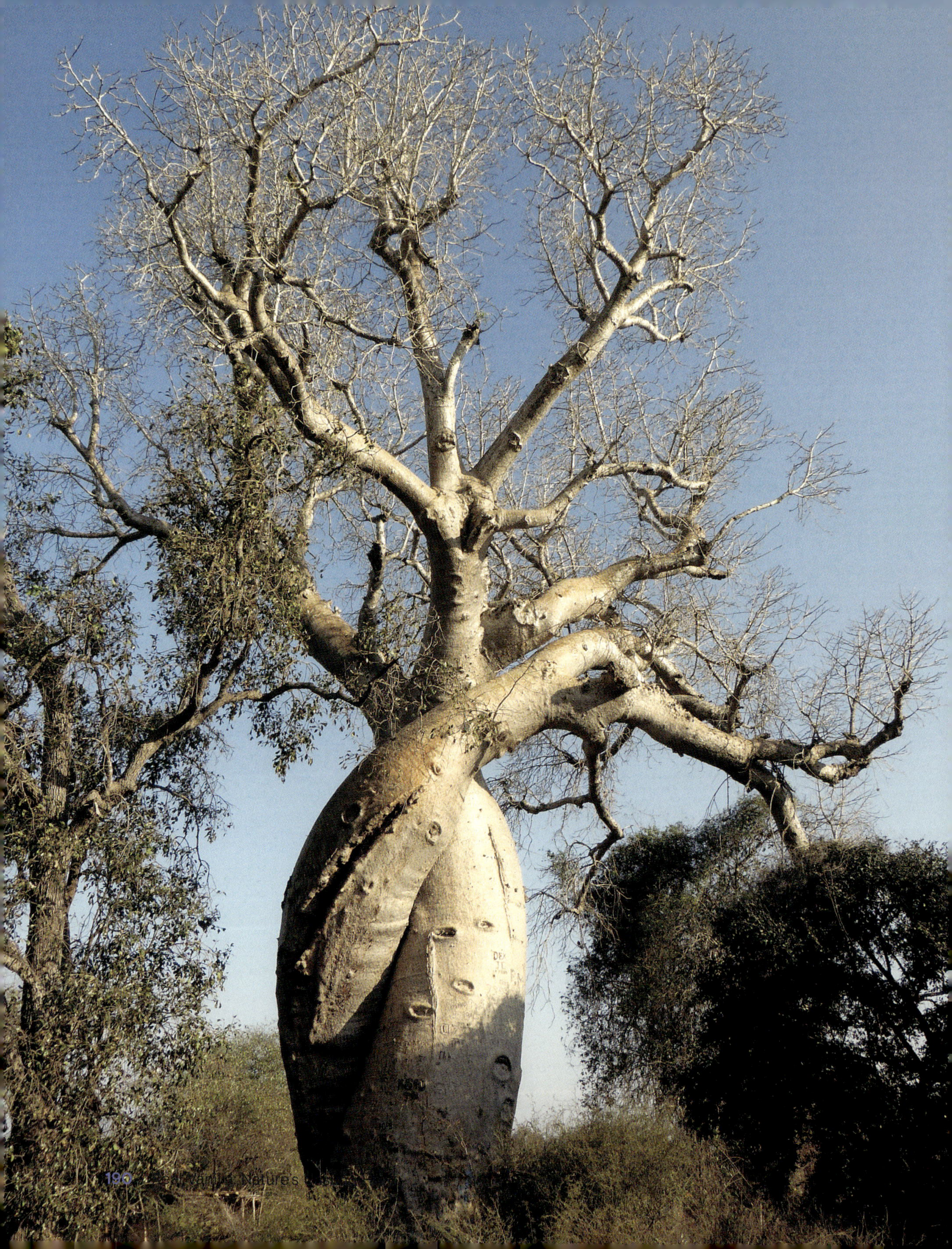

'Apparently in Madagascar the baobab tree is known to have been an iconic tree going back 21 million years. Baobabs were there along with the orchids and the dinosaurs. They hold water in their trunks, and the elephants love them.

'There were so many families of elephants. They are a keystone species that plays a vital role in the ecosystem. I love them. They are the symbol for the tree of life. They are so useful, too: medicine, food, clothing, rope and glue – this tree just keeps on giving. It is also the national tree of Tanzania.'

Patricia Rain, the Vanilla Queen, gave me an embroidery of the Tree of Life handmade by the Totonac people of Mexico. I have known this symbol since I was a child. My mother taught me that in Irish it is known as 'Crann Bethadi'. It is almost as old as humankind. It features in Christianity, ancient Egypt, Buddhist, African, Turkish and Celtic cultures. A unifying symbol of connection to the afterlife, strength and growth, the Tree of Life represents our ancestral roots and rebirth, our connection to the divine.

In 2011 when LittlePod was one year old I decided that I would hold a first-year anniversary celebration. The Vanilla Queen was visiting the UK from California, and I invited her to join the LittlePod team for a special birthday tea in London. I am a friend of the Chelsea Physic Garden, and I thought that would be an appropriate place to hold the event.

In my early days in London, I would cycle to the Garden to find solitude and safety away from the busy streets outside. London was exciting but also overwhelming at times and just knowing that I could walk on Hampstead Heath and also visit the apothecary's garden gave me a sense of escape. I often think I would not have stayed in London for twelve years without these significant places. It must have been the late 1970s or early 1980s when I first came upon the garden and experienced the agape feeling that filled my seeking soul at that time. I was thrilled when almost forty years later I was approached to become a Patron of the Garden. It was known as the Secret Garden, although in 2023 it turned 350 years old! Now it is thriving as an independent garden, sharing knowledge and offering courses for all. Its role is as important today as when the early botanists first brought their plants from expeditions all over the world.

I invited a special group of people to come to celebrate with us, including people who knew Patricia Rain, some of whom she had not seen for a long time. I invited Tim Ecott, BBC journalist and author of *Vanilla: Travels in Search of the Luscious Fruit*; Michael Macdonald of the Vanilla Pod restaurant in Marlow; Manju Malhi BEM, author and cook; and head chef Leonel Gouveia from Patisserie Valerie. Patisserie Valerie had been a very special gathering place for me when I was first in London and there I first met my friend Marika.

Opposite: The iconic Madagascan baobab tree

Leonel had met me when I launched LittlePod at the Speciality Food Show in London in 2010. He understood the quality of LittlePod's vanilla and wanted it for their cafés. But authority to purchase tends to reside with the accountant rather than the pastry chef, as it was in this case. I had to argue the virtues of LittlePod on Leonel's behalf with their head accountant. It was my first encounter with the hard reality of the hospitality world. I realised that this man was responsible for keeping costs down and had no idea of the quality of their cakes. He argued over every penny and pressed down heavily on the price I was offering, wanting it to be that of artificial vanillin. After an hour he could see from my body language that I had resolved to call it a day when he suddenly announced, 'OK, it's worth your PR to pay that extra price.' I learnt so much about business that day! I felt so happy for Leonel that he would have the best vanilla and be so proud of his bakes!

'There is a keystone tree at the entrance to the hotel where you are staying', says Syiraz. The others nod in agreement. 'I have seen it. It is magnificent. What is it called?' I ask. 'It is the banyan tree. Without it the forest would not exist. It is a fig tree.' 'What are those long roots that hang down?' I ask. 'The banyan starts life as an epiphyte. Those long roots are aerial roots that grow down from its branches. The tree has difficulty holding itself up, so it produces new roots to anchor it to the ground. It is a national tree of India as well.'

I say, 'I think banyans also grow in Nepal. LittlePod has a very special customer there, Marcus Cotton, who owns the Tiger Mountain Pokhara Lodge hotel.' The Lodge was first opened by Sir Edmund Hilary. Their head chef, Lalu, loves our LittlePod vanilla paste and orchard pods, and they have bought our vanilla for years. When Marcus comes to Devon he is always committed to purchase from LittlePod. LittlePod's filmmaker, Will Halfacree, was hiking in Nepal in 2018 when we won the Queen's Award for Enterprise in Sustainable Development. Will interviewed Marcus, and they sent a wonderful message on film congratulating LittlePod on its success.

LittlePod has individual customers in the most amazing places around the world – Diane at the Love Shop in Trinidad, Alicia at the Tuck Shop in Bermuda, Katy at Marcel Monsieur in the Los Angeles farmers' market, just to name a few. One day I hope to do a tour!

Opposite: LittlePod's pure bourbon vanilla extract

Keep it REAL   193

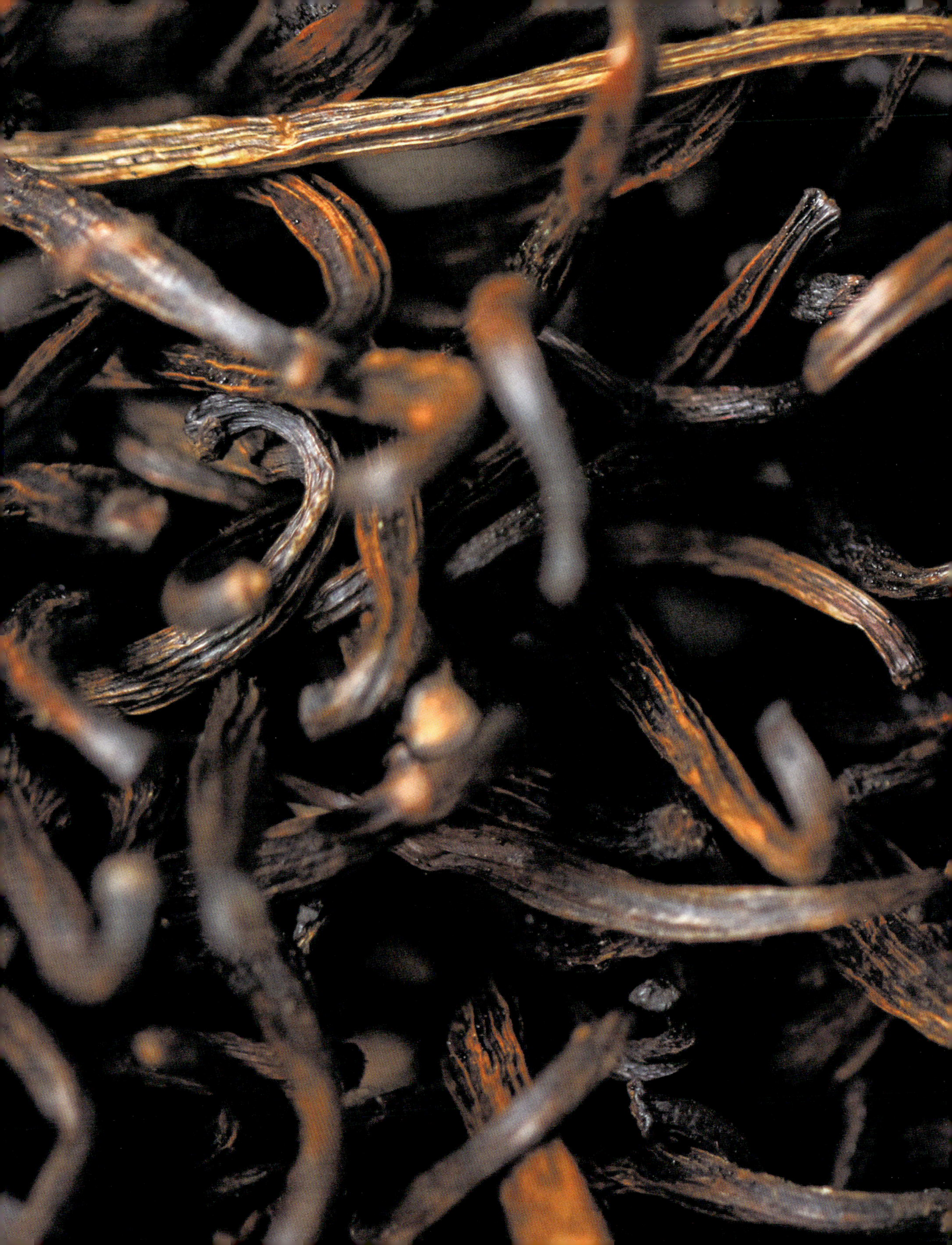

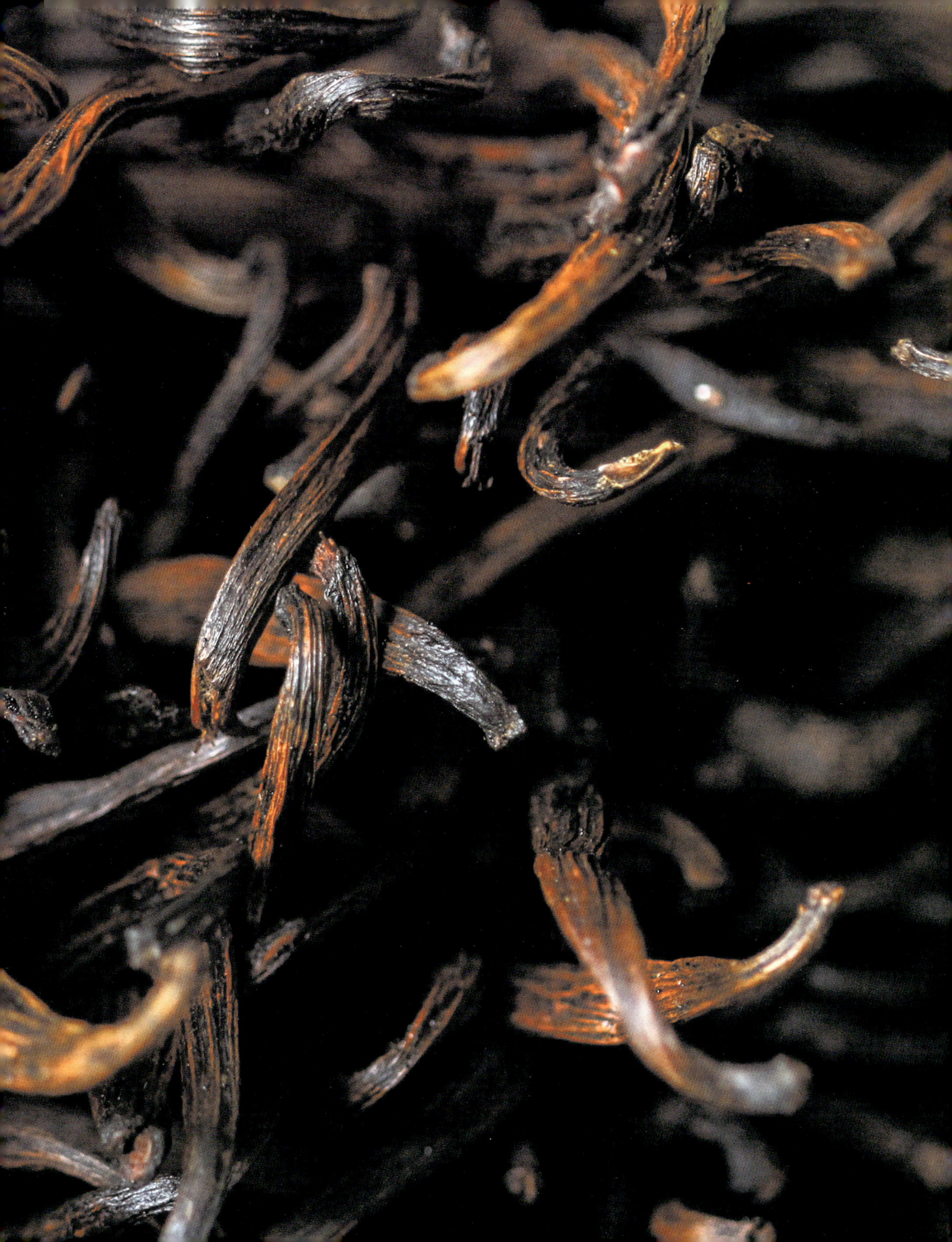

15
Our Man in Belém

LittlePod is a small company, but it has a wide appeal that reaches across generations and all over the world to people who share our concerns for the natural world.

While it is impossible to go to global conferences and to hear first hand what is being discussed, often behind closed doors, we are very fortunate to have a LittlePodder friend called William Wisden, who does attend these conferences and who can report to us what is being discussed.

COP30 will be held in November 2025 at Belém in Brazil. It will be the 30th United Nations Climate Change conference. Countries will be updating their NDCs (national climate action plans). Brazil will be highlighting the Amazon's role in climate regulation and will demonstrate its commitment to protecting indigenous rights and combating deforestation.

Paul has recently interviewed William, who told him about his relationship with Janet and LittlePod. Paul asked him,

'How do you know Janet, and were you surprised to find her running a business?'

William said, 'Janet was my neighbour many, many years ago. We had an affinity. Janet

Opposite: Catching up with William at LittlePod HQ in 2025

Our Man in Belém

used to come over for tea and we went to her house. We go back a long way, and we've kept up. I know how much energy Janet has got and how she gets inspired by things. When she told me about LittlePod and the concept at the beginning we were on the same wavelength. Janet's enthusiasm for getting something done and getting it well done – I can imagine how that rubs off on other people. Not just locally with the people around her in the UK, but abroad and overseas I'm sure it's the same. We all must deal with stresses and strains, but when you're running a company, in a close community, you have a lot of responsibility built in emotionally. The cutthroat world of business must be dealt with. Janet does it in a very human way, a very humane way. I'm sure that's part of the company philosophy.'

'What is your connection to this forthcoming conference?'

'I'm involved with the Climate Change COP in Belém. One of the areas we deal with that would be of obvious interest to LittlePod is that of food consciousness. More broadly we deal with biodiversity, sustainability, and many other areas of the climate agenda that would be of interest to LittlePod.

'I'm a researcher at the University of Pará in Belém. I look at indigenous people and their needs and help local communities to become involved in sustainable agriculture, which is something that overlaps with LittlePod and the work that is being done with the vanilla farmers.

'The head of the department, Professor Flavio, is concerned with family agriculture. It's all centred around small farmers doing their best, and it's a big fight to try to retain their legal rights to be able to produce food that is healthy, not sprayed and contaminated in various ways. We're trying to move in the direction of helping them – local farmers, local communities, indigenous people. That's why I'm tied in with the organisation that I'm currently working with, called the CIC, the International Council for Game and Wildlife Conservation.

'The organisation originated from the hunting community. It's eighty years old. That is the voice that gave rise to the IUCN (the International Union for Conservation of Nature). Hunters were thinking, "We have to keep the forests to keep the game," and that, if you like, has turned around, slowly, so that they've become a really switched on conservation organisation, working with traditional hunters, so that biodiversity in the Amazon is preserved by indigenous people who still need meat to survive. People are often a little suspicious – conservation and hunting are not usually used in the same sentence.'

'Have you followed the LittlePod journey?'

'I've always followed the LittlePod story, and I was delighted to hear that Janet has the opportunity now to put pen to paper and tell us all about it.

'Stories like LittlePod's are important and powerful. Through storytelling people who care about the environment can be brought together, making connections right through to chefs and consumers. It is about pride; it's not just added value commercially. It's also added value in a feelgood sense.

'People working together around the world put more pressure on governments to do the right things. It makes me so sad that there's all this frustration at not having funding coming out effectively from Cali and Baku. More generally, I lament the lack of a global narrative prioritising climate and biodiversity above arms sales.

'I wish it was more of an upbeat message. There are so many people doing really good things on a small scale, but the bigger picture is still grim. Whether we're talking about Brazil or somewhere else, the bigger agricultural industry machinery is still there and is poised to take out small agriculture. Mining interests – the whole thing is pretty difficult. You must really tough it out sometimes to see the light. There is a fightback at least, and the people fighting back are the good people, by and large. And then there's LittlePod – there are lots and lots of compelling stories. LittlePod's is certainly one of those stories.'

Paul asked, 'I believe you went to Cali in Colombia. What was that like?'

'I went to the biodiversity COP16 in Cali a couple of months ago, and there I met a man, Mark, who is running a super project using tropical fruits for high quality fruit wines for the Bogotá markets and restaurants. It is a story similar to Janet and the vanilla. These small-scale projects are working tirelessly to present the case for the preservation and restoration of the rainforests.

'My job over the next year is to make it obvious that there's a cross-continental movement of people, a network, a trading environment. If there were more political will and more funding, this could provide a platform for a paradigm shift. Think about food, and there's a shift in consciousness towards sourcing. There's still a time lag. In Brazil people still haven't gone into industrialised food quite to the extent that they have in the broader West, and this could be helpful. But at the same time there's a knowledge gap. There should be a greater understanding of natural foods. A lot of Brazilians who are now on rice and beans aspire to be on fast food and the industrial stuff. That's a learning curve that needs to be confronted. The more support for indigenous people on a local community level, for them to take pride in what they're doing and what they're eating, can contribute to change.

'The focus for COP16 in Cali was biodiversity, although we're trying to do as much as possible to underline that all these events are interlinked. The main thing that most people took from Cali is that there was no sign off for funding.

'The positives to take from Cali are that there are more people involved and there is more networking going on. I've been to Nairobi to speak to representatives of the indigenous people there, we've got an event coming up in Zimbabwe, and these are all excellent opportunities to raise the volume and encourage effective change.

Paul asked, 'What do you think needs to happen?'

'We need a holistic integrated approach to what is happening to the planet; we must not just keep parcelling it into climate and biodiversity and food and not making the links. These are huge events with a great deal of complexity.

'I was in Africa recently; I was at UNEP (United Nations Environment Programme), in Nairobi, and at least one of the conversations was regarding family farming and motivating people to go in that direction.

'I was with the co-ordinator of food consciousness for UNDP, the United Nations Development Programme, talking about their movement. Sometimes I just think there are too many things going on, and we're not knitting together the bigger picture. It's hard because there are geographic differences, different continents, but that's why Belém could be a springboard for various movements to acknowledge this and say "You know, we've got synergies here and those synergies could be tied far more effectively than they are at the moment." Indigenous peoples, for instance – at the COP in Cali they came out with a result. Now indigenous people are recognised as serious important actors around forests, not only in Brazil. Some of the momentum came from Brazil and the Amazonian countries, but there are going to be crossovers with Africa, crossovers with Asia, and wherever else there is indigenous interest in conservation.

There are good stories.'

'Do you think people feel hopeful?'

'I feel for the representatives of all the different countries who go to these events such as COP. They have high hopes that they'll be doing something effective; then at 2am, when they've been on their feet or sitting in meetings for twelve hours, some pedantic detail about some policy legislation gets in the way. That's frustrating. It was the case with the Pacific Islanders. They're crying out for direct financial aid because of the rising ocean levels, and it's all postponed again. It's the financial mechanisms, the financial priorities of governments, that are the biggest concern.

'But governments must listen, and with all the other issues going on globally, the environment is beginning to get pushed to the side again. There's a lot of talk, and efforts are being made. But the political football is continuing to be kicked around without the goals being scored.

'We've had the recent election in the United States, with what for many wasn't a good result. There's perhaps even more hostility towards environmental campaigners. We talk about the "bioeconomy," which started out as being a good word, but like "sustainability" it can be turned in the direction of greenwashing.

'We talk about these things a lot but taking action is something different, and it's difficult to knit these things together.

'There are a lot of people – individuals like Janet and companies like LittlePod – who know what needs to be done. But on a higher level, how to make that into an integrated, holistic, international movement is much more difficult and complex. Smaller companies and individuals like Janet must be encouraged.

'The UN Secretary General has so much to think about as he moves around the world, how does he keep his spirits up? Congratulations to him that he does, because the challenges are enormous. What a challenge. Wow.'

'What is the situation in Brazil?'

'There has been a change of government. Marina Silva is now the Minister of the Environment, and she has been ranked as one of the most important people on the planet in terms of conservation and the world's future. She has been in this area for decades, putting together all the pieces that, in theory, will work not just in Brazil but more broadly. It's a political thing. When public money gets involved there's an issue. COP in Belém is going to be very interesting. President Lula has been taking a lead, South Africa has been vocal, but there's still the notion that there's a polarisation between North and South on these questions. Smaller or less advanced areas of the world are saying that it should be turned around the other way, that the countries that have not developed their natural environment should be guided by those countries that historically have, to save the lungs of the planet and whatever else. Put your money where it's needed... But you try convincing your voters back at home. In Europe you might stand a better chance, but in other parts of the world no chance.

'I listened to Marina Silva speak a few months ago. Her supporters reminded her that, like them, she was a vocal activist on the ground, representing grassroots communities. The criticism that was levelled against her, politely, was that she should be doing something more vocal, more dramatic. She's obliged to follow Brazilian legislation as a minister and she sits down at the round table, as all ministers of the environment do, with the minister of mining and engineering and the minister of agriculture and the minister of petroleum or whatever, and President Lula, likewise obliged to follow Brazilian legislation, must listen to all the other sectors. The balancing act can go the other way. But there are plenty of good projects – a lot of good people and good things being done.

'It's about speaking the right language to get the people to do the right thing. It's hard sometimes to think other than through government. It's about more than short-term profit. It's long-term planning.

'The ethos I know from LittlePod and from visiting Janet is spot on. It's the challenges, though.

'We must go on doing what we're doing. The little companies like LittlePod and those I know in Brazil are doing their very best at subsistence level to integrate more effectively – people who are entrepreneurial, people who have good ideas of how to take these things forward. It's difficult because it can mean exposing yourself. The financial strains, labour laws, those kinds of things can affect companies and make this all more complicated.

'There are all sorts of areas of complexity, which if you're working on a small scale can become major headaches and take the focus not only off the bigger picture but also off life on the ground. Family agriculture is a big, tough battle.

'It's hard to scale up, but that doesn't mean it's not worth trying. You can lose the beauty, lose the feelgood of what you're doing with a smaller number of people, selling enough to support the whole community of families who have taken great pride and feel great relief that their income levels have gone up. But these small-scale projects can be replicated. There's a knowledge transfer that could put someone else in a position to do the same kind of thing.

'Janet writing a book – it's a wonderful story to be able to tell how someone else, working with something else, not necessarily vanilla, can apply the LittlePod-Janet model to make a difference in another part of the world. There is international support for these things.

'LittlePod has got a story to tell. I think it can be put into various environments. Vanilla is the product, real vanilla. I know about other people, other products, I know lots of different environments in which this works. People must be shown that there's an opportunity to go into a market and find a niche for themselves. Companies like LittlePod are doing this.

'LittlePod has got a story to tell. I think it can be put into various environments. Vanilla is the product, real vanilla. People must be shown that there's an opportunity to go into a market and find a niche for themselves. Companies like LittlePod are doing this.'

'The LittlePod vanilla story is fantastic. But I don't know to what extent Janet had sleepless nights about it all, the finances, the legislation, everything else that is involved. It shouldn't be this complicated. Cell phones, money transfers, all these other things – it's obvious that there must be a change from the traditional to the modern. We're all experiencing it. Subsistence farmers suddenly have cell phones in their hands. I've seen that generational change take place just in the time when I've lived out in the sticks in Brazil. From a little village with no energy suddenly everyone has energy, they've got piped water and cell phones. That's a huge technological leap in fifteen years from traditional subsistence. Now you're saying you're in a different world, and unless you get switched on to how the banking system works and the rest of it, eventually you'll be closed or there will be a generational dissatisfaction because the younger ones will want to pull in one direction and their grandparents will be backing the other. It is about connecting. That's a very local challenge that reflects a global one.

'Polyculture is part of the Brazilian agricultural shift towards something that is more sustainable. Trying to get that argument won is the challenge. I know from my own local community that they all know, because they drive past the fields and the stench of pesticides coming off the tomatoes is horrendous. Do those tomatoes get washed effectively? No. Eliminate the pesticides because they're killing off all the insects... They know that those tomatoes are poisoned, but the people in the city don't. If these things can be better articulated... It doesn't have to be scare tactics, more a case of realism and education.'

'How do you feel about the next COP conference? We will be interested to hear your thoughts.'

'"Peace with Nature" was the title, the theme, of the COP in Cali. Green diplomacy is something that we're going to be debating: this involves peace with nature. Planting trees is an effective way of educating children, educating people suffering from hardship and conflict in their lives. Providing inspiration that long-term aims can be met across generations at a local level and on a global scale that integrates us humanistically.'

16
A Promise Fulfilled

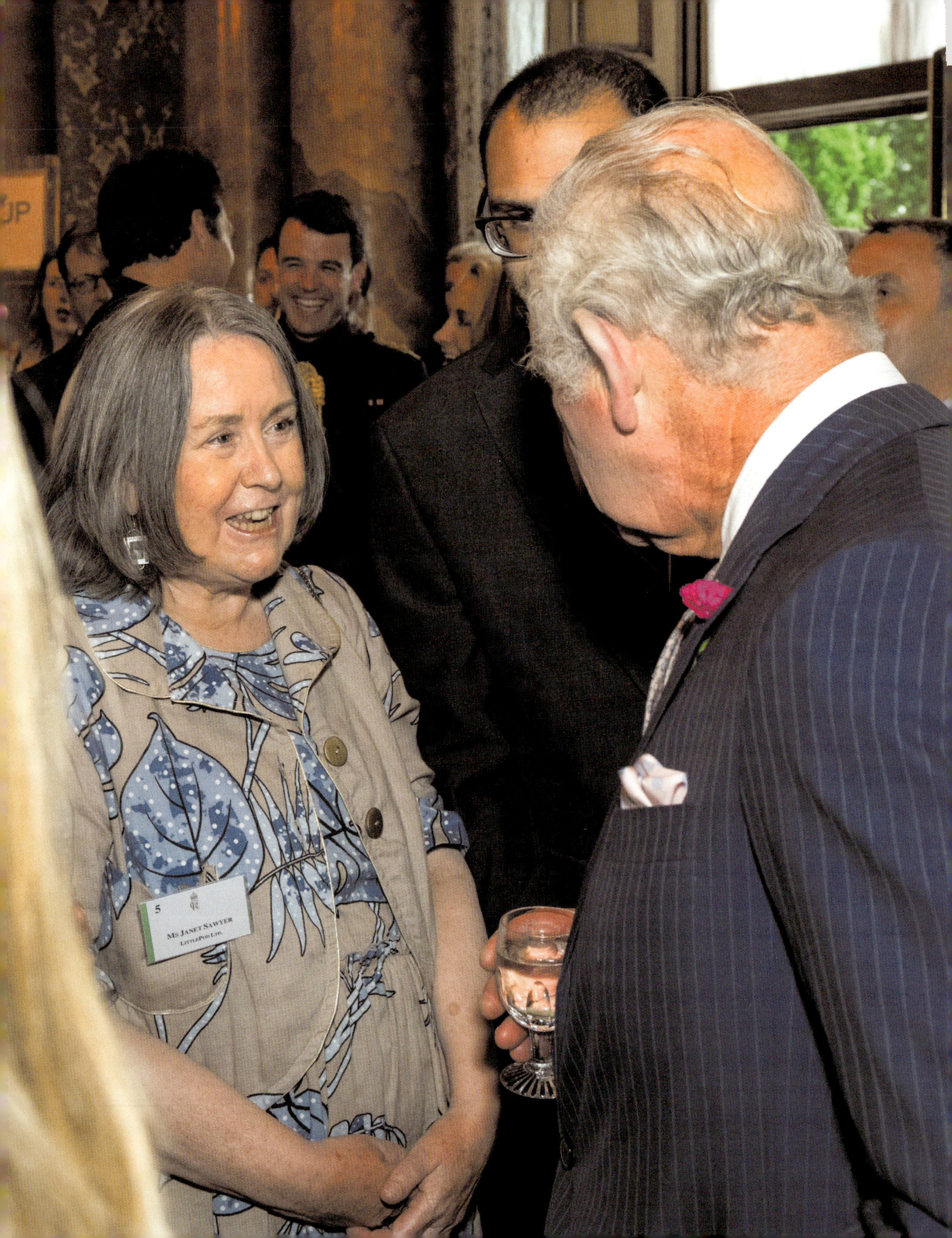
5
Ms Janet Sawyer
LittlePod Ltd.

> 'There they are.' It is Dr Made, wondering where we have been all this time. I wave at him. 'Hello, Janet', he says. 'Come and meet everyone.'

Opposite: Renewing acquaintances with King Charles at the King's Awards for Enterprise reception at Buckingham Palace in 2023

David and Paul are also back from their excursion to the plantation on the other side of the forest. 'How did it go?' I ask. 'Fantastic' says David. 'You should see the coconuts falling from the tree. It is so high. We were helping to shake them as others were climbing up to put the rope around. It was great fun.'

There are so many farmers here now. Dr Made introduces me to them one by one. There is a lot of high chatter and drinks being offered. The heat is just perfect, when the body needs to make no effort.

I ask David if he has the hats. He hands me the bag. 'I have a present for you all', I say as I pull out some black peaked caps with the LittlePod logo sewn across in white writing. All of the men (there are five Mades among them) don their new caps. Looking at us, they say 'We are family.' I am reminded of what Juan said about the vanilla farmers in Tanzania: they don't mention a supply chain, they say 'We are family.'

We are all seated on Made 2's concrete patio in the shade. It is now late afternoon. I am feeling tired, and my face is aching. I call Dr Made over.

'Made, please would you apologise to everyone and let them know that I want to smile as I am feeling so happy but that I just can't at the moment. I had a sinus operation, and I am still recovering.' Made explains the situation and there is a mumble of acknowledgement tinged with a little concern, but they don't seem unsettled. It must have been the way Made told them. Strange how now that I have told them about my pain I feel that I can make the effort to smile. I don't know if it was something in the tea or just the relaxation here.

A Promise Fulfilled

Nyoman, the elder of the men, is talking the most. He has a lot to say about the project and how it has gone. He is comparing things to the old days. He has always thought that the answer to the supply chain is to have a trusting partner. If we know that we can sell vanilla, then we can grow it. What is needed is the appreciation of the time involved.

We all chatter more. With lots of translation I understand that the harvest has gone particularly well and everyone is pleased.

We talk about the curing facility and the wonderful centre that Ketut has designed. 'We had a tour yesterday. I had a magical time in the forest orchard, Dr Made', I say earnestly. 'It was like walking in my woods but with different furniture. Furniture is what they called the trees in the woods when I sent them to auction.' Dr Made tells the farmers about walking in my woods and how precious they are. The farmers are interested to know that I owned woods of my own that I had to take care of. Dr Made translates when I say to them that when you start a company in the UK you need to find funding to get launched. Early on I was lucky enough to find an investor. Her name is Sally Sedgman; she wears rather large hats and is known to have the poshest voice in England. She has been a great friend to LittlePod. However, after a few years the company grows, and more investment is needed. The farmers nod in agreement. When LittlePod became about four years old it needed further investment to keep going, so I did a thing I never dreamed I would do. I decided to sell Ivy Woods and put the money into a manufacturing facility. I came to terms with the idea and felt sure that it was the best pragmatic decision. However, on the day of the auction I found that I couldn't go. Clara, LittlePod's administrative assistant, who was with me at the time, dealt with it by phone. I was in the dining room when she came in and told me 'The woods have sold.' I burst into tears!

The farmers know how I feel. I can feel their sympathy for what was a straightforward transaction but nonetheless painful.

A mobile phone starts ringing and I am called over by Sister (Dr Made says that everyone calls Made 2's wife 'Sister'). She smiles and shows me her phone. It's their son, Yoga. 'Hello, Yoga. How are you?' I ask. He speaks English because he is a manager in a hotel. 'Thank you. I am well.' 'Gosh,' I say, 'you were just a young teenager when this project started, and now I hear that you are about to be married soon.' 'Yes', he says. I can tell that he is happy to speak with me. Dr Made tells me in confidence, 'You see, Janet, you don't know, but in the early days when Made 2 was planting the vines and they were looking good the other villagers came to him to ask if they could buy a few metres of vine. Made 2 told them that he wanted to send Yoga to school; the other farmers said, "Oh, so that's why you want some money" – and that's how he sent Yoga to school.' 'I am so happy to hear this', I reply; 'it is how it should be.' 'Yoga has grown into a lovely young man', I say to Sister. She smiles a mother's proud smile.

'Come, come', one of the farmers calls out. We all rise and walk down a path into a wooded area where there is another concrete building on a plinth. (I know from my previous experience in Bali that it is important to build off the ground for safety when the rains come.) 'This building is like your village hall', says Dr Made. I point to a board: 'Oh, what's that?' Two of the farmers hold up a professionally printed board that pronounces ' The LittlePod Orchard'. It is the final affirmation of the trust that has been built between us all, and a sign of commitment on all sides for a future together.

'I must ask Will to come and film the forest now', I say to them all. 'Will, the filmmaker,' they say, 'how is Will?' They all remember him because he came out with Dr Made the first time and caught him on camera finding his father's old rootstocks; Dr Made was in bed for a week with poison ivy having climbed high to get them. There was much chatter about old times and the filming.

Dr Made tells the farmers that LittlePod won the King's Award and that I met the King again at Buckingham Palace a few months ago. I say, 'In fact two weeks after my operation. My consultant gave me some painkillers and said I could go. The day before, the palace phoned me at home to let me know that the King was going to speak with me. I thought "Oh no. I hope that I will be able to respond." I think it must have been the adrenaline, plus a glass of champagne – I did relax at the reception, and when the King spoke with me he was so keen to ask about you, the farmers, all the

Top: Enjoying treats in Tallin – with David at Pierre Chocolaterie.
Bottom: Yoga – Made 2's son – on his wedding day in 2024

Top: David Fursdon, the Lord Lieutenant of Devon, speaking to Dr Made and Ketut via video link in 2023
Bottom: The Dayak root from Borneo

farmers actually, and how the project was going. He is very interested in the work you are doing.' Dr Made reminded them of the Lord Lieutenant and what he had said when they zoomed in on the presentation day. 'Send our best wishes to the Lord Lieutenant,' they say, 'and tell him and the King they are very welcome to visit.' 'I will', I say.

It is time to leave. I turn to Dr Made and say, 'Don't forget you are coming to dinner with us this evening.' He smiles. 'We are going to Mosaic', I say. Mosaic is a French restaurant which has wonderful reviews. 'Ketut designed that restaurant', Made says. What I don't understand is why the farmers do not understand what we do with vanilla when there are all these restaurants in Bali. 'Here is a simple way of life, Janet. These people do not go to the town. They stay here.' I don't blame them. I turn to Made 2 and say with unequivocal sincerity, 'You have a lovely home amidst this wonderful orchard forest. To think this forest has been replenished by the vanilla vines we sponsored is so uplifting.'

We all hug and say our goodbyes. The bond of friendship has been reinforced.

The journey back to the hotel is a bit tortuous for me. It's been a long day, and the pain is telling me I have to rest. We have left it a bit late and are getting tied up in traffic jams. The driver is excellent and is taking much care. I am really appreciative, as I don't need a bumpy ride.

At last, we are at the hotel. It's getting dark, but we do have an hour or so before meeting for dinner. After some rest I am ready to face the restaurant. Luckily, we have decided to have the tasting menu, so I just have to eat small morsels at a time.

I say to David, 'Do you think that Made will turn up?' 'Of course he will', he says. 'I am not sure,' I reply, 'he is not comfortable in high end restaurants.' 'Oh, don't worry, he will be fine.' The restaurant building is made of glass and wood and is beautifully designed so that inside and outside feel as one. The waiter has told us that we will have the first three courses inside and the rest outside. The courtyard has a lovely garden.

'Hello, Made. I am delighted that you are here.' 'First and last time at this restaurant, Janet.' I laugh. I am aware of Made's tastes. Well, this is a very special occasion. We must celebrate him.

David is browsing the menu, which is pleasing his palette before we have even begun.

We reflect on what a wonderful, successful day it's been. We talk about the farmers, Yoga, ambitions, and the forest floor, as we dip into canapé-size treats. 'Do you remember in the early days, Made, that you went to Borneo to work with the Dayaks, the forest people?' I ask him. 'I laugh now', I say, 'that I wrote a letter to the Dayak people to introduce myself as a sort of guardian. I was worried that you were going to be far away from anywhere; I had read that the Dayak were still a head-hunting tribe in the 1960s, and I wanted them to know that someone was looking out for you.' We laugh at the idea.

'Then,' I continued, 'the Dayaks gave you a root to give to me, asking if I could find out what the active ingredients were, as it is an important medicine for curing cancers. I took the task very seriously on your behalf (just in case) and went to Dr Knight. Jan Knight told me that she could not do any tests on it in her lab, but she knew people who would know. She introduced me to all sorts of scientists, who confirmed her feelings that the machinery we would need to make an assessment of the root would be far too costly. In the end I phoned Glaxo Smith-Kline to ask about the procedures for borrowing machinery. Their simple reply was "We have so many tables with plants that are waiting to be examined. We simply do not have enough lab assistants or the right technical equipment." Think of all those potential cures sitting on desks in that room.

'I felt awful about it, particularly when you came into the Food Matters Live show that year by satellite link. Do you remember, you said, "Sorry to be late, we have walked five miles to get a connection." You pointed to me and said, "That is Janet," and they all waved. I do hope you told them how hard I had tried on their behalf. I still have the root in my cupboard at home just in case a new technology is developed that can identify it one day.

'Food Matters was attempting to make itself the voice hub of the food market. They had approached me because they said that they wanted to break the mould of static stands with no creativity: they would give me a discount if I could produce a lively stand. We had the best-designed stand in the show, with a whole series of events there, including the interactive fact finder that the winning students from the school I was working with as an Enterprise advisor had invented. Do you remember that Aisha came from Unilever to present the awards? When you and the Dayaks arrived online, there was a series of talks given by people in the food industry on the future of food. I introduced everyone to Aisha and they asked if you had any requests she could take back to Unilever. The Dayaks said, "Send us some food." Here were the voices of reality, that were not heard in the conference room where industry guest speakers were giving their talk on the future of food.'

We carry on eating through one course after another, and we are all feeling pretty tired. 'What a full-on day we have had, but I would not have missed it. This memory will last forever. When I came to Bali the first time, Made, I was taken by a friend to a very picturesque French restaurant that had gained the title of the best restaurant in the world. It was called Warisan. Did you know it?' 'I knew of it', says Made; 'it was run by two Swiss ladies. They brought the vegetables in every day fresh from France.' 'Imagine paying for those airmiles,' I say, 'but I have to admit it was wonderful food.'

Made says, 'Ketut wants Syiraz to take you with him to the government forest tomorrow. Can you do it?' 'Oh no, not this time, Made. The long journey today was challenge enough. I am so glad though that the Indonesian government have seen the progress with the orchard forest and want to emulate your work.'

'Yes, they are committed to regenerating the rainforest and are planning to plant two per cent with NTFP (non-timber forest products), with vanilla being number one.'

'I can't wait to tell the Vanilla Queen that vanilla is saved for the next generation,' I reply happily, 'so long as the Indonesian government don't destroy the forest in Borneo. If they just chop down the palm tree plantations to restore the soil and grow food, then we will be happy.'

I tell Made that Juta and her family are intending to holiday in Bali. 'Who is Juta?' he asks. 'Juta is the owner of a distribution company in Estonia. She and her family spent a year travelling around the world with the intention of finding fine foods that they could import. Juta came across LittlePod and loved us. They have been selling our products in Estonia for many years now. In 2014 when my book came out Juta invited me to do a signing, and I visited the beautiful city of Tallinn. It was in Tallinn that David and I tasted the 'Drink of the Gods' in a beautiful café called Pierre Chocolaterie. They have researched the Aztec recipe of chocolate and vanilla and made their own and called it 'Montezuma's Desire'. Tallinn is also the place where Walt Disney sent his imagineers when he was looking for inspiration for Disneyland. 'Oh,' said Made, 'she must see the vanilla growing at the Pita Maha Hotel.' 'Yes,' I say, 'we are planting the saplings tomorrow.

'It has been such a long journey, Made. I don't know how we could tell our story, do you?' After a pause, he says, 'It is a story of a promise made and a promise fulfilled, Janet.' 'Shall we toast to that, Made?' We raise our glasses and make a little clinking sound.

'What next?' I say to Made. He turns to me with a twinkly smile in his eyes and replies, 'Next chapter, Janet!'

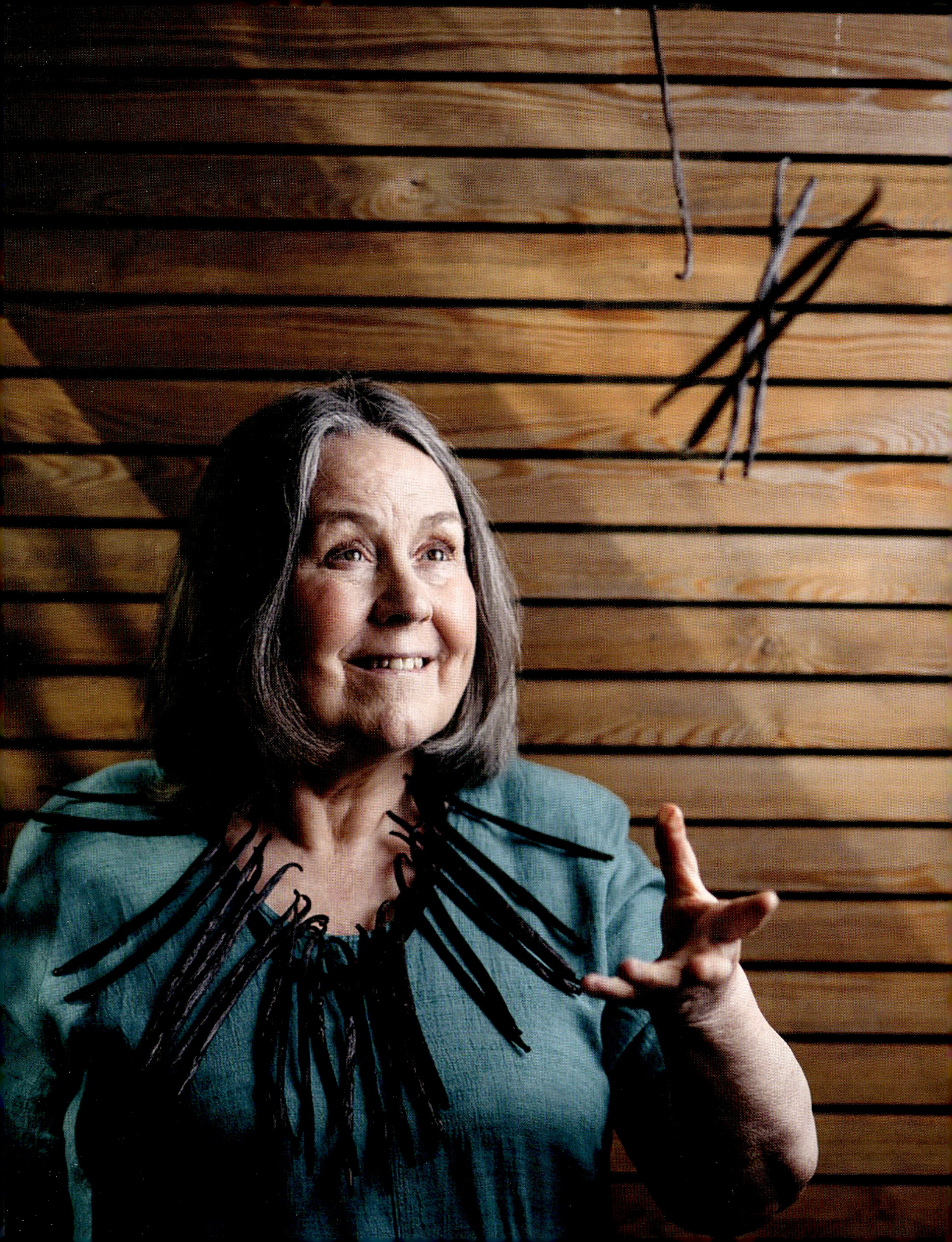

ACKNOWLEDGEMENTS

I would like to thank the following people for their help and support in writing this book.

Firstly, to Judi Burnett who invited me to one of her luncheon events as a guest speaker. It was here that I met Simon Perks, the Sales and Marketing Director for Unicorn Publishing, who was a hearer and heartener of my story. Simon gave me his business card and said that he felt I had a unique story to tell. Thank-you both.

Thank-you to Ian (Lord) Strathcarron at Unicorn Publishing for commissioning the book, to Ryan Gearing for overseeing the process, to Emily Lane for all her patient editing and proofreading and to Lauren Tanner.

The design of the book was committed to the capable and trusted hands of Harriet Beesley/Ferguson, who has been a devoted and talented LittlePodder since day one of this story. Thank-you for bringing our story to life, Harriet.

Thank-you to Dr Vik Mohan for his much-valued foreword to this book.

Huge appreciation to Paul Gilder, LittlePod's media manager, for his patient sub (and sensory) editing and proofreading to make sure that the book would make sense and meet its deadline for production, and for using his journalistic skills to research facts and interview those whose voices feature in this story.

My great thanks to those people whose reflections and expertise proved to be valuable inclusions and who agreed to be interviewed; to Mike Curtis, Juan Guardado and Muhammad Syirazi – Syiraz; to William Wisden, Dr Vik Mohan and Naushad Lalani, whose long and treasured friendship was to some extent responsible for this story.

My heartfelt thanks to my longtime friend Catherine McGowan, who was prepared to read the first draft and tell me honestly that my writing style is indeed readable!

A debt of gratitude is owed to Dr Made Setiawan and to Ketut, Made Suartika – Made 2 – and all the farmers who have worked so tirelessly to make this a story to be continued.

Special thanks to the LittlePod team for bearing up whilst I squirreled myself away to write this book, especially Richard Morris, our Operations Manager, for keeping everything running smoothly.

Thank-you to all the special people who have given myself and LittlePod an endorsement for this book; to Dame Prue Leith, Sue Medway MBE at the Chelsea Physic Garden and David Fursdon, the Lord Lieutenant of Devon; to Patrick Devine-Wright, Oliver Coysh of Exploding Bakery, Aisha Stenning and the amazing Patricia Rain – the Vanilla Queen!

Thank-you to Yoga in Indonesia for giving me permission to use the beautiful photograph taken on his wedding day.

Just prior to starting to write this story, I received the sad news that Nyoman Mudiarta had passed away. One of the elders amongst the farmers at the LittlePod orchard, Nyoman had believed in LittlePod and this project from the beginning and it was a great pleasure to meet him in Bali in October 2023 and to share our mutual appreciation of vanilla and everything that it means to so many. We are pleased that Nyoman was able to see LittlePod's collaborative orchard come to fruition and to experience the revival of vanilla production in his village – something that he had long advocated.

Just prior to completing this story, it was a great shock to hear that Achim Rohr – a dear friend, colleague and long-time LittlePodder – had also passed away. Achim was a devoted LittlePodder from way back in the early days and contributed a great deal to LittlePod and our endeavours. Achim was always a fantastic cheerleader for LittlePod and as a colleague, as a friend and as a man, I shall miss him greatly. He was one of the good guys.

This book is a tribute is Nyoman and Achim. Thank-you both.

Finally, thank-you to LittlePodders everywhere, to our distributors and customers at home and abroad who have chosen to support our Campaign for Real Vanilla by promoting our REAL vanilla products and sharing the vanilla story to a wider audience, who have become educated about vanilla's special properties and value, not just in the kitchen, but also for the regeneration of the rainforest.

Thank-you.

littlePod
RESPONSIBLY SOURCED
organic
coffee
extract
100ml e
vanilla
paste

littlePod
RESPONSIBLY SOURCED
pure
chocolate
extract
100ml

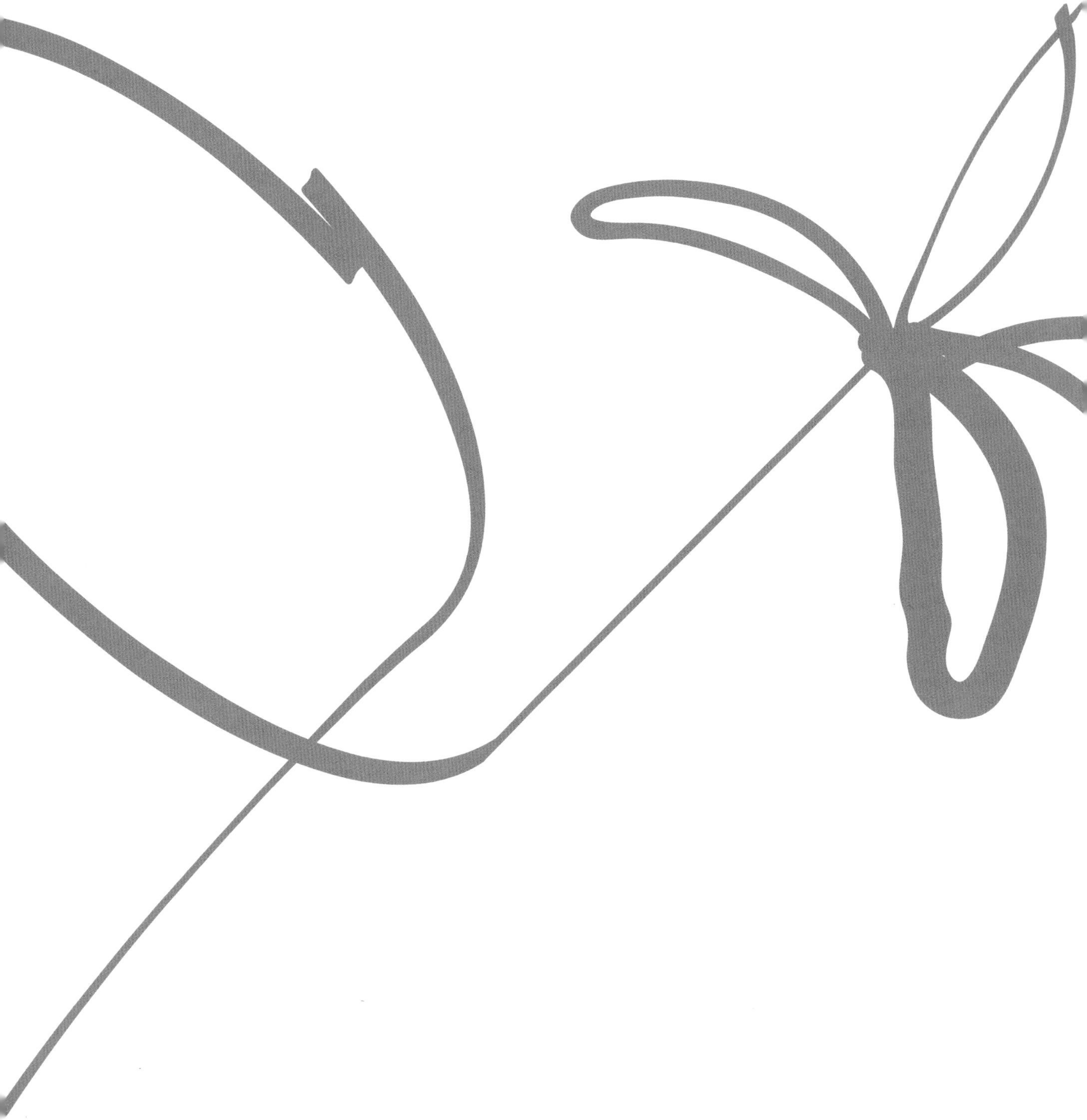

Picture Credits

Page 32: Photograph by Steve Painter, taken from Vanilla, cooking with one of the world's finest ingredients, copyright Ryland, Peters & Small
Pages 3 & 217: SGHaywood Photography

Other imagery taken by: Janet Sawyer, Paul Gilder, Wayan Martino, Nick Hook, Olly Aplin, Will Halfacree, Dr Made Setiawan, Dr Vik Mohan, Irine Hendry, Tom Hales, David Wornham, Matthew Surridge, Emmanuel Hammond, Naushad Lalani, Austin Robison, Bickleigh Castle, I Gede Sayoga Mahayana & Buckingham Palace.

Many thanks to all contributors. Every effort has been made to trace copyright holders and acknowledge the images. The publisher welcomes further information regarding any unintentional omissions.

Full Page Image Descriptions

Pages 18-19: Made 2 at the LittlePod orchard in Bali
Pages 40-41: Seeing polyculture in practice during our time in Tanzania
Pages 54-55: Made 2 and Putu sorting vanilla pods in Bali
Pages 64-65: The LittlePod orchard from above
Pages 78-79: Visiting a village during our time in Bali
Pages 102-103: Hand pollinating the vanilla orchid
Pages 160-161: Rice terraces at the LittlePod orchard
Pages 170-171: Made 2 and the LittlePod farmers
Pages 178-79: Balinese children's drawings
Pages 194-95: Vanilla pods from Indonesia
Pages 220-221: LittlePod's responsibly-sourced ingredients range

Published in 2025 by Unicorn, an imprint of
Unicorn Publishing Group
Charleston Suite, Meadow Business Centre
Lewes, East Sussex
BN8 5RW

www.unicornpublishing.org

Text © LittlePod Ltd

Author: Janet Sawyer MBE BEM

All rights reserved. No parts of the contents of this book may be reproduced, stored in or introduced into a retrieval system, or transmitted, in any form or by any means (electronic, mechanical, photocopying, recording or otherwise), without the prior written permission of the copyright holder and the above publisher of this book.

ISBN 978-1-917458-03-0

Design: Beesley/Ferguson Design

Printed in Malta by Gutenberg Press